MW00829851

# SURVIVAL GUIDE
## FOR THE MARINER

# SURVIVAL GUIDE
## FOR THE MARINER

### ROBERT J. MEURN
*Master Mariner*

## CORNELL MARITIME PRESS
*Centreville, Maryland*

Copyright © 1993 by Cornell Maritime Press, Inc.

All rights reserved. No part of this book may be used or reproduced in any manner whatsoever except in the case of brief quotations embodied in critical articles or reviews. For information, address Cornell Maritime Press, Inc., Centreville, Maryland 21617.

Figures 3-2, 3-3, 5-1, 5-2, and 5-3 are reprinted, with permission, from *Dr. Cohen's Healthy Sailor Book* by Michael Martin Cohen. Copyright © 1983 by International Marine, an imprint of TAB Books, a Division of McGraw-Hill, Inc., Blue Ridge Summit, PA 17294-0850 (1-800-233-1128).

Library of Congress Cataloging-in-Publication Data

Meurn, Robert J.
    Survival guide for the mariner / Robert J. Meurn. — 1st ed.
      p.  cm.
    Includes index.
    ISBN 0-87033-441-1
      1. Survival after airplane accidents, shipwrecks, etc.    I. Title.
VK1259.M48   1993
   363.12′3— dc20
                                               93-7990
                                              CIP

Manufactured in the United States of America
First edition, 1993; second printing, 1997

*To John C. Carrothers*
[1905–1991]

A shipmate and friend, in appreciation
for a life dedicated to safety of life at sea

Life's battles do not always go
To the stronger or faster man,
But sooner or later the man who wins
Is the man who thinks he can.

—reprinted from
*How to Survive on Land and Sea,*
a 1943 U.S. Navy publication.

# Contents

# Figures

# Tables

# Preface

This book was written to help the seafarer survive safely at sea. By choice as well as by tradition the seafarer is a rugged individualist. No other profession or venture demands a higher degree of ruggedness. The perils of the sea are many but nowhere else is there the self-satisfaction and the fulfillment of dreams.

The greatest obstacle that is faced at sea is fear of the unknown. Thousands of seafarers have survived the sinking of their vessels. They have been rescued or have made their way to land. Fear is natural, but it can be controlled and overcome. Survival at sea depends on three things: *knowledge, equipment,* and *morale.* Part of the responsibility is that of the master or captain of the vessel who has the duty to see that crew members fit their roles in the safety organization of their vessel. Responsibility also lies with each seafarer. The best possible safety devices will be worthless if you don't know how and when to use them.

*Survival Guide for the Mariner* is primarily a guide and refers to SOLAS regulations. It does not purport to cover all of the SOLAS regulations, and readers are advised to read the SOLAS regulations Chapter III and all the amendments. The survival guidelines are applicable to seafarers abandoning a ship, yacht, or any type of vessel at sea. Seafarers must keep in mind, however, that the best conditions for survival are not in the lifeboat or life raft but aboard their vessel. All necessary action should be taken to save the vessel. There should be no hesitation, however, in abandoning the vessel when the master issues the order. This book should help such persons confront the fear of the unknown. It will provide information and illustrate the knowledge, equipment, and morale required in order to survive safely at sea.

Acknowledgment is gratefully made for the permissions granted by authors to quote passages from their publications and by manufacturers of safety equipment to utilize their photographs and illustrations. In addition, there are many mariners whose experiences at sea are drawn upon for this book. For these experiences I am extremely grateful. I am very fortunate to have known John C. Carrothers, retired chief engineer and shipmate, to whom this book is dedicated. John was truly concerned for the safety of seamen and that history record the true accounting of tragedies at sea. His efforts to clear the name of Captain Lord of the SS *Californian,* accused of failing to come to the aid of the passengers on the *Titanic* during her fateful 1912 voyage, are well documented and have resulted in Captain Lord's recent vindication. The Titanic Historical Society's cooperation in clearing Captain Lord through their excellent magazine, *The Titanic Commutator,* in support of John Carrother's findings, is greatly appreciated. I am grateful to Captain George Sandberg, U.S. Merchant Marine Academy, and Captain Alex Baranov, State Maritime Academy, St. Petersburg, Russia, who both read every page of this manuscript. Their advice and recommendations were immensely helpful.

Last, but not least, I gratefully acknowledge the assistance of my wife, Christine, who despite the constraints of a full-time job and our active six-year old Cathryn, typed, proofread, and edited my third manuscript. I am thankful for her faithful support, encouragement, and patience.

# SURVIVAL GUIDE

## FOR THE MARINER

# CHAPTER ONE

# Before You Sail

Only fools do not fear the sea. Anyone who goes to sea is exposed to some degree of risk. Just falling into relatively warm water can shortly cause hypothermia, cooling the body core temperature to a point where the heart can no longer function. It is not necessary to fall overboard in order to find yourself quickly abandoning your vessel. The capsizing of the *Herald Of Free Enterprise* in 1987 and the sinking of the Epirotiki Lines ship *Oceanos* off the South African coast on August 3, 1991, reveal that even though seafaring has become progressively safer, it can still be a hazardous venture. Safety, however, is purely relative and in every walk of life there is an element of risk. How can we reduce these threats to life? How can we prevent a tragedy such as that aboard the fishing vessel *Aleutian Enterprise*? This account by Captain James Drahos, FNI, appeared in the October 1991 *Seaways* magazine :

> On 22 March 1990, the *Aleutian Enterprise,* a fish processing trawler, was operating in the Bering Sea. Of the 31 crew, nine were missing and presumed dead, when the ship capsized and sank in ten minutes while hauling a large catch of fish on board. The net failed, releasing the large volume of fish on deck. The quick shift of weight increased an existing port list. Rapid and progressive flooding resulted when through-hull openings (for fish processing purposes) were submerged.
>
> Serious safety concerns are raised by this casualty. This class of vessel is uninspected, which means that legal safety requirements are minimal. In recent years, increased casualties in the fishing industry have highlighted many problem areas. Initial Coast Guard and industry efforts focused on voluntary standards. The *Aleutian Enterprise* sinking does not appear to validate the effectiveness of that approach.
>
> The U.S. Coast Guard Marine Board of Investigation report thoroughly details events leading to this tragedy. Although Coast Guard licenses were held by the master, who survived, and the mate

and chief engineer, who did not, there is ample evidence that the responsibilities vested in those certificates of competency were not fully understood, much less discharged. No license was required, but persons holding a license must be held to a higher standard.

Among the contributory causes were the lack of a loadline, which would have required through-hull openings to be fitted with non-return devices. No significant safety training was conducted, nor were drills held aboard the vessel. The general alarm was inoperative. *Although exposure suits were aboard, many crew did not understand how to use them.* In fact, some surviving crew stated that they thought the suits were for "one-time" use only and should not be donned for training or practice! The list is, unfortunately, too long and indicates a complete disregard of the realities of safety at sea.

For too long, the fishing industry has experienced loss of life due to lack of safety and training. Industry and the Coast Guard have put forward the idea that self-regulation could overcome the problems. It has not. Regulation may not be the answer, but it is better than repeating casualties like the loss of the *Aleutian Enterprise*.

In 1987 a U.S. federal judge in Portland, Oregon, ruled that the owner of a fishing vessel that sank off the Oregon coast was negligent in failing to provide a survival suit for every man on board and an inflatable life raft. According to the ruling the 73-foot trawler F/V *Lasseigne* was therefore unseaworthy when she went down on November 15, 1985. Hypothermia and drowning were listed as the causes of death for the two crewmen. Still on board the vessel when it sank was the only survival suit. An inflatable life raft had never been part of the vessel's equipment.

During World War II, when many U.S. merchant ships sailing in convoy were sinking as a result of enemy action, the medical division of the War Shipping Administration published a manual entitled *Safety For Seamen*. Within the manual there were "Ten Commandments for the Merchant Marine." Before you sail it is relevant to review these commandments since they outline the purpose of this book.

1. Keep physically fit.
2. Know how to swim.
3. Be expert in first aid.
4. Make sure all emergency gear is okay and know how to use it.

5. Drill until action is automatic.
6. Stay with your vessel—your responsibility—your best bet unless there is no other alternative.
7. Take the lead if necessary. Get your bearings—plan—then act.
8. Learn how to help survivors.
9. Know how to live if castaway.
10. Understand your fears and anger. Learn how to handle them.

### KEEP PHYSICALLY FIT

In an emergency your life may well depend on your strength and stamina. The time to get in shape is on the beach. You must exercise and eat a well-balanced diet with an emphasis on fresh fruit, vegetables, and fish or poultry. Roughage and plenty of water along with moderate exercise should get you in fairly good shape before you sail. In today's society many people overeat and smoke and have reduced strength and stamina as a result. To survive at sea it is necessary also to be drug free, which means all drugs, including alcohol. Moderation in all things is a good rule of thumb. It is paramount that every seafarer obtain regular medical checkups, especially before going to sea. The night before sailing, ensure you obtain plenty of rest. Too many seafarers believe it is traditional to stay up drinking for one last binge before sailing. An emergency can happen anytime once you board your vessel. You must be alert and vigilant in order to respond properly.

### KNOW HOW TO SWIM

This commandment cannot be overstressed. Swimming is the most important requirement for any seafarer, particularly those who go down to the sea in small vessels. To comply with the first commandment of physical fitness there is no better exercise than swimming. But even with the ability to swim you may not have sufficient strength to save yourself without the help of a life jacket and/or immersion suit. You must be able to take advantage of all measures to improve your buoyancy. You must keep in mind that the number one threat to survival at sea when in the water is hypothermia. Heat loss is 25 percent faster in the water than in the air. If a clothed person can remain still in cold water the survival rate is about 30 percent longer than if engaged in swimming. In this regard the *HELP* position (Heat Escape Lessening Posture, figure 3-2, page 58), will reduce heat loss, since parts of the body in direct contact with the water are minimal.

## BE EXPERT IN FIRST AID

Take advantage of all opportunities to become an expert in first aid. In addition to many books on the subject there are courses offered by community colleges, adult education programs, and the Red Cross. Courses are also offered in handling medical emergencies at sea by the continuing education departments at the U.S. Merchant Marine Academy in Kings Point, New York, and several state maritime academies. Maintain your proficiency in cardiopulmonary resuscitation (CPR) and emergency cardiac care through courses offered by the Red Cross or American Heart Association. Such courses in CPR are valid only for a year and must be taken annually to maintain proficiency. The U.S. Coast Guard recognizes the importance of these courses and has made First Aid and CPR qualification from approved courses a requirement when taking an original marine license or renewing such license. This training is also required in order to earn an Able Seaman endorsement on a U.S. merchant mariner document (i.e., Z-card). This qualification is not only valuable at sea but also ashore since you never know when you may be the only one who can save a person's life. Advanced training in emergency medical technician (EMT) courses could be very useful at sea and are strongly recommended for the seafarer. The manufacturers of life rafts and lifeboats provide instruction and survival manuals with each of their survival craft. Within these manuals are sections devoted to first aid. By reading such sections before you sail you will be in a better position to render first aid immediately when the emergency occurs.

## MAKE SURE ALL EMERGENCY GEAR IS OKAY
## AND KNOW HOW TO USE IT

Before sailing read all instruction manuals for each item of emergency gear that is aboard your vessel. This would include, but is not limited to:

> *Personal Equipment*
> Life buoys
> Life buoys with attached water lights and smoke floats
> Work vests
> Life jackets (personal flotation devices)
> Immersion (survival) suit
> *Lifeboats and/or Life Rafts*
> Launching method and inflation of life rafts
> Equipment on board and when and how to utilize it

*Free-float Arrangements*
*Escape Slides*
    How and when to actuate
*Rescue Boats*
*EPIRBS (emergency position-indicating radio beacons)*
*VHF Radios*
    Emergency frequencies and how to use them
*SAR (Search and Rescue)*
    Methods utilized (see chapter 7)

## SOLAS Regulations

Aboard your vessel, before it sails, ensure all lifesaving equipment is in accordance with SOLAS requirements and that all required safety inspections are up-to-date. If the opportunity presents itself, take part in the inspection and manufacturer servicing of equipment so as to familiarize yourself with the equipment's operation. Practice getting into your immersion suit. It should take a maximum of 60 seconds to don your suit. The immersion suit is a protective suit which reduces loss of body heat by a person in cold water. Since the heat loss from the head and hands is substantial, a suit with a well-insulated hood and good gloves is recommended. Chapter III of the Intergovernmental Maritime Organization (IMO) Regulation which came into force on July 1, 1986, requires that certain types of ships be provided with immersion suits. The Viking "Musk Ox" immersion suit (figure 1-1) is a waterproof, cold-protective suit that complies with this regulation. It has a boiler suit shape and an adjustable harness system based on the elevator principle that ensures it will fit persons from 4'7" up to 6'7" (145-200 cm). It is made of a nylon fabric coated with polyurethane with a layer of Thinsulate for insulation. The orange suit has built-in buoyancy and the gloves are fitted so that they can be taken off without water intrusion. It comes with a harness for helicopter hoist, buddy line, light, whistle, and reflective tape. There is a zipper for narrowing of the legs and the suit comes in its own transportation bag. The total weight of the suit and bag is 13.5 lbs. (6.1 kgs). Your name and the vessel's name should be clearly marked on the suit.

    Hypothermia is a lowering of body core temperature which occurs when a person is immersed in water which is colder than body temperature. As body core temperature drops, the individual gradually loses muscular control as the body tries to conserve warm blood for the brain and other vital organs. At this point, an individual without flotation or

Fig. 1-1.Viking "Musk Ox" immersion suit, SOLAS 1986. Courtesy of Viking USA MIA.

even with flotation in rough water may swallow water and drown. The critical water temperature seems to be around 59°F (15°C). To the unprotected person, water at this temperature is painful and hypothermia seems to progress much faster than in warmer waters.

The U.S. Coast Guard Authorization Act of 1984 added specific requirements to the United States Code (46 U.S.C. 3102) for immersion suits on certain vessels operating in the Atlantic Ocean north of 32°N or south of 32°S, and in all other waters north of 35°N or south of 35°S. Immersion suits were formerly called exposure suits and are sometimes called survival suits. These latitudes were intended to include waters where water temperatures dropped below 15°C at some time during a typical year. This law originally applied to cargo vessels, tank vessels, and mobile offshore drilling units. The statutory notes explain that this law does not limit the authority of the U.S. Coast Guard to require immersion suits on vessels not specifically required under the law to have them. With the passage of the Commercial Fishing Industry Vessel Safety Act of 1988, Congress specifically extended the application of this law to documented commercial fishing vessels operating beyond the boundary line and vessels with more than 16 individuals on board. Casualty records indicate that there have been deaths from hypothermia in accidents involving small vessels which have not been required to carry lifesaving equipment that provides survivors with out-of-the-water flotation. New regulations address this by requiring inflatable life rafts or inflatable buoyant apparatus on certain of these vessels operating in cold waters (i.e., 15°C or less). Because many of these vessels operate seasonally, the regulations are written so as to require this additional equipment only when the vessel is operating in cold water areas. Cold water areas change throughout the year with seasonal water temperature variations. The determination of these cold water areas can be found in the *U.S. Coast Guard Navigation and Vessel Inspection Circular No. 7-91* of 20 May 1991.

Immersion suits are invaluable and knowing how to get into one quickly is well worth the time. The controversy over whether to keep the immersion suit in one's room or on the boat deck in a container can be resolved by having one in each location. Wherever the immersion suit is stowed it must be readily accessible during an emergency. You must keep in mind that the suit is bulky and may hamper your egress if donned in your room, particularly if your room is deep down in the vessel. Wherever located, the suit must be donned before entering the lifeboat or life raft.

## DRILL UNTIL ACTION IS AUTOMATIC

There is no substitute for proper planning in preparing for any possible emergency aboard your vessel. While it is true that out of ten troubles coming down the road at you, nine will run into the ditch before they reach you, the tenth will strike those who are not prepared. All personnel aboard vessels must be ready to respond to a potential emergency. Those traveling aboard passenger vessels should be required to go to their emergency station and abandon ship station before the vessel sails, not merely within 24 hours of sailing. Ship owners, crew, and passengers should not be concerned about disrupting a good time aboard. The Russian passenger vessel, *Admiral*

*Nakhimov,* sank in 1986, one and a half hours after sailing from the port of Novorossiysk on the Black Sea. A collision at 11:12 PM on August 31 with the inbound bulk carrier, *P. Vasev,* resulted in the sinking of the *Admiral Nakhimov* and the drowning of over 400 passengers who had had no time for drilling in emergency procedures. Passengers should be thoroughly instructed in what is required of them during emergencies. Seafarers should rehearse in their minds what they would do for various emergencies that may occur aboard their vessel. Reading instruction manuals, the many publications on safety of life at sea, and the contents of this book should help them in this regard.

As an illustration, the author, while on active duty with the U.S. Navy aboard a destroyer in the Black Sea, had a man go overboard while he was officer-of-the-deck during the midwatch. Constant drills and rehearsal of action to be taken during previous dull watches resulted in all the correct orders and maneuvering required to bring the vessel around on a Williamson turn to make a shipboard recovery possible and save the man from hypothermia and possible drowning. All seafarers should rehearse what they would do and constantly drill until action is automatic.

Knowledge can save your life. It is the best life preserver you can have and one that you can't lose if you keep drilling. It gives you confidence and diminishes fear and anxiety. It is the know-how that is all important. Acquire as much of this knowledge as you can on the beach before you sail. Knowledge includes what the emergency signals are. For larger vessels these signals should be ingrained in every seafarer's mind and the action should be automatic. These emergency signals are:

> *Fire/emergency*—a continuous blast of the ship's whistle supplemented by a continuous ringing of the general alarm bell for *not less than 10 seconds.*
> *Dismissal from fire/emergency stations*—sounding the general alarm bell *three times* supplemented by *three short blasts of the whistle.*
> *Abandon ship*—*seven short and one long blast* on the ship's whistle and the same signal on the general alarm bell.
> *For lifeboats*—
> > Lower boats—*one short blast* on the whistle.
> > Stop lowering boats—*two short blasts* on the whistle.
> > Dismissal from boat stations—*three short blasts* on the whistle.
> > Note: On river boats the ship's bell may be used instead of a whistle.

*Man overboard*—Immediately throw a life buoy preferably with smoke float and water light attached. Hail and pass word to bridge "man overboard port/starboard" and keep man in sight. On some vessels three short blasts of the whistle (Morse code for "O" Oscar) may be used to signal man overboard.

The master of a vessel may establish any other emergency signals in addition to those above to give all officers, crew, and passengers notice of an existing emergency. The master must conduct drills as required and give such instructions as necessary to ensure all hands are familiar with their duties as specified in the station bill (figure 2-1, page 19). It is a sign of courage and intelligence to face possible emergencies and then figure out what you would do and how you would do it, if they should happen. Before you board your vessel figure out what you would be able to do in any of these emergency situations.

## STAY WITH YOUR VESSEL—YOUR RESPONSIBILITY—YOUR BEST BET UNLESS THERE IS NO OTHER ALTERNATIVE

There have been countless cases at sea of a vessel thought to be sinking but remaining afloat while the seafarers went overboard and did not survive. A decision to abandon your vessel is taken only when the master or captain is convinced that everything has been done to save the vessel and losing the vessel is imminent. The saying that "you should never leave the ship until it leaves you" is a wise one since the best lifesaving unit is your own vessel until its loss is obvious and leaves you no other alternative. Before abandoning your vessel, send a distress signal giving your vessel's position, close all watertight doors, stop the propeller, and close all hatches. Collect extra clothing and take a portable radio and extra survival rations to your life raft or lifeboat. Charts and navigational instruments should be brought if time permits. Immersion suits or life jackets should be donned. A muster must be taken to account for all personnel assigned to each abandon ship station. Once the order is given it will be the master's responsibility to have the crew and passengers safely abandon the vessel as quickly as possible. It must be reiterated that many lives have been lost by premature and unnecessary abandonment of vessels. Many seafarers have safely reboarded their abandoned vessels. Ensure all measures have been taken to save the vessel. A crew well trained in damage control and firefighting will ensure that the master or captain makes a wise decision when he orders the abandoning of his or her vessel. The master and ship's officers should discuss damage stability prior to departure as part of their contingency planning. Many of the new computer stability programs have a damage stability feature which will speed the task considerably. However, there is no time for calculations during an emergency, and the master should not hesitate to give an order to abandon the vessel pending such calculations.

## TAKE THE LEAD IF NECESSARY—GET YOUR BEARINGS—PLAN—THEN ACT

Rehearse in your mind before you sail what you would have to do if you had to abandon your vessel and you were the most senior or experienced person in a life raft or lifeboat. Take inventory, stand back, and take a look at the whole picture. Be calm, but then lead. Follow the steps outlined in chapter 4. Basically, you must assign all aboard duties according to their capabilities, however small. Assign watches. Everyone must have a job to do and establish a definite routine. Enforce discipline vigorously if necessary. Even if resented it will benefit all aboard. Locate your position, set goals and a definite objective, and stick to it. This will bring about reassurance. The desire to live can keep all alive. A calm frame of mind is contagious. It improves the chances of surviving to an extraordinary degree and actually will keep you in better physical condition. Hope is as important as food and water. It helps you to follow the few simple rules on which life depends and prevents destructive behavior. Begin discussions, no matter how trivial the subjects. Find something to talk over in order to divert the minds of all aboard. For survival, nothing can take the place of people who keep up their spirits, who are fair in the distribution of rations, and who preserve a certain sense of discipline which keeps up self-respect. Tolerance and patience make life more endurable but sometimes bullying helps. Anger can give people strength. Leadership is the key to survival and as a leader you must lead. All one has to do to reinforce this concept is to read the account of Captain William Bligh and his heroic leadership while navigating a longboat 4,000 miles. Mutiny on his vessel, H.M.S. *Bounty,* led by his mate Fletcher Christian, resulted in Captain Bligh and 17 loyal crew members being cast adrift on April 28, 1789, near the Friendly Islands in the southern Pacific. Through his leadership and seamanship skills he navigated his open boat 4,000 miles westward and landed in Timor in the East Indies. In May 1866 the clippership *Hornet* sank on a passage from New York to San Francisco via Cape Horn. The master,

Captain Mitchell, navigated his longboat and 15 crew members over 4,000 miles in 43 days from near the equator to the islands of Hawaii. All survived, which is a tribute to Captain Mitchell, an experienced seaman who recognized the need to take command and give hope and courage to those with him. It shows the leadership needed by any seafarer in a similar situation. In most cases today, with present search and rescue capabilities, these long voyages are not advocated. It is best to stay in the area for the most rapid rescue.

## LEARN HOW TO HELP SURVIVORS

Your vessel may pick up survivors. Some of them may be nervous and upset. Treat them gently and quietly. They may want someone to stay with them for reassurance—they can't believe they are safe. They often wake up terrified, thinking that they are still on the life raft/ lifeboat. Speak quietly. Convince the survivor that he or she is being taken care of. Don't try to stop anyone from weeping, or yelling— encourage the survivor to get it out of his or her system. Stop aggressive behavior only if it is disturbing or becomes too exhausting for the survivor. In that case give the survivor a half-grain of phenobarbital and talk reassuringly. Being rough with a survivor who has been through an ordeal does not help. It will only make the survivor angry or increase his or her nervousness. Some survivors may feel guilty because they survived and their shipmates did not. They may feel that they should have done more to help the mates that perished. Be comforting, telling them that they did all that was possible. Keep a close watch, since a deep depression may set in and suicide is possible.

A survivor who has been in a life raft or lifeboat for some time where water intake was low may easily go into shock due to poor blood circulation. If the survivor suddenly rises to his or her feet the blood pressure will drop suddenly and fainting will result. Help and support the survivors during the rescue. Bring them to a horizontal position as soon as possible in order to keep up blood pressure. Administer liquids in small quantities. Food should be light until the bowel again functions normally. Other conditions may need attention. Examine each survivor carefully and look for:

General condition—shock, effects of thirst, hunger, and exposure
Injuries
Burns

Frostbite
Swellings
Numb or paralyzed arms, legs, fingers, or toes
Unusual pain when touched

If the case is beyond you, ask for help by radio. It may be possible to have a doctor flown in. Otherwise, advice can be obtained by radio. Describe as in this example:

Male, age 48, in life raft two weeks, on ship two days, emaciated, pulse is weak, temperature 103° for two days or longer, cough, pain in chest, second degree burn over most of one leg, infected for two weeks, request advice.

In addition to physical care it is important to maintain the psychological care of all the survivors.

## LEARN HOW TO LIVE IF CASTAWAY

Before you sail read accounts of survivors who were castaways. Go through the procedures outlined in chapter 6. Your priorities become shelter, water, food, and rescue with the equipment available to you. You must set up camp, organize, and maintain the same leadership exhibited in the life raft or lifeboat. Action will be taken according to the type of climate and the region in which survivors have made landfall. Activities, as far as the strength of the survivors will allow, should be encouraged in order to build morale and prepare for the ultimate rescue. Build at least three fires to signal searching aircraft or vessels. It may be advisable to travel if you are convinced that rescue is not coming. You must maintain the will to survive. Survivors never give up.

## UNDERSTAND YOUR FEARS AND ANGER— LEARN HOW TO HANDLE THEM

### Fear

Everyone in danger is afraid—even more while the danger threatens than before it arrives. This is normal and natural. Society has conveyed the opinion that to admit it to oneself makes one a coward. That is simply not true. The strain of feeling afraid and hiding it can be tremendous. The body and mind must carry a double load. Heroes feel afraid and admit it. To carry on in spite of fear is courage. The first principle of psychological first aid is to admit, at least to yourself, what you are feeling. This goes for all feelings, not fear alone. The second principle is to know what to do about it. There is nothing like confidence to fight fear. You can obtain confidence from a lot of things. If you have drilled until you can *act without thinking* you begin to feel better as soon as you get going. There is also the knowledge that a lot of other survivors have made it. Experience tells you that your chances with present-day equipment are excellent. If you are not afraid of being afraid you will be able to think through any situation and make decisions. This gives you a feeling of control and that is an improvement. As soon as you begin to plan and act you immediately feel better and you really are better. Feelings are as much a part of the body as heat is part of a burning log. No matter what you feel, the body goes through a corresponding change. When you are frightened the heart beats faster, more blood is pumped through it, the muscles get tense, more sugar for fuel is sent into the blood, and you breathe faster so that more oxygen will be sent around the body. You may be paralyzed just for the moment or longer or you may find yourself doing something about the situation in a hurry. It is natural to be nervous. Getting accustomed to such emergencies is a help and this experience will make it easier to endure the next time. For the present emergency know that you will be afraid, admit it to yourself, and with training, rehearsals, and drills you can *act without thinking*.

## Anger

It is natural to become irritable and explode with minimal provocation when under strain. Fear and anger are first cousins. There are two ways to handle anger: directly by confronting it and possibly fighting it out, or indirectly with competition. Even trying to win at cards relieves a lot of tension. Share troubles and be concerned with problems your shipmates may be having. A trouble shared with someone is no longer so difficult. Do not allow personnel to turn anger inward resulting in desperation and hopelessness to the point where suicide may be contemplated. Do not allow inner rage to take over. Immediately get going on something active and constructive. Fight the wind and seas. Cast overboard loss of faith, anxiety, overfatigue, fear, and anger. Keep aboard common sense, understanding, talking it over, and confidence. Rehearse these things before you sail.

## CONCLUSION

Maintain the will to survive. Never give up. Before you sail know anticipated duties on the station bill. On smaller vessels promulgate a float plan with estimated times of arrival, estimated times of departure (ETAs, ETDs), and locations for various parts of the voyage along with communication capabilities. The Pacific Vessel Owners Association promulgated these seven steps to survival in a video of 1987 entitled "Safety Equipment and Survival Procedures":

1. *Recognition*—Recognizing sources of dangers and potential emergencies.
2. *Inventory*—Stand back, take stock, and look at the whole picture—then act.
3. *Shelter*—Vessel is best shelter, then survival suit, then life raft or lifeboat—remember cold is a killer.
4. *Signals*—Alert someone by any means: VHF, beacons, dyes, flares, smoke, mirror, etc. Ensure signals are bigger and/or brighter and/or different.
5. *Water*—Drink fresh water.
6. *Food*—Don't eat without fresh water.
7. *Play*—Keep morale up—survivors never give up.

Finally, think in terms of your own *Personal Survival Kit*. Items to carry in a duffel size waterproof bag could include the following:

| | |
|---|---|
| Watch cap | Candles |
| Extra clothing | Extra glasses |
| Spare blanket | Fishing kit |
| Plastic garbage bags | Food supplies |
| Whistle | Seasick pills |
| Mirror | Medicine |
| Flashlight | First aid kit |
| Survival handbook | Extra line |
| Waterproof matches | Folding/pocket knife |
| Lighter | Aluminum foil |
| Fire starter | |

There are other items that should be included but are not safe or feasible if your survival kit is in your room. In another kit near the abandon ship station you could include:

Water in a one-gallon or one-liter container
EPIRB
Handheld radio
Flares and rockets
Navigational kit

With the knowledge and equipment above, in addition to what is provided on your vessel, all you need is morale and the will to survive (and good luck!).

# CHAPTER TWO

# On Your Vessel

The steps which follow depend on the type of vessel that you will sail on. They apply to larger vessels but can be modified to any size vessel.

## CHECK STATION BILL

Once aboard your vessel consult the station bill (figure 2-1) which will give the alarm signals and emergency duties for every member of the crew. With reduced crews on many vessels it will be necessary to consolidate emergency duties and responsibilities. An emergency squad and a support squad should be designated for fire and emergency. For abandon ship the crew on cargo vessels may utilize a lifeboat or life raft from either side of the vessel depending on the most favorable side. The lifeboat or life raft number may therefore not be indicated on the station bill. *Memorize* the signals and your duties. The corresponding number and duties along with the signals should be fixed to each bunk as a crew station card or bunk card (figure 2-2) in a frame into which the card can be easily inserted. This card may be issued when signing on. Ensure the duties match with the station bill. If you are assigned the duty of being in charge of a lifeboat or life raft, a muster list should be provided giving the name and abandon ship duties of each member of your crew. These duties, set forth in the station bill and muster list, include assembling and guiding the passengers (if on a passenger vessel) and assisting them with the adjustment of their life preservers or personal flotation devices. Usual procedure is to have lifeboat or life raft muster lists typed and pasted on smooth wooden forms, then covered with plastic or a clear varnish to protect them from moisture. One should be at each station and it is recommended you keep one in your room. If you are in charge it is also your responsibility to keep them current to reflect all crew changes. In consulting the station bill memorize any other signals the master may have prescribed which he deemed necessary, such as signals for assembling the emergency squad. The station bill should indicate the channel for all those in charge of various emergency or abandon ship stations to switch to for

# EMERGENCY STATION BILL

## M/V JULIUS HAMMER

**SIGNAL:** CONTINUOUS SOUNDING OF THE SHIPS GENERAL ALARM BELLS ACCOMPANIED BY ONE LONG BLAST ON THE SHIPS WHISTLE FOR AT LEAST TEN SECONDS

### EMERGENCY SQUAD

MUSTER AT EMERGENCY GEAR LOCKER PORT SIDE OF BARGE MACHINERY SPACE

CHIEF MATE - IN CHARGE FOR DECK AND ACCOMMODATION EMERGENCIES

1ST ASST. ENGINEER - IN CHARGE FOR ENGINE ROOM EMERGENCIES

BOSUN

ABLE SEAMAN OFF WATCH

ABLE SEAMAN OFF WATCH

ORDINARY SEAMAN

### SUPPORT SQUAD

MUSTER ON BOAT DECK

SECOND MATE - IN CHARGE

SECOND ASST. ENGINEER

ORDINARY SEAMAN

STEWARD/COOK

UTILITY

WIPER

CADET

### SPECIAL DUTIES

MASTER - IN COMMAND ON BRIDGE

CHIEF ENGINEER - ENGINE CONTROL ROOM IN CHARGE

THIRD MATE - ON BRIDGE, RELIEVE THE WATCH

THIRD ASST. ENGINEER - ENGINE CONTROL ROOM RELIEVE THE WATCH

ABLE SEAMAN ON WATCH - HELMSMAN

DECK ENGINEER - BARGE MACHINERY SPACE, START GENERATOR, HYDRAULIC SYSTEM, STANDBY FIRE PUMP AND FOAM SYSTEM

CADET - ENGINE CONTROL ROOM, ASSIST AS DIRECTED

SUPERNUMERARIES - MUSTER ON BOAT DECK

THE FOLLOWING LICENSED PERSONNEL ARE RESPONSIBLE FOR THE READINESS OF ALL SAFETY EQUIPMENT
### THIRD MATE

## ABANDON SHIP STATIONS

**SIGNAL:** 7 OR MORE SHORT BLASTS FOLLOWED BY 1 LONG BLAST ON THE SHIPS WHISTLE ACCOMPANIED BY THE SAME SIGNAL ON THE SHIPS GENERAL ALARM BELLS

| | |
|---|---|
| MASTER IN OVERALL COMMAND | CHIEF ENGINEER |
| CHIEF MATE IN CHARGE OF LOWERING BOAT | 1ST ASST. ENGINEER START LIFEBOAT ENGINE |
| SECOND MATE BRING NAVIGATION GEAR | 2ND ASST. ENGINEER START LIFEBOAT ENGINE |
| THIRD MATE BRING LIFEBOAT RADIO & EPIRB | 3RD ASST. ENGINEER ASSIST AS DIRECTED |
| BOSUN LOWER BOAT | WIPER ASSIST AS DIRECTED |
| ABLE SEAMAN RELEASE FWD GRIPES | CADET ASSIST AS DIRECTED |
| ABLE SEAMAN RELEASE AFT GRIPES | CADET ASSIST AS DIRECTED |
| ABLE SEAMAN ASSIST AS DIRECTED | STEWARD/COOK BRING BLANKETS AND WATER |
| ORDINARY SEAMAN LEAD OUT SEA PAINTER | UTILITY ASSIST SUPERNUMERARIES |
| ORDINARY SEAMAN LEAD OUT SEA PAINTER | DECK ENG ASSIST AS DIRECTED |

Fig. 2-1. Station bill. Courtesy of Captain George Sandberg, USMS.

**CENTRAL GULF LINES, INC.**

**CREW STATION CARD**

S. S.___GREEN ISLAND___

Date___DECEMBER 5, 1988___

Name___Capt. Robert Meurn___

Rating_____

Article No.___N/A___

Boat Station___NUMBER TWO___

__Assist as Directed__

__Fire or__
Emergency Station__Windward wing of__

__Bridge. Assist as Directed.__

__(See other Side)__

INITIALED_____ Master

INITIALED_____CHIEF OFFICER

CG-1617 (R7/85)

**EMERGENCY SIGNALS**

REPORT TO FIRE STATIONS — Continuous ringing of ship's bell and general alarm bell.

DISMISS FROM FIRE STATIONS — Three rings on general alarm and three blasts on whistle.

REPORT TO BOAT STATIONS — More than six short and one long blast on whistle supplemented by same signal on general alarm.

LOWER BOATS — One short blast on whistle.

STOP LOWERING BOATS — Two short blasts on whistle.

DISMISS FROM BOAT STATIONS — Three short blasts on whistle.

SIGNATURE

Fig. 2-2. Crew station card. Courtesy of U.S. Coast Guard.

communications by walkie-talkie. Check how to get to these stations quickly and in the dark. Learn alternative routes in case your route is impeded by fire, smoke, or the ingress of water. A watertight door en route may be jammed or the passageway may be obstructed in any number of ways. Therefore, all alternative routes to your stations should be explored.

## STOW PERSONAL SURVIVAL KIT

The next step will be to stow your personal survival kit, described at the end of chapter 1, in an area of easy accessibility. Contemplate carefully whether it would be best to stow your kit in your room or at the abandon ship station. Depending on the type of vessel, it would probably be best to stow it in the vicinity of your bunk or where it is readily accessible. This kit, with a walkie-talkie for those crew members designated, should be taken to all abandon ship drills.

## CHECK LIFE JACKET

Check your life jacket/preserver. The general U.S. requirements and markings are shown in figure 2-3. There must be one approved life preserver for each person carried on board distributed throughout cabins and additional numbers provided for personnel on watch in the engine room, bridge, and bow lookout on larger vessels. Many foreign vessels have the life jackets placed in storage boxes on the boat deck. If children are carried a suitable number of children's life preservers should be provided. Each preserver should be stamped with the word "PASSED," inspector's initials, port, and date. Failures must be removed from the vessel. Each life preserver should have at least 2000 square centimeters of retroreflective material attached to front, back, and sides. Kapok and fibrous glass life preservers, which do not have plastic covered pad inserts, are not allowed. There should be an attached light and whistle (ensure they both work). The light should comply with the IMO requirement for eight hours' duration. The light may be automatically activated on entry into the water or have a dry cell activated by a short lanyard. These dry cell life jacket lights should have a "press to test" faculty to ensure the light will work. The best lights available are of the strobe type.

Although personal flotation devices may look similar there are considerable differences between them. The differences go far beyond color, style, comfort, wearability, and other marketing considerations and are summarized as follows:

*Type I* (wearable)—Provides the greatest buoyancy and protection. Designed to turn most unconscious persons in the water from a face-down position to a vertical or slightly backward position. Adult size provides a minimum of 22 pounds of buoyancy; child size a minimum of 11 pounds of buoyancy.

*Type II* (wearable)—Designed to turn its wearer to a vertical or slightly backward position, but the action is not as pronounced or effective as a Type I. The adult size provides a minimum of $15\frac{1}{2}$ pounds of buoyancy while the child size provides a minimum of 11 pounds buoyancy, and an infant size provides 7 pounds of buoyancy.

*Type III* (wearable)—Designed so wearers can place themselves in a vertical or slightly backward position. Although this type of personal flotation device has the same buoyancy as a Type II, it provides a smaller turning moment. However, it is more comfortable to wear.

# LIFE PRESERVERS

## GENERAL REQUIREMENTS (46 CFR 160.001)

- Of such construction, materials and workmanship that it can perform its function in all weathers and temps. which may be expected in its normal usage.

- Capable of supporting in fresh water for 48 hours a minimum of 16.5 lbs.

- Must not depend on air compartments, inflation or loose granulated material.

- Must be simple in design, reversible and capable of being quickly adjusted to securely fit the wearer.

- Shall be of highly visible color such as Indian Orange.

- Shall support the wearer in an upright or slightly backward position, and support the head so that the face of an unconscious person is held above the water.

- Shall be capable of turning the wearer in the water to the safe flotation position described above.

- Shall not be deteriorated or rendered unable to perform its function by oils.

# LIFE PRESERVERS

## MARKINGS (46 CFR 160.002 AND 160.005)

Each life preserver must have the following clearly marked in waterproof lettering on a front section:

In letters three-fourths of an inch or more in height:

1. Adult (for persons weighing over 90 lbs.); or
2. Child (for persons weighing less than 90 lbs.).

In letters capable of being read at a distance of 2 feet:

the type of personal flotation device, that it is inspected and tested in accordance with U.S. Coast Guard regulations, the type of buoyant material used and the minimum buoyant force in pounds, a warning not to tear or snag the inner plastic cover, persons it is approved for Adults (90 lbs or more) or Child (less than 90 lbs.), the U.S. Coast Guard approval number, model number, name and address of manufacturer or distributor, and the lot number.

Fig. 2-3. Life preserver general requirements and markings. Courtesy of Captain Richard Beadon.

*Type IV* (throwable)—This type is designed to be thrown to a person in the water; it must be kept available for immediate use.

*Type V* and new Type V Hybrid (wearable)—Special personal flotation devices accepted for use only in a particular context—for example, a harness/personal flotation device for windsurfing, or a vest with head protector for canoeing. Since August 1986, a variation of this category, called a Type V Hybrid, is acceptable for use on all recreational craft. Consequently, having a Type V Hybrid aboard your boat, safely stowed away in a locker, does not satisfy any U.S. Coast Guard requirements. The Type V Hybrid contains a small amount of flotation material, and can be inflated orally or with a $CO_2$ cartridge to increase flotation to roughly Type II flotation levels.

One Type I, II, III, IV, V, or V Hybrid is required for each person aboard any vessel less than 16 feet in length. If it is a Type V Hybrid it must be worn, not carried. For vessels 16 feet and not more than 65 feet in length one Type I, II, III, or V Hybrid is required for each person aboard. For commercial vessels, charter boats, and U.S. merchant vessels one Type I vest with reflective tape, personal flotation device, light, and whistle is required for each person. Finally, follow the donning instructions (figure 2-4), which should be posted in each cabin.

### CHECK IMMERSION SUIT

The immersion suit is the next important item to check once you board your vessel. One approved-type suit is required for each person on board vessels operating between 32°N and 32°S in the Atlantic Ocean or between 35°N and 35°S in all other waters. U.S. requirements along with required drills and stowage are found in figure 2-5. The SOLAS 1983 Amendments, Chapter III, to SOLAS 1974 have different requirements for covered and open lifeboats as they pertain to immersion suits and thermal protective aids (figure 2-6). Vessels with totally enclosed lifeboats on both sides do not require immersion suits or thermal protective aids as stipulated in Regulation 27.3.2. Thermal protective aids are required for only 10 percent of each boat's rated capacity. For any open boats, however, the number of immersion suits and thermal protective aids are determined by Regulation 27.3.2, which is calculated as follows on non-U.S. flag vessels:

$$x - 3 = y$$

where x = rated capacity of open boat, 3 = number of immersion suits, and y = number of thermal protective aids.

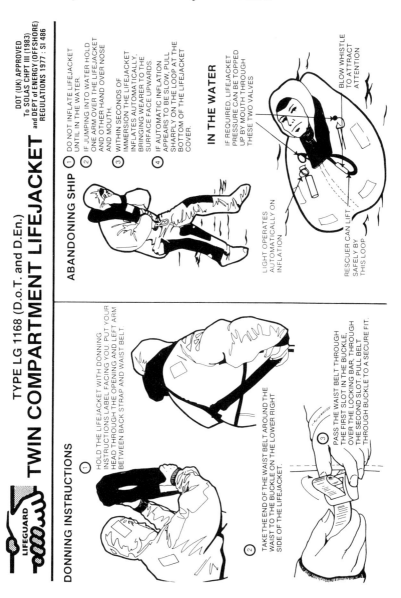

Fig. 2-4. Life preserver donning instructions. Courtesy of ML Lifeguard Equipment Limited, UK.

**SUMMARY OF MAIN REQUIREMENTS (46 CFR 160.171)**

**Construction**

- Must cover wearer's entire body except nose and eyes. Must be capable of being worn inside-out or obviously in only one way.
- Must allow the wearer to jump into the water from a height of at least 4.5 m (approx 15 ft.) without injury, or damage to the suit. Each seal or closure must be designed so that following a jump into the water from a height of 4.5 meters there is no undue ingress of water into the suit.
- Primary color must be vivid reddish orange. Exterior must resist tearing and abrasion when tested. Hardware must be capable of being easily operated by the wearer.
- Arm gloves must allow sufficient dexterity for wearer after being immersed in water at 5 C for an hour. Legs must have enough room for a work shoe to be worn inside and designed to minimize free air in legs when wearer enters water head first.
- Must be capable of being worn comfortably over clothing. Sizes - child, adult and oversize.
- Must be fitted with retroreflective material and an approved light.

**SUMMARY OF PERFORMANCE REQUIREMENTS (46 CFR 160.171)**

**Instructions.**

- Must be designed so that person can don the suit correctly within two minutes of reading instructions.
- Each suit must have instructions for donning and use. Instructions in English and not more than 50 words. Instructions must be on exterior of storage case or on waterproof card attached to case or suit.
- Instructions must also be available for mounting on bulkhead. Placard must be in English, must include illustrations, and must include warning as to risk of entrapment in a compartment due to buoyancy of suit.
- Instructions, together with instructions for care and repair and other information must be available aboard vessel in loose leaf format suitable for inclusion into training manual.

**SUMMARY OF PERFORMANCE REQUIREMENTS (46 CFR 160.171)**

**Performance.**

- Must turn unconscious person in the water from any position to one where the mouth is clear of the water in five seconds without any assistance. Must have means of preventing water spray from entering wearer's mouth.
- Must have a stable floating position in which wearer's head is tilted to a position between 30 to 80 degrees above the horizontal with the mouth at least 4.75 inches above the water, or, if inflatable bladder worn then 2 inches above the water without the bladder being inflated.
- In standing position the wearer must have unrestricted vision 60 degrees on either side of straight ahead. Must allow a standing wearer to move head and eyes up and down far enough to see both feet and a spot directly overhead.
- Following one jump into water from height of 4.5 m, wearer's body core temperature must not fall more than 3.6 F after being immersed in calm circulating water at a temperature of 32 - 35.6 degrees F.
- Must not be damaged by storage in temperatures from - 22 F and 149 F. Must prevent sustained burning after it is totally enveloped in fire for a period of 2 seconds. Must be useable after 24 hours exposure to diesel oil.

Fig. 2-5. Immersion suit requirements. Courtesy of Captain Richard Beadon.

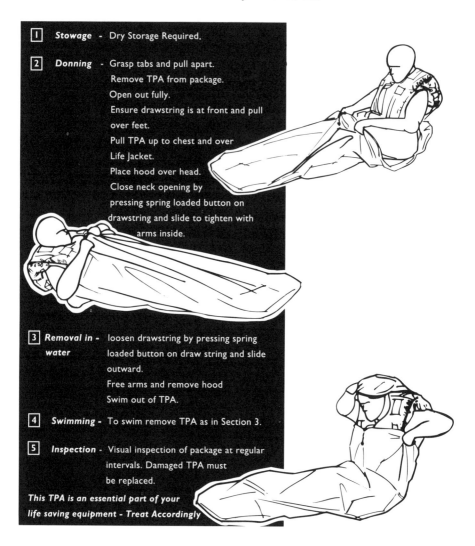

1. **Stowage** - Dry Storage Required.

2. **Donning** - Grasp tabs and pull apart.
   Remove TPA from package.
   Open out fully.
   Ensure drawstring is at front and pull
   over feet.
   Pull TPA up to chest and over
   Life Jacket.
   Place hood over head.
   Close neck opening by
   pressing spring loaded button on
   drawstring and slide to tighten with
   arms inside.

3. **Removal in - water** loosen drawstring by pressing spring
   loaded button on draw string and slide
   outward.
   Free arms and remove hood
   Swim out of TPA.

4. **Swimming** - To swim remove TPA as in Section 3.

5. **Inspection** - Visual inspection of package at regular
   intervals. Damaged TPA must
   be replaced.

*This TPA is an essential part of your
life saving equipment - Treat Accordingly*

Fig. 2-6. Thermal protective aid. Courtesy of R. Perry and Company Ltd., UK.

If the opportunity presents itself, test your suit on deck, or, even better, in the water. Ensure that the size is correct as they come in child/ small adult, adult, and adult/oversize. All suits must be maintained in good and serviceable condition. This means operable waterproof zippers, valves, seams which do not leak, and no unrepaired holes. Maintenance instructions are provided with each approved suit. The date of the last inspection should be indicated on the outside of the storage bag.

The U.S. Coast Guard does not approve inspection and repair facilities for immersion suits. However, manufacturers recommend that inspections be performed by one of their representatives in a facility equipped to do a complete inspection, including leak testing. Repairs can be made, as long as they restore the suit to a condition equivalent to the originally approved state. This requires the use of materials and methods recommended by the manufacturer. Repairs should be made by persons with the experience or training to work with those materials and methods. Most problems with immersion suits involve the following:

1. *Zippers*—Zippers can corrode if not properly maintained. The manufacturer's recommended zipper lubricant should be used. Paraffin should be avoided, especially in cold climates. The teeth that actually secure the waterproof zipper are the small teeth on the "inside" of the zipper. A little corrosion on these teeth can block the slider, or damage the teeth so the zipper does not operate. If a closed zipper can be separated when probed with a dull table knife, the zipper needs to be replaced.
2. *Seams*—Immersion suit seams are stress points and are often the source of leaks. Suits should be leak checked periodically, and leaking seams repaired.
3. *Inflatable collar*—If a suit has an inflatable collar, it should be inflated periodically and allowed to stand overnight. If the collar does not stay firmly inflated overnight, it should be repaired or replaced. Inflation tubes should be complete, securely attached, and not have kinks which would prevent the wearer from inflating the collar.
4. *Drying*—When suits are used in the water or become wet for any reason, they should be rinsed with fresh water and not be stowed until completely dry. This usually requires hanging the suit in a dry well-ventilated area, first turned inside out and then right side out. Complete drying may take two days.

*Stowage.* Immersion suits are intended for abandon ship use. The regulations require that they be stowed so they are readily accessible to the individuals for whom they are intended, from both the individuals' normal workstation and berthing area. This is to prevent searching throughout the vessel to find them in an emergency. The stowage container for immersion suits must *not* be capable of being locked.

1. Immersion suits are often stowed in or near berthing areas. Duplicate immersion suits may be required for persons whose normal workstation is not near their berthing area.

2. Suits should not be stacked more than a few high, or be kept on the bottom of a stack of any other equipment. Excessive stacking can compress suits at the bottom of the pile, eventually damaging the buoyant insulating foam.

*Marking.* Each suit must have a waterproof marking identifying the vessel and/or the individual to whom the suit is assigned or belongs. The manufacturer's recommended methods and materials should be used for this marking, since not all inks and paints are compatible with immersion suit materials.

*Retroreflective material.* Approved suits are equipped with retroreflective material when they are manufactured. The material is positioned on the suit to make a person wearing the suit in the water as visible as possible under nighttime search conditions. The pattern is not necessarily the same as that used on a life jacket or other personal flotation device.

1. If the retroreflective material deteriorates or must be replaced for some other reason, new material should be positioned in the same place as the old material.
2. Unapproved suits should also be equipped with retroreflective material. An approved suit of a similar type should be used as an example for the placement of material.
3. Only Coast Guard approved retroreflective material should be used. This material is tested for flexibility, adhesion, and optical performance under cold, wet, and oily conditions. The application directions supplied with the retroreflective material should be carefully followed.

*Recommendations.* The U.S. Coast Guard makes two recommendations for immersion suits. They are:

1. Carriage of immersion suits should also be considered for warmer waters, especially if the vessel will operate far offshore in winter where prompt rescue may not be available.
2. Immersion suits are often designed to carry small items of equipment. Whistles, dye markers, aerial flares, and small Class B emergency position-indicating radio beacons (EPIRBs) can all help attract attention and are recommended.

## SECURE ROOM FOR SEA

Be sure to secure your room for sea. Unsecured books, luggage, furniture, radios, cassette, and compact disc players, etc., become dangerous missiles when the vessel commences to roll heavily. If the vessel is stiff with a rapid roll the acceleration of these missiles increases. Prepare for the worst. Experienced seafarers can always be found securing their rooms before the vessel sails because they know the tremendous force the sea can impart. Do not overload any circuits. Ensure that any equipment to be plugged in is checked by the vessel's electrician.

## TOUR YOUR VESSEL

A tour of the vessel is a must. The time it will take is determined by the size and number of spaces aboard. Inspect all areas that you will normally be standing watch or working in. In all compartments find two ways of egress and the quickest route to your emergency station and life raft or lifeboat. Get in the habit early on of carrying with you a working *flashlight, sharp knife, white handkerchief,* and *whistle* (in case you get lost or fall overboard). Let someone know that you are going on a tour. This also applies when working in any enclosed area aboard. Do not go into any compartment that may have been closed for a long period of time, i.e., a chain locker where rusting might have depleted some of the oxygen or a refrigerated/chilled compartment where there may be an increase of $CO_2$. Deep tanks and forepeak tanks that have been sealed up for a long time may also be deficient in oxygen. On your tour, as well as when the vessel is underway, do not wear loose clothing, rings, gold chains, long hair, or anything that can snag. Remember the motto "One hand for yourself and one hand for the ship." Hold onto both ladder handrails in case a rung is loose. Go down steep ladders backwards facing into the steps. Wear safety shoes on deck—do not wear shower clogs anywhere except in the shower. Watch for tripping hazards such as pad eyes and door sills. Look out for low overheads. Do not step on piping. Watch out for slipping hazards and remember oil and water don't mix but are very slippery on deck. During any cargo operations walk on the offshore side to stay out of the way of slings or pallet loads. On a tanker avoid the hose connection areas. On a container vessel do not walk under containers being loaded or discharged and watch out for lashings being cast off by longshoremen or crew members. Stay out of the bights of mooring lines; don't step over taut lines or step on them. Be careful of nylon lines stretching.

## INSPECT SAFETY EQUIPMENT

Next, inspect safety equipment aboard—if not as soon as possible in port, make your inspection soon after the vessel gets under way. Appliances to be inspected include lifeboats, life rafts, escape slides (if utilized aboard), life buoys, distress signals, and emergency gear or repair lockers.

## Lifeboats

The inspection of types of lifeboats will begin with the increasingly historical relic: the open lifeboat, the hand-propelled lifeboat complete with mast and sail, and the open motor-propelled lifeboat. From July 1, 1986, all new built vessels of 85 meters in length are required to have totally enclosed lifeboats on board. For most merchant vessels now in service these requirements went into effect on July 1, 1991. SOLAS Regulation III/6.1 states, "Every lifeboat shall be propelled by a compression ignition or diesel engine." Therefore, the backbreaking chores of rowing or hand propelling a lumbering lifeboat away from a sinking vessel may soon fade away. Experienced mariners complain that an open boat is difficult to launch, exposes occupants to physical injury when being lowered down the side of a listing ship, may be damaged from bashing against the hull, and may be capsized or swamped once in the water. Crew members lowering the boat, moreover, are left on deck, faced with climbing down a Jacob's ladder, climbing down lifelines to the lifeboat, or diving overboard. Open boat passengers may be exposed to frigid weather and cold seas and if the portable cover aboard is not erected may suffer hypothermia. Newer, totally enclosed lifeboats, free-fall boats, rescue boats, survival capsules, and partially enclosed lifeboats are described briefly following general requirements.

General U.S. requirements for lifeboats include:

1. Normally being *pointed* on both ends to make it more seaworthy,
2. Capability of maintaining *positive stability* when fully loaded (including persons) and open to sea,
3. A *maximum capacity of 150 people*—Capacity = length × breadth × depth × .64 ÷ 10.
4. *Construction* of steel, aluminum, or fibrous glass reinforced plastic. No wood was permitted after 1963. Due to electrolysis, steel and iron tools should never be left in aluminum boats.
5. *Buoyancy* or *stability* to be provided by built-in independent air tanks, buoyant material such as fiberglass, or buoyancy units of polystyrene or unicellular plastic foam.
6. *Rudder* made of wood or metal; watertight and hollow so it will float.

7. *Automatic plug* to ensure complete drainage of boat and provided with a cap and chain to attach to the boat.

8. *A disengaging apparatus* designed to release both ends of a lifeboat simultaneously under tension, affected by partially rotating a shaft (usually 180°) which shall be continuous and extend from point of contact with the hooks. The control shall be readily accessible and painted bright red with the letters "DANGER—LEVER DROPS BOAT" or "DANGER—LEVER RELEASES HOOKS." Area in way from keel to side benches painted white in a 12-inch-wide strip to provide a contrasting color.

9. *Grab rails* for one-half the length of the boat or grablines festooned in 18-inch bights with a seine float in each bight if grabline doesn't float.

10. *Markings:*

   (a) On *both* bows:
   1. Boat number even to port, odd to starboard in 3-inch numbers.
   2. Name of vessel in 3-inch letters.
   3. Port of registry in 3-inch letters.
   4. Cubical contents in $1\frac{1}{2}$-inch letters.
   5. Number of persons in $1\frac{1}{2}$-inch letters.

   (b) Name of vessel and port of registry on each stern in 3-inch letters.

   (c) On *two thwarts* number of persons in 3-inch letters.

   (d) International orange painted on footings, side benches, and thwarts.

   (e) *Oars* to be marked with vessel's name.

   (f) *Builder's plate* on bow inscribed with manufacturer's name, serial number, approval number, boat dimensions, cubic capacity, air tank capacity, number of persons, date approved for, weight, and inspector's initials.

The nomenclature of an open and hand-propelled lifeboat is shown in figures 2-7a and 2-7b. The automatic drain and Rottmer releasing lever and associated hook are shown in figure 2-8. On your inspection ensure the drain(s) is (are) open and the releasing lever is in the secure position with safety pin inserted and associated hooks secure and preventer bar in its proper place. Hand-propelled or fleming gear is required in boats carrying between 60 and 100 persons. The gear should be tested ahead and astern for five minutes each week and should be examined for condensation in the gear box in cold weather. In the water, the hand-propelled boat

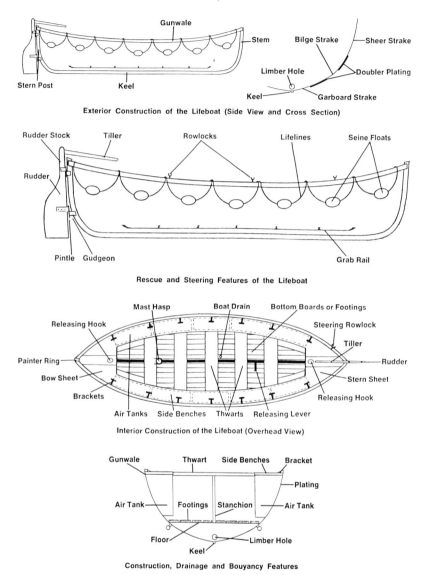

Fig. 2-7a. Lifeboat nomenclature. Courtesy of U.S. Coast Guard.

must be capable of making three knots in both light and load condition. Motor lifeboats are required on all U.S. passenger vessels and on vessels of 1600 tons and over on an international voyage. The number and class are determined by the U.S. Coast Guard, but minimally they must be readily started in all conditions and have sufficient fuel for 24

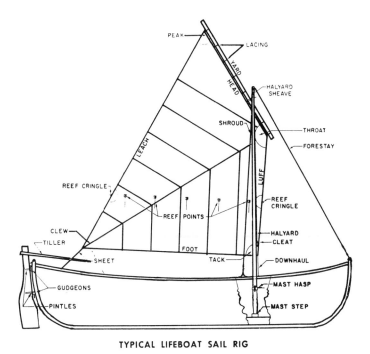

TYPICAL LIFEBOAT SAIL RIG

Fig. 2-7b. Lifeboat nomenclature. Courtesy of U.S. Coast Guard.

hours' operation with a speed ahead of six knots when loaded with persons and equipment. Class 2 motor lifeboats have, in addition, a searchlight and class 3 motor lifeboats have a searchlight and radio installation in a cabin. All classes have a compression ignition engine which must be tested ahead and astern for not less than 5 minutes at least once a week. It shall be launched once every three months and the crew shall demonstrate their ability to work the engine and handle the boat under power. The fuel shall be changed annually.

The *totally enclosed lifeboat* has already been provided for tankers and offshore installations. These boats provide better protection against the cold and sea. They have extra top buoyancy so that they are self-righting. Some of these boats have provision for a mist of seawater around them if proceeding through burning oil, an internal air supply, and an ability to resist flames up to eight minutes. Examples of such lifeboats are shown in figure 2-9.

The *free-fall boat* is a totally enclosed lifeboat that is used for offshore installations as well as for merchant ships. To minimize shock of impact

*Survival Guide for the Mariner*

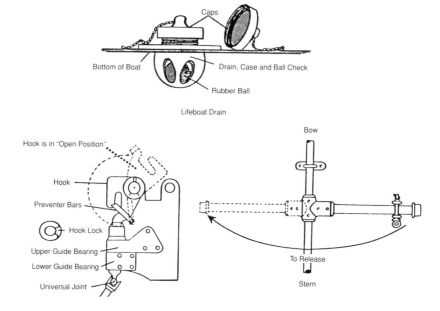

Fig. 2-8. Automatic drain and Rottmer releasing hook and lever. Courtesy of U.S. Coast Guard.

from the fall, all passengers and crew have safety belts fastened in rear-facing seats. Spaceship experience has been utilized to provide protection against the impacts of falls from up to 40 meters. The boats are self-righting and are capable of being launched mechanically or by a float-free system. The coxswain's cubical provides for 360° vision. Free-fall boats are generally launched from aft, as illustrated in figure 2-10.

*Rescue boats* are designed to rescue persons in distress and marshal survival craft. They come in a variety of shapes and forms. They can be semirigid with a fiberglass hull and have inflated rubber buoyancy chambers to provide extra stability or be an inflatable rescue boat as shown in figure 2-11. The rescue boat should be designed to be launched quickly from a vessel in case of a man overboard. SOLAS rules require three immersion suits for persons manning rescue boats.

*Survival capsules* (figure 2-12) first appeared in the 1960s in the United States to appeal to the offshore oil industry. The circular shaped, reinforced plastic, totally enclosed sphere has a skirt near the bottom to act as a keel and prevent the craft from spinning like a top. Capsules seat up to 54 persons in a circular configuration. Regardless of size, all of the self-righting capsules are launched and recovered with a single wire rope

2-9. Totally enclosed lifeboats. Courtesy of Schat Watercraft.

fall attached to a hook centered on the capsule overhead. The capsules are usually powered with a marine diesel engine that is liquid cooled using a seawater–fresh-water heat exchanger. They are able to withstand temperatures up to 2000°F and are equipped with an exterior water spray system and an interior oxygen supply for the engine and occupants.

On *passenger ships* the revised chapter III of the Safety of Life at Sea Convention permits *partially enclosed lifeboats* (figure 2-13) built with a rigid cover over the bow and stern sections and equipped with a flexible

Fig. 2-10. Free-fall lifeboat. Courtesy of Harding Safety A.S., Rosendal, Norway.

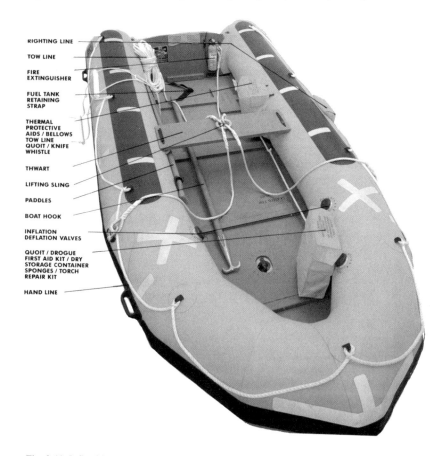

RIGHTING LINE

TOW LINE

FIRE EXTINGUISHER

FUEL TANK RETAINING STRAP

THERMAL PROTECTIVE AIDS / BELLOWS TOW LINE QUOIT / KNIFE WHISTLE

THWART

LIFTING SLING

PADDLES

BOAT HOOK

INFLATION DEFLATION VALVES

QUOIT / DROGUE FIRST AID KIT / DRY STORAGE CONTAINER SPONGES / TORCH REPAIR KIT

HAND LINE

Fig. 2-11. Inflatable rescue boat. Courtesy of ML Lifeguard Equipment Limited, UK..

**Survival capsule**

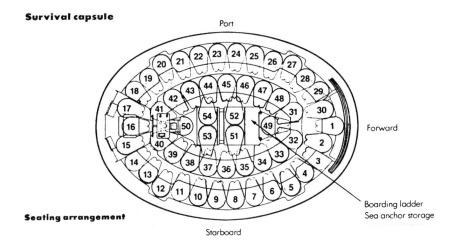

Port

Forward

Boarding ladder
Sea anchor storage

**Seating arrangement**

Starboard

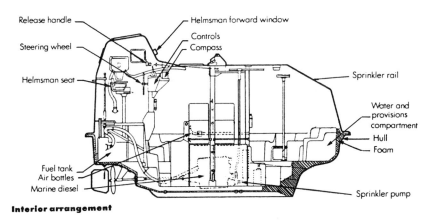

Release handle
Steering wheel
Helmsman seat

Helmsman forward window
Controls
Compass

Sprinkler rail

Water and provisions compartment
Hull
Foam

Fuel tank
Air bottles
Marine diesel

Sprinkler pump

**Interior arrangement**

Fig. 2-12. Survival capsule. Courtesy of Survival Systems Int., Valley Center, CA.

cover that can be deployed over the open areas. This lifeboat is lighter and less expensive than a totally enclosed craft carrying the same number of occupants, a vital factor due to the number of boats carried on a passenger ship compared to cargo vessels manned with a crew of twenty to forty seafarers.

Lifeboat *survival and signaling equipment* are listed and described in Appendix A.

Lifeboats may carry equipment in addition to the required amounts only if it does not interfere with seating, seaworthiness, or operation of the boat, and does not overload the davits. A fully equipped lifeboat has very little remaining space, and that space must be used for embarking and seating passengers and carrying out all of the activities associated with the launching.

You should prepare a checklist to assure that all required equipment is actually aboard your lifeboat.

2-13. Partially enclosed lifeboat. Courtesy of Schat Watercraft.

## Life Rafts

A secondary lifesaving appliance aboard a majority of vessels is the life raft. On some vessels they may be the primary appliance. Inflatable life rafts which comply with the 1974 SOLAS Convention are made in sizes from 6 to 25 persons. For small vessels there are 4 to 6 person life rafts and for special purpose high-density passenger vessels on short international voyages life raft capacity can range from 35 to 45 persons. The general U.S. requirements, markings, and servicing requirements are shown in figures 2-14a through 2-14c. Inflatable life rafts must:

1. Not weigh more than 400 pounds.
2. Be provided with an inflatable floor and have water pockets for stability.
3. Have a lifeline festooned in bights, a boarding ladder, and towing connection.
4. Be provided with an Indian orange canopy.

5. Be boardable 30 seconds after pulling the painter.
6. Be able to be towed at five knots.
7. Not be damaged by an adult jumping on the canopy from a height not less than 15 feet.

---

## INFLATABLE LIFERAFTS - GENERAL

### STOWAGE (46 CFR 33.20)

Stowed in such a way that they:

- can be launched in the shortest possible time even under unfavorable conditions of trim and list.
- will float free in the event of vessel sinking.

Decks on which rafts are stowed must be kept clear of freight and other obstructions which will impede launching.

### HYDRAULIC RELEASE (46 CFR 160.062)

Automatically releases liferaft from cradle at depths of 5 to 25 feet above a sinking vessel. Must be diaphragm spring plunger type designed to operate with spring tensioned gripes.

---

## INFLATABLE LIFERAFTS - GENERAL

### INSTRUCTION PLACARD (46 CFR 160.051 - 6)

Each manufacturer of inflatable liferafts must provide appropriate number of instructions placards to master or operator of vessel on which his rafts are carried.

Placard size - not less more than 14 inches by 20 inches and contain simple instructions and illustrations for launching and operating the raft.

### POSTING OF INSTRUCTION PLACARD (46 CFR 35.10 - 9)

Every vessel equipped with inflatable liferafts shall have posted in conspicuous places which are regularly accessible to the crew and/or passengers, approved placards containing instructions for the launching and inflation of inflatable liferafts.

Number and location of such placards shall be determined by the Officer in Charge, Marine Inspection.

Fig. 2-14a. General U.S. requirements for life rafts. Courtesy of Captain Richard Beadon.

If at all possible, witness the annual servicing of the life raft to observe the survival equipment aboard and how the raft inflates by its $CO_2$ cylinders. The stowage requirements aboard the vessel are illustrated in figure 2-15. Provision should be made to have a nonskid deck around the

---

## INFLATABLE LIFERAFTS - MARKINGS

**(46 CFR 160.051 - 8)**

**NAMEPLATE**

Each inflatable liferaft and container shall have permanently attached a substantial nameplate of compatible material on which is embossed or imprinted the following:

- name of manufacturer
- the approval number
- the manufacturer's model number and serial number
- the number of persons for which the raft is approved to carry
- the lot number

In addition, the container shall be marked "Ocean Service Equipment" or "Limited Service Equipment" together with the Marine Inspection Office identification letters, the date, and the letters USCG.

---

## INFLATABLE LIFERAFTS - MARKINGS

**(46 CFR 160.051 - 8))**

**MARKING**

Following information must be clearly and legibly marked in a color contrasting to its background, using materials which are permanent for the life of the inflatable liferaft:

- instructions for inflating; directions for righting; directions for boarding; position and use of items stowed outside equipment containers; contents of equipment containers, and warnings against tampering.

**RECORD OF INSPECTIONS**

Raft container must have a stainless steel plate showing a stamped record of the data of the annual inspections and gas inflation tests.

**NUMBERING AND MARKING (46 CFR 33.25 - 10)**

Stenciled in a conspicuous place in the immediate vicinity of each inflatable liferaft "Inflatable Liferaft No. _____, _____ Persons Capacity.

Fig. 2-14b. Markings required on U.S. life rafts. Courtesy of Captain Richard Beadon.

---

## INFLATABLE LIFERAFTS - SERVICING

---

### (46 CFR 160.051 - 6)

**FREQUENCY**

All inflatable liferafts must be inspected and serviced every twelve months by an approved servicing facility. In addition, every fifth year it is to undergo special inflation tests.

**RECORDING**

Service facility shall maintain a complete record of each inflatable liferaft serviced.

**SERVICING CERTIFICATE**

Certificate shall be issued by the servicing facility for each inflatable liferaft inspected and serviced. Certificate must be retained aboard and will include following information:

- serial number of the raft.
- date of inspection.
- initials of marine inspector.

---

Fig. 2-14c. Servicing requirements for U.S. life rafts. Courtesy of Captain Richard Beadon.

cradle so that at the most crucial time of launching the raft personnel are not slipping on a slippery and probably angled deck. Once inflated, the components of a life raft are illustrated in figure 2-16. The survival equipment required in an approved ocean service or "SOLAS A" life raft is illustrated in figures 2-17a through 2-17d.

Approved life rafts are designated as "SOLAS A," "SOLAS B," and "coastal." Older approved life rafts are designated as "ocean" service, which is equivalent to SOLAS A, and "limited" service, which is equivalent to SOLAS B. Ocean service and limited service life rafts may be used interchangeably with SOLAS A and SOLAS B life rafts, respectively.

SOLAS B life rafts carry no food, water, or fishing kits. They carry only half the number of flares and smoke signals found in SOLAS A life rafts. A SOLAS B life raft may be used to meet the requirements for any survival craft required in the commercial fishing industry vessel regulations, except where a SOLAS A life raft is required.

The smallest approved SOLAS A and SOLAS B life rafts are of the six-person size, in order for the life raft to be sufficiently large for open ocean use. Reductions in food and water are allowed in SOLAS A life rafts, in order to equip them for fewer persons. This will result in a lower

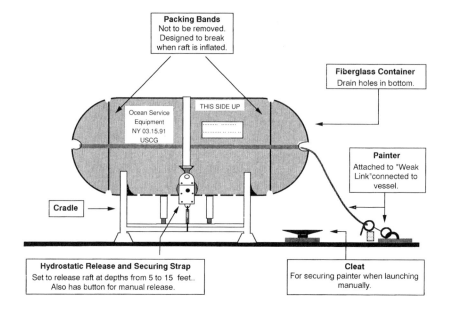

Fig. 2-15. Stowage requirements for life rafts. Courtesy of Captain Richard Beadon.

capacity which must be clearly indicated on the container. Such reductions only eliminate some of the food and water carried in the life raft and are not recommended, since they result only in minimal cost and weight savings.

Coastal service life rafts have less equipment than SOLAS A or SOLAS B life rafts, and are not required to have all of the intrinsic design features of SOLAS life rafts. Therefore, while a servicing facility can normally upgrade SOLAS B life rafts to SOLAS A, and limited service life rafts to ocean service *approved*, coastal service life rafts can generally *not* be upgraded to a higher service level. An exception would be a life raft built to SOLAS standards, but only equipped with a coastal survival equipment pack. A coastal life raft may be used to meet the requirements for any survival craft required in the commercial fishing industry vessel regulations, except where a SOLAS A or SOLAS B life raft is required.

The owner may specify equipment in addition to the required equipment to be carried in the life raft. The additional equipment must be packed in the life raft in accordance with the instructions of the manufacturer to ensure that the additional equipment does not interfere

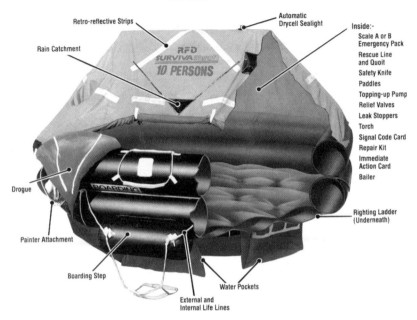

Retro-reflective Strips

Rain Catchment

Rescue Line

Automatic
Drycell Sealight

Inside:-

Scale A or B
Emergency Pack

Rescue Line
and Quoit

Safety Knife

Paddles

Topping-up Pump

Relief Valves

Leak Stoppers

Torch

Signal Code Card

Repair Kit

Immediate
Action Card

Bailer

RFD
SURVIVA
10 PERSONS

BOARDING

Drogue

Righting Ladder
(Underneath)

Painter Attachment

Boarding Step

Water Pockets

External and
Internal Life Lines

Fig. 2-16. Life raft components. Courtesy of R. Perry and Company Limited, UK.

# LIFERAFT EQUIPMENT (OCEAN)

### Hand-Held Rocket Propelled Red Flare Distress Signals

- 2 hand-held rocket propelled parachute red flare distress signals.
- Expires not more than 42 months from date of manufacture.
- Must be stamped with date of manufacture and instructions.
- Minimum altitude 500 feet.
- Minimum burning time 30 sec.
- Maximum rate of descent 15 ft. per sec.
- Must be stowed in watertight container.

### Hand Red Flare Distress Signals

- 6 hand red flare distress signals
- Expires not more than 42 months from date of manufacture.
- Must be stamped with date of manufacture and instructions.
- Must burn for not less than 2 minutes.
- Must be stowed in watertight container.

Fig. 2-17a. Survival equipment aboard an approved life raft. Courtesy of Captain Richard Beadon.

## LIFERAFT EQUIPMENT (OCEAN)

**Boarding Ladder**
- One at each entrance to raft.
- Handholds on each side of entrance.

 **Lifelines**

- Two. One around outside periphery and one around inside of raft.
- 9/16 inch nylon tubular webbing.
- Outside lines festooned in bights not more than 24 inches long and fastened at intervals not exceeding 18 inches which hang within 3 inches of the waterline when raft fully loaded

 **Jackknife**
- Fitted in pocket near forward entrance.
- If raft carries more than 13 pers. then another jackknife packed inside raft.

 **Towing Connection**
- A suitable towing connection at each end of the raft.

**Buoyant Heaving Line.**
- Not less than 100 feet long
- One end attached to buoyant quoit.
- Other end attached to raft near after entrance.

## LIFERAFT EQUIPMENT (OCEAN)

 **First Aid Kit**

- 1 Compressed bandage - 4 inches
- 4 compressed bandage - 2 inches
- 16 waterproof adhesive compress
- 3 eye dressing packets
- 2 compressed gauze bandages
- 1 tourniquet
- 1 forceps
- 1 pair scissors
- 12 safety pins
- 1 wire splint
- 10 ammonia inhalants
- 10 iodine applicators
- Aspirin, phenacetin and caffeine
- 4 sterile petrolatum gauze

 **Emergency Fishing Tackle Kit**

- 1 kit consisting of fishing rigs, accessories and instructions packed in a sealed container

 **Daylight Signalling Mirror**

- 1 signalling mirror of approved type.

 **Signal Whistle**

- 1 ball type whistle of corrosion resistant construction, with a 36 inch lanyard attached.

Fig. 2-17b. Survival equipment aboard an approved life raft. Courtesy of Captain Richard Beadon.

# LIFERAFT EQUIPMENT (OCEAN)

 **Water**

- One and a half quarts of drinking water for each person raft is certified to carry.
- Packed in approved hermetically sealed containers.
- Date of manufacture must be stamped on container. Service life 5 years from that date.
- One pint per person of this requirement per person may be replaced by an approved desalting kit.

 **Provisions**

- One pound of hard bread or its approved equivalent for each person raft is certified to carry.
- Packed in hermetically sealed cans of approved type.

 **Can Openers**

- Three means of opening the hermetically sealed containers.
- Special blades on the jackknife can be counted as a can opener.
- Blades or cutting edges must be sheathed to prevent damage to raft and its equipment.

# LIFERAFT EQUIPMENT (OCEAN)

 **Paddles**

- Two. Each 4 feet long.

 **Sea Anchors**

- Two. One stowed inside the raft ready for use and the other stowed outside the raft which will stream automatically without entanglement when raft is inflated

 **Instruction Manual**

- Printed on water resistant film.
- Suspended in clear envelope inside raft.

 **Lights**

- Two. One fitted outside on top of canopy . Other one inside.
- Must be watertight and operate automatically when raft is inflated.
- Must be powered by dry cells or water activated batteries which can operate the light for 12 hours. Outside light must:
- be visible at least 2 miles.
- Have means of interrupting power to light.

 **Pump**

- One inflation/deflation pump with hose.

Fig. 2-17c. Survival equipment aboard an approved life raft. Courtesy of Captain Richard Beadon.

## LIFERAFT EQUIPMENT (OCEAN)

**Anti-Seasickness Tablets**
- 6 tablets for every person the raft is certified to carry.

**Balers**
- One if <12 pers.
- Two if >13 pers.
- Flexible material. Not less than 6 inches in diameter.

**Sponges**
- Two Type 1 Size 10 cellulose sponges.

**Repair Kit**
- Six sealing clamps.
- Five 2 inch tube patches and cement compatible with the raft fabric.
- Cement to show date of manufacture. Must be manufactured within 18 months of the time it is packed in the raft.

**Flashlight**
- One.
- Three spare cells.
- Two spare bulbs.

Fig. 2-17d. Survival equipment aboard an approved life raft. Courtesy of Captain Richard Beadon.

with the proper inflation of the life raft. When an EPIRB is carried in the life raft, the life raft container must be suitably marked to indicate that it contains an EPIRB. The marking must indicate the category or type of EPIRB, last date of test, and date of battery expiration.

The free-float arrangement required by IMO 1986 regulations is possible through the hydrostatic release unit. If the raft cannot be launched manually the hydrostatic release unit will automatically release the container lashings at a depth between 5 and 15 feet. The buoyance of the life raft in its container will bring the raft to the surface where it will be inflated by its painter line before the wink link breaks the attachment of the painter to the vessel.

### Escape Slides

The marine adaptation of aviation escape slides is becoming very popular aboard high-density ferries with high freeboard. They are quick to release, easy to operate, comfortable for passengers, and with two track slides can evacuate up to 360 passengers within 30 minutes up to 15 meters above water level. These requirements comply with SOLAS and are in accordance with chapter III of IMO. The Viking system (figure 2-18) consists of four main components:

1. One stowage box individually dimensioned within certain limits to fit into the ship. Stowing height up to 15 meters above water level.
2. One inflatable dual-track escape slide consisting of 12 tube chambers divided into four independent sections.
3. One inflatable boarding platform with a capacity of 96 passengers.
4. Eight inflatable marine life rafts, each with a capacity of 45 passengers, available with or without canopy.

Pulling one handle inflates the system in two to five minutes, and evacuation down the slide can begin. The embarkation platform functions as a buffer zone until the first life rafts have been thrown or lowered overboard and marshaled to the platform. The two-slide platform can absorb 96 passengers, thus leaving the crew ample time to launch the life rafts. There are up to eight 45-person life rafts for each slide. Escape slides would probably not be found on your type of vessel.

## Other Items

Other items that would be on your inspection tour are buoyant apparatus, life buoys, and rescue lines. Examples of such lifesaving equipment are shown in figure 2-19. Aboard U.S. vessels there should be at least the

Fig 2-18. Escape slide. Courtesy of Viking, Denmark.

number of ring life buoys prescribed by the U.S. Coast Guard. They should be placed so as to be readily accessible and plainly indicated to persons on board. They must not be permanently secured and must always be capable of being cast loose. Requirements for throwable

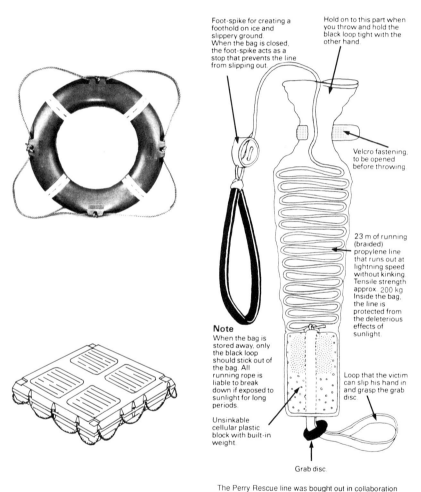

Foot-spike for creating a foothold on ice and slippery ground. When the bag is closed, the foot-spike acts as a stop that prevents the line from slipping out.

Hold on to this part when you throw and hold the black loop tight with the other hand.

Velcro fastening, to be opened before throwing.

23 m of running (braided) propylene line that runs out at lightning speed without kinking. Tensile strength approx. 200 kg Inside the bag, the line is protected from the deleterious effects of sunlight.

**Note**
When the bag is stored away, only the black loop should stick out of the bag. All running rope is liable to break down if exposed to sunlight for long periods.

Unsinkable cellular plastic block with built-in weight.

Loop that the victim can slip his hand in and grasp the grab disc.

Grab disc.

The Perry Rescue line was bought out in collaboration with the Swedish Life-Saving Association-Swimming Support League (SLS), which is a member of the Trygg-Hansa Accident prevention organisation, this line is approved and imported by

Fig. 2-19. Buoyant apparatus, life buoys, and rescue line. Courtesy of R. Perry and Company Limited, UK.

flotation devices/ring life buoys are shown in table 2-1. Know the location of distress signals and emergency gear or repair lockers. Know how and when to use all of the equipment found therein. Ensure that your EPIRBs will work when needed by following these steps:

1. Collect the EPIRB, a small FM radio, a half-filled bucket of water, and a watch.
2. Check the EPIRB's battery by operating the test switch.
3. Turn on the FM radio and tune it to 99.5 MHz.

**TABLE 2-1**

Throwable Flotation Devices/Ring Life Buoys*

*Each vessel must be equipped with a throwable flotation device or ring life buoys as in the following table:*

| Length of vessel in feet (meters) | | Approved devices required | | | | Lifeline length on one ring life buoy in feet (m)[4] |
|---|---|---|---|---|---|---|
| *At least* | *Less than* | *Number* | *Description* | *Color* | *Minimum Diameter - in inches (mm)* | |
| | 16 (4.9) | None | | | | None |
| 16 (4.9) | 26 (7.9) | 1 | Any Type IV PFD | Any | Any | None |
| 26 (7.9) | 65 (19.8) | 1 | Ring Life Buoy Approval series 160.050/. . . [1] | Orange[2] | 24[3] (600) | 60 (18.3) |
| 65 (19.8) | | 3 | Ring Life Buoy Approval series 160.050/. . . [1] | Orange[2] | 24 (600) | 90 (27.4) |

[1] Cork or balsa ring life buoys approved under former approval series 160.009/ . . . may continue to be used as long as they are in good and serviceable condition.

[2] White ring life buoys on board the vessel on or before September 15, 1991, may be used to meet these requirements as long as they are in good and serviceable condition.

[3] Ring life buoys at least 20 inches (500 mm) in diameter and on a vessel less than 65 feet (19.8 meters) in length on or before September 15, 1991, may be used to meet these requirements as long as they are in good and serviceable condition.

[4] The lifeline required on one of the life buoys on a vessel 26 feet (7.9 meters) or more in length, should be:
    a. Buoyant
    b. Non-kinking
    c. At least $\frac{5}{16}$ inch (8 mm) in diameter

* Courtesy of U.S. Coast Guard.

4. Check the time. The full-power test can only be made during the international distress frequency test period—from 00 to 05 minutes of any hour.
5. When the time is right, dunk the bottom of the EPIRB into the water, watch the indicator lamp, and listen to the radio.

If the EPIRB is working properly, the indicator lamp will light and you will hear the EPIRB signal—an oscillating tone—on the radio. Pull the EPIRB out of the water as soon as you hear the signal. This full-power test transmission *must not* last longer than one second or three audio sweeps. If you don't hear the signal on the radio, then your EPIRB is in need of service. Perform this test each month and enter the results in the radio log.

## HOLD DRILLS, INSTRUCTION, AND SAFETY MEETINGS

### Drills and Instruction

The most difficult operation in handling lifeboats is launching, including embarkation of passengers and crew. It may be advisable to embark passengers on the boat deck instead of the embarkation deck, with some shipboard modifications to ensure safe boarding by passengers and crew. To achieve this safely and efficiently, frequent drills are necessary so that each crew member learns his or her duties and the order in which they must be performed. Training should be so thorough that the crew performs correctly despite any confusion or excitement. Alternating responsibilities of the crew assigned during drill would ensure a safe launching if a key crew member does not appear. For these reasons, weekly drills are required by U.S. laws which can be summarized as follows:

1. Passenger vessels—
   (a) At least once a week: fire and boat drills. [Note: if voyage exceeds one week, then conduct fire and boat drill before vessel leaves port.]
   (b) All vessels on international voyage (other than short international voyage) shall muster passengers for fire and boat drill within 24 hours after leaving port and weekly thereafter.
2. Cargo and miscellaneous vessels—
   (a) At least once a week.
   (b) At least within 24 hours of leaving port if more than 25 percent of crew replaced at that port.

All drills should be conducted in accordance with SOLAS regulations and as if an actual emergency existed: *All* hands report to station, prepared to carry out assigned duties:

1. Fire pumps started, system checked by opening sufficient number of outlets.
2. All emergency gear brought out and ability to use demonstrated.
3. Watertight doors operated.
4. Weather permitting: lifeboat covers (if any) removed, plugs/caps in place, boat ladders secured in position, painter led forward and tended.
   —motor operated at least five minutes ahead and astern.
   —hand propelling gear, at least five minutes.
5. In port, all boats (if practicable) swung out, unobstructed ones lowered to water, crew exercised at oars or hand propelling gear.
   —each boat must be lowered to water at least once every three months.
6. Under way (weather permitting) all boats shall be swung out.
7. Person in charge of boat/raft to be provided with list of its crew and observe that they are acquainted with duties; all passengers encouraged to participate fully and be instructed in use of life preservers.
8. Lifeboat equipment shall be examined at least once a month.
9. Each member of the crew drilled and exercised at oars at least once every three months; additionally, crew of motor or hand-propelled lifeboat demonstrate ability to handle boat under power. If possible, launch lifeboats with the ship having a headway of two to four knots.

Although there may be little opportunity to command a lifeboat under oars, except during required drills every three months, the person in charge (coxswain) should be aware of the standard commands. The coxswain will be using a larger oar called the sweep oar. This oar should be painted white to make it more easily recognized among all the oars. When handling such a boat under oars all rowers shall keep their eyes on the back of the person in front and the aftermost starboard oarsman will set the pace as the stroke oarsman. Oars should be feathered on the recovery part of the stroke to reduce wind resistance and prevent "catching a crab." Commands should be given at the start of a stroke to permit oarsmen to complete the stroke and execute the new command in unison. Refer to table 2-2.

**TABLE 2-2**

## Lifeboat Commands*

| Command | Instruction |
|---|---|
| 1. Stand by the stern | Prepare to let go line. |
| 2. Cast off the stern | Throw off after line. |
| 3. Stand by the bow | Prepare to throw off forward line. |
| 4. Shove off forward | Throw off line, shove off the bow with a boat hook (rounded end). |
| 5. Stand by the oars | Lifelines out, rowlocks in sockets, put oars on the gunwales, blades flat and pointed towards the bow and resting against rowlock of man behind in order from aft forward. |
| 6. Out oars | Lift oars with crook of arm and place them in rowlocks with blades trimmed fore and aft (flat), wrists under. |
| 7. Stand by to give way (may or may not be given) | Follow the man in front of you, lean forward, push wrists over and dip blades halfway into the water slightly beyond the perpendicular. |
| 8. Give way together or give way | Follow man in front of you, pulling blade through the water, making sure it doesn't cut too deep into the water. |
| 9. Hold water port, give way starboard | Gradual port turn. |
| 10. Back water port, give way starboard | Sharp port turn. |
| 11. Hold water starboard, give way port | Gradual starboard turn. |
| 12. Back water starboard, give way port | Sharp starboard turn. |
| 13. Hold water all or hold water | Drop blades in the water together, vertically. This command slows the boat. |
| 14. Trail oars | This command is given when passing an obstruction of another boat. The oars are dragged alongside of the boat with the tips of the blades opposite the motion of the boat. |
| 15. Oars | Blades are brought temporarily out of the water, blades flat trimmed fore and aft. Command is given after a turn is made and after rowing in an astern motion, to get oarsmen together, given between every command, except way enough and trail oars. |
| 16. Stern all or backwater all | Oarsmen row in astern (backward) motion. |
| 17. In bows | Two oarsmen in the bow of boat, boat the oars and help fend off or pick up a man in the water. |
| 18. Way enough | Complete stroke, swing oars into the boat together, take rowlocks out of sockets, bring lifelines into boat. |
| 19. Stand by the bow | Man closest to landing in the bow prepares to fend off or hold boat alongside, whatever is necessary. |
| 20. Stand by the stern | Man closest to landing in the stern prepares to fend off or hold boat alongside. |
| 21. Bank oars or cross oars | Draw the oar through the rowlock until the handle rests on the opposite gunwale. This command is given after the command "oars." |
| 22. Boat the sweep oar (Note: this command is not given by the coxswain but by an instructor or inspector to the coxswain during boat drills) | The sweep oar is brought directly into the boat with the handle on the first thwart in front of the coxswain. |
| 23. Boat the oars | All oars brought into the boat with the handles aft and blade forward in order from forward aft. |

* Courtesy of U.S. Coast Guard.

During weekly fire and emergency drills the emergency squad of 6 to 24 men should be exercised. If the size of the crew permits, such a squad should be organized under the command of the chief mate. They form the nucleus damage control party aboard and should be knowledgeable about their vessel and trained in the fundamentals of damage control. On some vessels there may be an emergency squad and support squad. On Military Sealift Command vessels where crew sizes are larger, several emergency squads or repair parties can be organized for each section of the vessel. An example of such drills and instruction is shown in figures 2-20a and 2-20b.

Cross-training is the training of crew members to carry out critical duties which are not their normal assignments in an emergency: during fire, man overboard, or abandon ship drills.

The starting of lifeboat engines, the operation of lifeboat portable radios and the emergency radio transmitter in the radio room, the operation of the fixed foam and $CO_2$ fire-fighting systems, the changeover to aft steering, and the launching of lifeboats and life rafts are all good examples of critical duties where the absence of one officer or seaman must not prevent or delay the operation.

Emergency drills and instruction periods should emphasize cross-training within various teams. Members of one department should never assume that they will not need to perform a critical operation normally carried out by crew from another department.

Identify the critical emergency operations which only one or a few people are now trained to perform. Ask yourself, "What if the 'expert' is missing at a critical time?" Then, provide sufficient training to others so that the ship has an effective backup capability.

There must be a requirement to hold damage control instruction. This instruction is intended to drill the crew members in each part of the emergency organization in the use of safety equipment and emergency procedures. This individual instruction is just as important as the emergency drills. Without personal familiarity with safety equipment and procedures, the performance of the crew during an actual emergency cannot be effective. This instruction becomes especially important when a new crew is shipped or when changes are made in crew assignments, procedures, or equipment. It is vitally important after each drill to hold a thorough debriefing so that all hands may better perform their duties in a real emergency.

DEPARTMENT OF THE NAVY
USNS MARIAS (T-AO 57)
FPO MIAMI 34092

IN REPLY REFER TO.

22 NOVEMBER, 1981

MEMORANDUM

FROM: CHIEF OFFICER, USNS MARIAS

TO: ALL HANDS

SUBJ: FIRE & BOAT DRILL

1. SUBJECT DRILLS WILL BE HELD AT 1020 ON MONDAY 23 NOVEMBER, 1981.

2. FOR THE FIRE DRILL THE FOLLOWING FIRES EXIST:

| LOCATION | CLASS OF FIRE | REPAIR PARTY/ ZONE TEAM |
|---|---|---|
| CARPENTER SHOP (1-98-2) | C | REPAIR I |
| PAINT LOCKER (1-100-1) | B | ZONE I |
| FUEL TEST LAB (1-72-2) | B | ZONE II |
| MACHINE SHOP (2-35-2) | B/C | REPAIR II Assisted by ZONE III |

3. UPON COMPLETION OF THE FIRE DRILL THERE WILL BE AN ABANDON SHIP DRILL. FOR THE ABANDON SHIP DRILL REPORT MISSING PERSONNEL BY NAME.

4. AFTER DRILLS ALL HANDS ASSEMBLE ON THE FOREDECK (MAIN DECK), STARBOARD SIDE FOR INSTRUCTION IN THE USE OF AN EDUCTOR.

5. DECK DEPARTMENT WILL HAVE THEIR SAFETY MEETING IN THE CREW'S LOUNGE FOLLOWING ALL MORNING DRILLS.

H.J. MEURN C/O

Fig. 2-20a. Drills and instruction with feedback to master. Courtesy of Military Sealift Command.

## Safety Meetings

The more information everyone has in common the more confidence you will have in each other and the better you will act if in danger. Discussions accomplish this. They are particularly important when inexperienced crew members are aboard, but every person can profit from them. Each head of department should hold a safety meeting at least monthly with his or her personnel. There is nothing trivial when it comes to safety and everything of concern should be discussed. The proceedings should be noted in minutes. The master should then hold a monthly meeting with

*On Your Vessel*

DEPARTMENT OF THE NAVY
USNS MARIAS (T-AO 57)
FPO MIAMI 34092

IN REPLY REFER TO.

3 DECEMBER 1981

MEMORANDUM

FROM: CHIEF OFFICER
TO: MASTER, USNS MARIAS

SUBJ: STATUS OF REPAIR II IN COMBATING MAJOR FIRES DURING FIRE DRILLS

1. REPAIR II CONTINUES TO BE UNSATISFACTORY DURING MAJOR FIRE DRILLS.
AS OF NOW REPAIR II WILL NOT PASS THE REINSPECTION OF THE PHASE
III MAJOR FIRE DRILL. LEADERSHIP OF THE PARTY IS NOT FIRM , GEAR
IS NOT BROKEN OUT AS REQUIRED AND THE PROCEDURES ARE NOT CORRECT.
PERSONNEL ASSIGNED TO BREAK OUT AND OPERATE GEAR DO NOT KNOW HOW
TO DO SO NOR DO THEY DISPLAY THE ENTHUSIASM NECCESSARY.

2. AS A RESULT PERMISSION IS REQUESTED TO HOLD TWO DRILLS A DAY, UNREP
OPERATIONS PERMITTING, UNTIL RETURN MAYPORT, FLA. AND TO REQUEST FIRE
FIGHTING SCHOOL IN MAYPORT AS SOON AS POSSIBLE AFTER ARRIVAL FOR
ALL PERSONNEL IN REPAIR II AND ZONE III.

VERY RESPECTFULLY,

R.J. MEURN   C/O

FROM: MASTER, USNS MARIAS
TO: CHIEF OFFICER

1. PERMISSION IS GRANTED TO CONDUCT TRAINING AS NECCESSARY.

R.E. HAYNES

Fig. 2-20b. Drills and instruction with feedback to master. Courtesy of Military Sealift Command.

department heads to review all minutes from their various areas and to
discuss performance at drills and any other items of concern to the safety
of the vessel. These meetings should have minutes which are promulgated to the entire crew. All discrepancies should be noted along with a
corrective action to be taken and when. The crew appreciates a master
who is concerned with their safety. A safe ship is not only a productive
vessel but also a happy ship.

## CONCLUSION

Adhere to these eight steps: (1) check station bill, (2) stow personal
survival kit, (3) check life jacket, (4) check immersion suit, (5) secure
room for sea, (6) tour your vessel, (7) inspect safety equipment, and (8)
hold drills, debriefings, instruction, and safety meetings.

By complying with these rules, as modified for your vessel, you
will then be better prepared to abandon the vessel if need be. The
alternative to proper preparation is panic.

CHAPTER THREE

# Leaving the Vessel

There are two ways a person can leave a vessel: voluntarily and involuntarily. In this chapter the involuntary leaving of the vessel will be explored in the discussion of man overboard procedures. The voluntary leaving of the vessel will encompass the procedures involved in the abandonment of your vessel.

## MAN OVERBOARD

Before any discussion of procedures to follow once a person goes overboard, let's see what can be done to prevent it. Here are some preventative measures:

1. Avoid the exposed decks in rough weather.
2. Avoid walking around the exposed decks at night.
3. Wear appropriate attire on deck, e.g., layered clothing in cold weather, watch cap, safety shoes, and work vest (figure 3-1).
4. Carry with you at all times a knife, whistle, white handkerchief, and flashlight.
5. Utilize railings, handrails, and any safety lines rigged.
6. If you have to go out on deck in rough weather, wear a life jacket with attached light, whistle, and reflective tape, and use your own safety line with snap hook attached.
7. Comply with the master's orders to stay clear of exposed decks during rough weather; use interior passageways.
8. Do not, if at all possible, go out on deck alone. If alone, let someone, including the bridge watch, know of your whereabouts, preferably with a walkie-talkie in hand.
9. Avoid drinking aboard.
10. Remember the old sailor's adage: "One hand for the ship and one hand for yourself."

There is one rule for man overboard and that is: "Don't be the man." If you go overboard the hazards include being injured by the fall or being

Fig. 3-1. Perry work vest. Courtesy of R. Perry and Company Limited, UK.

struck by the vessel and your disappearance not being noticed.
Once in the water remember these procedures:

1. Yell "help" and blow your whistle.
2. Remember flotation is the key.
3. Turn on flashlight and life jacket light if wearing one.
4. Let the vessel come to you—do not swim towards the vessel and let fatigue or numbness from exposure weaken you.
5. Conserve your strength for the rescue. Remain calm. A calm body floats better than a tense one.
6. Assume the HELP position (figure 3-2) to reduce loss of body core temperature and the onset of hypothermia. If several people went overboard assume the HUDDLE position (figure 3-3).
7. Only swim to a life buoy, rescue line, or buoyant bag with heaving line thrown by vessel personnel.
8. Stand by for ship recovery; or,
9. Stand by for rescue boat recovery; and,
10. Know the hazards in the water:
    hypothermia

# HELP  H̲eat E̲scape L̲essening P̲osture

Fig. 3-2. Heat escape lessening posture. From *Dr. Cohen's Healthy Sailor Book.* Courtesy of International Marine Publishing Co., Camden, ME, and TAB Books, Blue Ridge Summit, PA.

**HUDDLE**
**50% Increase in Survival Time**

Fig. 3-3. HUDDLE position for small groups. From *Dr. Cohen's Healthy Sailor Book.* Courtesy of International Marine Publishing Co., Camden, ME, and TAB Books, Blue Ridge Summit, PA.

    drowning
    psychological effects
    ingestion of oil, burning oil
    hazardous marine life.

The vessel response to man overboard should encompass the following steps:

1. Hard rudder port/starboard. Order to swing stern with the propeller away from the person in the water. Many mariners may

feel that the person overboard will be well past the stern before the ship's propeller passes, and it does not matter in which direction to turn. With a right-handed propeller, however, it would be best to order hard left.

2. Release a life buoy with water light or smoke signal.
3. Post lookout(s) to keep the person or life buoy in sight. The lookout(s) should continually raise their arm and point to the person in the water. Punch "HERE" key on Loran C receiver.
4. Commence round turn in clear weather or Williamson turn in restricted visibility or nighttime. Some mariners believe it is always best to execute a Williamson or Sharnoff turn to ensure returning to the same area where the person went overboard.
5. Inform master/engine room.
6. Stand by engines and sound three prolonged blasts of whistle.
7. Have key personnel in the recovery turn on their walkie-talkies. Have crew member standing by to assist in case of shipboard recovery. If possible, a crew member should be provided a wet suit. For shipboard recovery, lower a cargo net or accommodation ladder.
8. Assemble rescue-boat crew with walkie-talkie and ready boat. Use a boat that will eventually be on the lee side.
9. If there is a radio room on board, keep the vessel's position available to the operator.
10. Maneuver the vessel to launch rescue boat. Place the vessel between the wind and the victim.
11. Keep the man overboard forward of vessel's propeller.
12. If other vessels are in the area make a VHF call on channel 16 with PAN, PAN, PAN to clarify maneuvers or request assistance.
13. Once the victim is back on board treat for hypothermia.
14. If necessary, call the U.S. Coast Guard or local government authority and request medical advice. A list of agencies to call depending on the vessel's location should be posted in the wheelhouse.

## ABANDON SHIP

The vessel is our best shelter but it may become obvious that we must leave the vessel before it leaves us. While the decision to abandon the vessel is the responsibility of the master, the safety of the vessel depends to a very large degree on the planned on-board safety arrangements and training. Damage control and fire fighting must be efficient and the crew must be well trained in the maintenance and use of all the vessel's lifesaving equipment. The importance of crew drills and training cannot be emphasized too much because now it is time to leave the vessel. Apart from the use of free-fall lifeboats and escape slides there are three main methods for leaving:

1. Boarding lifeboats or life rafts at the embarkation deck level and being lowered to the water.
2. Going down shipside ladders into inflatable life rafts.
3. Getting off the ship on your own.

Before abandoning the vessel, every person should be in his or her immersion suit or wearing a life jacket that is properly donned. Wear as much warm clothing as possible. Board the survival craft dry, but if necessary you may have to jump directly into the water. The signal on the whistle and general alarm of seven short blasts and one prolonged blast is sounded.

### BEFORE LEAVING

1. Don survival suit or life jacket.
    *Survival Suit*
        Layered clothing on
        Watch cap on
        Insert feet.
        Tie arms of suit at waist if you must operate radio or
            perform other duties.
        Weak arm in first.
        Arch back and zip up front.
        Cover with face cover.
        Inflate inflation pillow only if in water.
        Ensure light, whistle, and mini-B EPIRB are ready.
    *Life Jacket*
        Layered clothing on
        Watch cap on
        Follow donning instructions.
        Ensure strap is fastened around crotch to prevent riding up.
        Ensure life jacket light, whistle, and mini-B EPIRB are ready.
2. Handle vessel properly.
        Maneuver to provide lee for survival craft.

Stop engines.
Stop overboard discharges.
Obtain accurate position to nearest land for radio room and survival craft commanders.
3. Make distress call as soon as possible.
Use VHF channel 16 (good up to a 20-mile range) and single sideband 2182 kHz (good beyond 50-mile range).
Speak slowly, clearly, and calmly after making sure transmitter is ON.
MAYDAY, MAYDAY, MAYDAY (derived from French for "help me").
Say vessel name *three* times.
Give position three times (ensure it's correct).
Describe position relative to land.
State nature of distress (e.g., taking on water, need pumps).
Give number of crew/passengers and injuries, if any.
Estimate seaworthiness of vessel.
Describe vessel: color, length, house forward, etc.
End by stating on which channel you are standing by and your schedule of communication updates, e.g., every 15 minutes, etc.
4. Activate emergency position-indicating radio beacons (EPIRB) and take one to the lifeboat.
5. Get emergency radio to lifeboat along with:
*Nautical Almanac*
*H.O. Pub. No. 229*
Plotting tools
Charts, including pilot chart
Sextant
Accurate timepiece
Portable VHF radio
Extra water and rations
Blankets
6. In addition to MAYDAY and SOS, require assistance from other vessels or from ashore. (See figures 3-4a and b, and Appendix C.)
7. Throw over as many buoyant objects as possible.
8. When muster of all aboard is complete and everyone has their personal survival kit, abandon the vessel. However, do not go back to get the kit.

## INTERNATIONAL SIGNALS OF DISTRESS

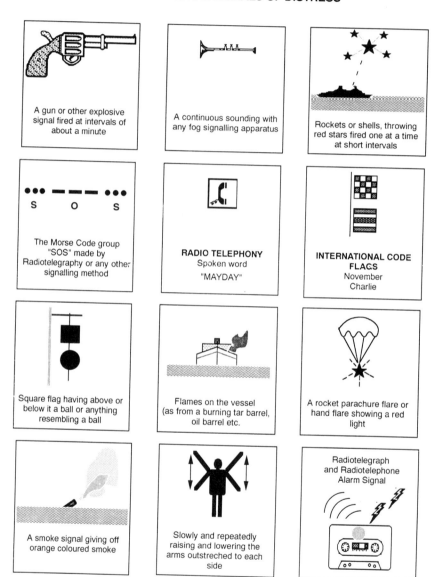

Fig. 3-4a. International signals of distress. Courtesy of Captain Richard Beadon.

## INTERNATIONAL SIGNALS OF DISTRESS - 2

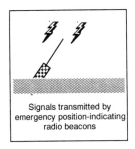

Signals transmitted by emergency position-indicating radio beacons

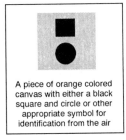

A piece of orange colored canvas with either a black square and circle or other appropriate symbol for identification from the air

Supplementary Signal

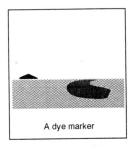

A dye marker

Supplementary Signal

## INLAND SIGNALS OF DISTRESS

Same as International signals plus additional

signal below

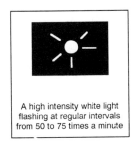

A high intensity white light flashing at regular intervals from 50 to 75 times a minute

The use or exhibition of any of the foregoing signals except for the purpose of indicating distress and need of assistance and the use of other signals which may be confused with any of the above signals is prohibited

Fig. 3-4b. International signals of distress. Courtesy of Captain Richard Beadon.

The number of survival craft on board depends on the type of vessel and must be in accordance with regulatory requirements. Regulations for the United States can be found in Title 46 of the *Code of Federal Regulations.* General U.S. requirements follow.

1. *Cargo vessels* (over 500 gross tons, international/ocean):
   a. Enough lifeboats on each side to accommodate 100 percent of vessel's complement.
   b. If 1,600 gross tons and over, at least *one* motor-propelled lifeboat—class 1.
   c. Enough life rafts to hold 50 percent of people on board if widely spaced accommodation and/or working spaces—then one life raft in each such location.
2. *Passenger vessels* (international voyage):
   a. Enough lifeboats on each side to accommodate 100 percent of people on board (50 percent on each side).
   b. Enough life rafts for 25 percent of persons on board.
   c. Enough buoyant apparatus for 3 percent of persons on board.
   d. Life raft substitution for lifeboats:
      —Enough boats on each side for 37½ percent (75 percent total).
      —Enough life rafts to make up the difference (25 percent).
      —An additional 25 percent life rafts (type that float free on sinking) and 3 percent buoyant apparatus.
3. *Passenger Vessels on Short International Voyage:*
   a. Lifeboats 50 percent each side, *unless* this requirement is relaxed by commandant, U.S. Coast Guard.
   b. 10 percent life raft; i.e., 10 percent the capacity of lifeboats required, plus buoyant apparatus for 25 percent of those on board.
4. *Tankers* (3,000 gross tons and over, international):
   a. Shall carry *not less than four* lifeboats
      —Enough on each side to accommodate all on board.
      —Two boats aft and two midships, unless all superstructure is aft, then all four boats aft, or,
      —Two boats aft only, each with 100 percent capacity.
      —If four is not feasible, number is subject to U.S. Coast Guard approval.

The method used to launch the two main types of survival craft will now be described along with a brief description and figures to illustrate how they are launched.

### LAUNCHING A LIFEBOAT

A lifeboat may be launched by means of radial or round bar davits, mechanical davits, gravity davits, or by the MIRANDA system. The following means of launching apply mostly to open lifeboats. The totally enclosed lifeboat may be launched by davits that are unique and the manufacturer's instructions for launching must be followed.

## Types of Davits

### *Radial or Round Bar Davits*
In moving the boat from the inboard to the outboard position, the heads of the davit arms on *radial* or *round bar* davits (figure 3-5) swing out in horizontal arcs. The boat is swung aft until the bow clears the forward davit arm; then the boat is swung outboard and forward to the lowering position. Hand turning-out gears may be attached to each davit arm to ensure that the boat can be swung outboard when the ship is listing heavily. The boats are lowered by paying out the rope over cruciform bitts or cleats provided for this purpose.

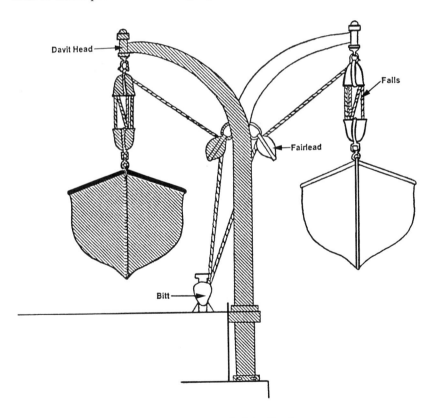

Fig. 3-5. Radial or round bar davit. Courtesy of U.S. Coast Guard.

The falls on radial davits are always made of fiber rope. Although radial davits are easily designed and manufactured, the difficulty of swinging out a heavy boat with these davits prevents their use on large ships. Only small vessels are allowed to carry radial davits.

### Mechanical Davits

The common mechanical davits are the quadrantal and the sheath screw types. For both types, the davit arm is cranked outboard by screws, gears, or other mechanical means. It moves outboard in a plane which is perpendicular to the side of the ship. The falls may be made of fiber line if the distance to the waterline is less than 20 feet at the lightest seagoing draft. Where wire falls are used a winch must be provided.

With *quadrantal* davits (figure 3-6), the lifeboat is carried on chocks under the davits. Chocks are heavy wooden or metal fittings which are secured to the deck of the ship. They are shaped like cradles and hold the hull of the lifeboat. The davits themselves stand upright, with the tops curved in towards each other so that the ends come directly above the hoisting hooks of the lifeboat.

In operation, the davit, which is pivoted near the foot so that it will turn in an arc at right angles to the vessel's side, is rotated outboard by

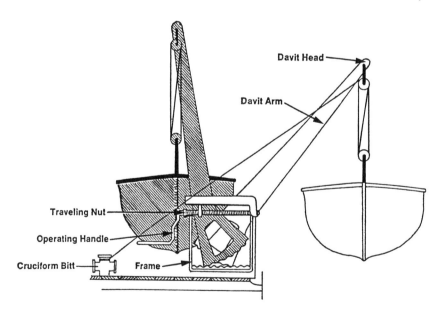

Fig. 3-6. Quadrantal davit. Courtesy of U.S. Coast Guard.

a crank operating a worm gear. When the boat is suspended over the side, a rope is then put around the falls so that it encircles them. The boat can then be pulled in toward the embarkation deck. This operation (putting a rope around the falls and pulling the boat toward the deck) is called frapping.

There are two variations of the sheath screw davit:

1. *Straight boom sheath screw davit* (figure 3-7)—the lifeboat is carried on chocks under the davit.
2. *Crescent sheath screw davit* (figure 3-8)—the lifeboat is cradled between the davits.

Like quadrantal davits, sheath screw davits are pivoted near the foot so that they will turn at right angles to the vessel's side. Sheath screw davits are rotated outboard by a crank operating a sheath screw.

When sheath screw davits are used, the lifeboat is suspended over the side of the vessel and frapped into the embarkation deck in the same manner as quadrantal davits.

In summary, there are two differences between quadrantal and sheath screw davits: (1) crescent sheath screw davits cradle the lifeboat between the davits (quadrantal davits and straight boom sheath screw davits have the lifeboat carried on the chocks); (2) sheath screw davits are operated using a sheath screw; quadrantal davits are operated using a worm gear. Both the sheath and quadrantal types are mechanical davits.

The lifeboats on both quadrantal and sheath screw davits are lowered in the same manner. Davit arms are hand-cranked out by the designated crew members. The crew member assigned as winchman/brakeman then releases the brake in the winch and the boat is lowered. The boat's descent is stopped at the embarkation deck by applying the brake. Releasing the brake again then lowers the boat to the water.

When using boats handled by mechanical davits, the following would represent a typical sequence of operations necessary to swing the boat over the side. As individual ship installations may vary in detail, study the equipment as found aboard your ship for possible differences. The principles of launching will hold true for all installations.

1. Remove the lifeboat cover and its supporting ridgepole. Put cap on drain. Lead sea painter forward, inboard of the forward falls, and make fast forward as low as possible, outboard and clear of all obstructions.
2. Release outboard gripes first so that a man assigned to this task cannot be knocked over the side by the swinging of the boat.

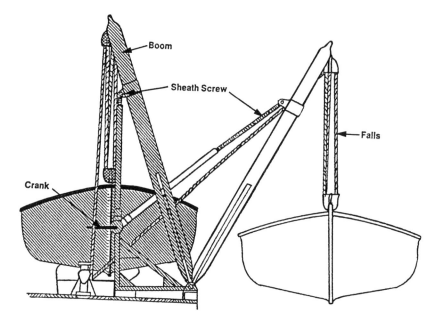

Fig. 3-7. Straight boom sheath screw davit. Courtesy of U.S. Coast Guard.

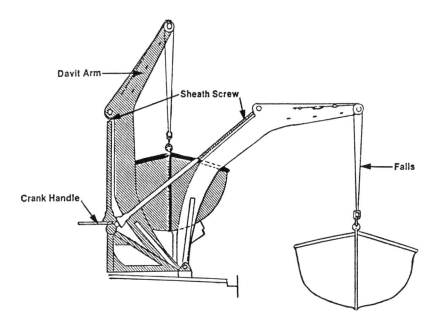

Fig. 3-8. Crescent sheath screw davit. Courtesy of U.S. Coast Guard.

3. With falls taut and secured to cleats, cruciform bitts, or winches, release inboard gripes and keel locking lug on chocks.

4. The davits with the boat suspended may now be swung out. Chocks are built high enough above the deck so that if the falls are taut no hoisting of the boat to clear the deck edge is necessary.

5. When the boat is in outboard position, lower to embarkation deck. With mechanical davits, it is often desirable to swing the davits back inboard so that the boat can be frapped-in snug. This will allow people to get in the boat without jumping space between boat and deck.

6. If the ship is pitching as well as rolling, frapping lines should have a fore and aft as well as athwartships lead. With boat complement aboard, davits are again swung outboard. Frapping lines are eased as necessary, and the boat lowered away on falls. In rough weather, the boat crew may have to fend off from the ship's side as the ship rolls, and use fenders made of mattresses or other available material to cushion impacts.

7. When the boat is in the water, the lifeboatman in charge should turn the releasing gear. With a swell running, the releasing of the boat should be timed to place the boat on the crest of the swell. The boat can then be held alongside with painter so crew members who remained aboard to lower it can climb down a ladder into the boat. If the boat cannot be kept alongside because of rough weather, these crew members can throw heaving lines to the boat; then with one end secured to themselves they can jump into the water and be pulled aboard the boat.

8. Shear away with rudder or steering oar and sea painter. When the boat is at a 45° angle to the vessel, release the sea painter.

### Gravity Davits

The most common type of davit is the *gravity* davit (figure 3-9). The use of gravity davits with electric or air-activated motor-driven winches has simplified rapid lifeboat launching and hoisting.

The most common gravity davit consists of two davit arms. These ride down fixed trackways to the outboard position on rollers.

Another type of gravity davit has two davit arms which move outboard through a system of mechanical linkages. They are pivoted at their lower ends to facilitate the launching of the boat.

Upon release of the gripes, the stopper bars simultaneously slide clear of the trackways. Gravity davits move from the inboard to the outboard position with no application of force except that needed to lift the winch brake handle. Using these davits, one man can lower a lifeboat from the secured position to the water. These davits are required for larger lifeboats (fully equipped lifeboats which exceed 5,000 lbs.) and are found on merchant ships. Their falls are always made of wire rope. These almost-automated davits require care and skill in their maintenance and routine inspection.

For boats handled by gravity davits, a different sequence is necessary, as follows:

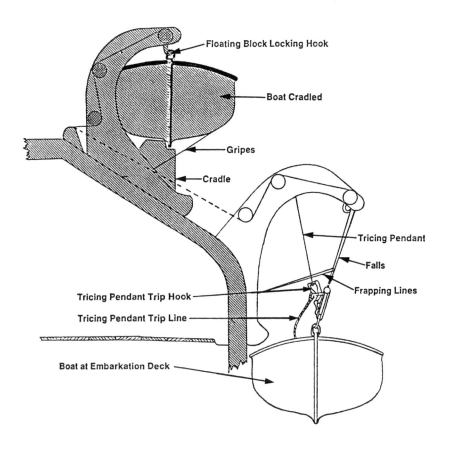

Fig. 3-9. Gravity davit. Courtesy of U.S. Coast Guard.

1. If necessary, remove boat cover and its supporting ridgepole. Put cap on drain. Lead sea painter forward, inboard of the forward falls, and make fast forward as low as possible, outboard and clear of all obstructions.
2. Release gripes.
3. Raise winch brake handle, and davits with suspended boat should roll to the outboard position. Lower away to embarkation deck. The tricing lines will bring the boat to the side of the ship. The brake must be put on before the tricing lines take all the weight.
4. Before passengers and crew enter the boat at the embarkation deck, pass frapping lines and heave taut. When all are aboard, the tricing pendant can be released. The frapping lines are *then* eased out. On non-U.S. vessels bowsing tackles are utilized in place of frapping lines.
5. Once the boat is in the outboard position, lower it by lifting up on the brake handle. The remaining sequence is similar to that for mechanical davits.

Mention should be made here about the possibility of recovering a lifeboat in case the vessel remains afloat and can be reboarded.

Picking up a boat at sea may present as many problems as launching it. It is best done by maneuvering to place the boat ahead and to leeward of the ship with the wind about broad on the bow of the ship. If the ship now overtakes the boat with both making way through the water on parallel courses, a sea painter can be passed to the boat. After the painter is fast, the boat's propeller is stopped or oars boated, and then the boat is brought alongside with rudder or steering oar. The ship can make slow way through the water. The sheer off can be overcome by a strap about the painter from the stem, hove close. After the falls are hooked and the boat is hoisted clear of the water, most of the crew can climb the ladder (figure 3-10); those remaining in the boat should grip the man-ropes for safety.

On ships with gravity davits, the boat is hoisted to a position where the tricing lines can be made fast. It is next lowered to the embarkation deck where frapping lines are secured and people in the boat debark. Before hoisting the boat into the stowed position release frapping lines and when hoisting check the operation of the limit switch (figure 3-11) by pushing down the lever arm to see whether the winch motor stops. Limit switches are in the control or power circuit for the motor. An emergency disconnect switch, which can stop flow of all power to the

Fig. 3-10. Crew members climbing on ladder from lifeboat. Courtesy of Welin Davit and Boat Company.

winch motor, must be manned when the boat is hoisted. Shipmasters must inspect limit switches and emergency disconnect switches every three months. Electric motors for lifeboat winches are powerful enough to easily break the wire rope falls if the motor is used to pull up the davit against the stops. Davits should always be hand-cranked for the last foot or more to the stowed position. Winch hand cranks have couplings which automatically disengage the crank if the electric motor starts. To further reduce possibility of injury, the emergency disconnect switch should always be in the off position when hand cranking.

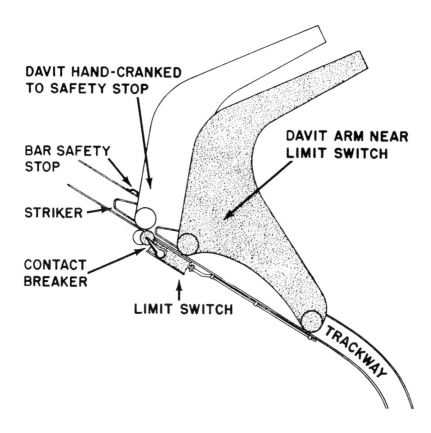

**DAVIT HAND-CRANKED TO SAFETY STOP**

**BAR SAFETY STOP**

**DAVIT ARM NEAR LIMIT SWITCH**

**STRIKER**

**CONTACT BREAKER**

**LIMIT SWITCH**

**TRACKWAY**

Fig. 3-11. Gravity davit limit switch. Courtesy of U.S. Coast Guard.

Serious injury may occur with the hand crank. One midshipman at the U.S. Merchant Marine Academy during his sea year was in the area of the hand crank when the chief mate lifted the brake handle to bring the lifeboat davit back down to the stopper bar. The hand crank spun and hit the cadet in the eye. As a result he lost sight in that eye and was disfigured for life.

### Miranda Davit
In October 1975 leading manufacturers of lifesaving equipment, in conjunction with the British Department of Trade, carried out extensive and successful sea trials of a prototype launch/recovery system aboard the fishery support ship *Miranda*.

The *Miranda* davit (figure 3-12), named after that vessel, is the result of years of experience in the development of davit systems. The Miranda system comprises fixed ramp arms, winch, motor, and a survival craft in its own launch/recovery cradle. The craft is stowed at the embarkation deck position in its cradle. It is this cradle which is lowered down the face of the fixed ramp arms, at the bottom of which the craft is released. The cradle with its rollers provides protection for the boat when it is being lowered, making it unnecessary to turn the craft out clear of the ship's side. This arrangement eliminates the need for a davit which turns or rolls from an inboard to an outboard position and all the constant maintenance which is associated with that type of equipment.

One of the most important features of the new davits is that they do not require that any crew member remain on deck and descend later to the boat by means of a ladder or man-rope—thereby adding to the hazard of the evacuation. In an emergency, all personnel can exit the ship in the lifeboat together.

In addition to the protection it affords the survival craft during launch and recovery, the Miranda system offers other advantages:

1. The lifeboat can be launched with the parent vessel in a 30° high or low side list accompanied by 15° trim either fore or aft. This exceeds International Maritime Organization Regulation III/48 requiring davits to function at a 20° list and 10° trim in either direction.

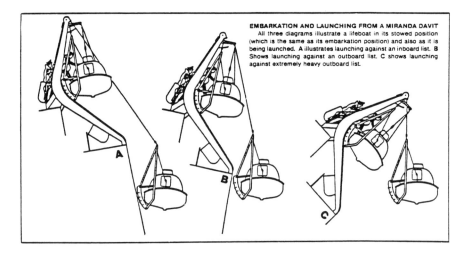

**EMBARKATION AND LAUNCHING FROM A MIRANDA DAVIT**
All three diagrams illustrate a lifeboat in its stowed position (which is the same as its embarkation position) and also as it is being launched. A illustrates launching against an inboard list. B Shows launching against an outboard list. C shows launching against extremely heavy outboard list.

Fig. 3-12. Miranda davit. Courtesy of U.S. Coast Guard.

2. The cradle allows personnel to embark while the boat is in a fully stowed position. The helmsman then controls launching from within the craft. Passengers do not have to wait for the lifeboat to be lowered to a different embarkation deck before they can climb aboard.

3. Other than the rubber-tired wheels on the cradle, the Miranda system has very few moving parts. The wheels enable the cradle, with the craft mounted on it, to move down the trackways, over the side of the ship, and into the water.

4. The lifeboat's gripes automatically disengage themselves as the boat moves down the trackways and do not have to be removed manually. Personnel inside the lifeboat disengage it from the cradle by actuating a lever inside the craft to simultaneously operate the release hooks at each end.

5. Because of the reduced number of moving parts, the maintenance required to keep a Miranda-type system in first-class working order is less than that needed for conventional mechanical or gravity davit systems.

6. Since the craft is protected by the cradle, a lifeboat can be launched while the parent vessel still has some way on and before it comes to a complete stop.

## Immediate Action

After lifeboats have been launched and the full complement is aboard, the boat must be maneuvered clear of the ship. If there is way on the ship, the sea painter is used to sheer the boat clear of the ship's side. The sea painter is then released by pulling the toggle pin (figure 3-13).

With the ship dead in the water, the boat must be fended off with the boat hooks and then rowed away. If engine or hand propelling gear is used, care is needed to prevent the propeller from being fouled by lines hanging over the side.

Once the boat is clear of the ship's side, it should remain in the vicinity to ensure that all survivors are picked up. It is likely that a distress signal has been sent by radio and the position given to other vessels. The task of rescue vessels will be made easier if lifeboats stay in this position and keep together, particularly when at least one boat is fitted with emergency radio signaling equipment on which radio bearings may be taken. Lifeboats should be tied together bow to stern by the full length of their painters.

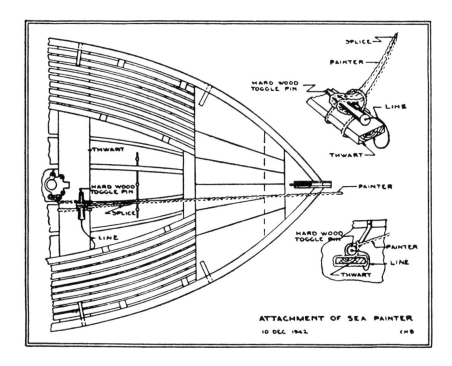

Fig. 3-13. Sea painter attachment. Courtesy of U.S. Coast Guard

## LIFE RAFTS

Inflatable life rafts have now, for the most part, replaced the older rigid life rafts. Rigid life rafts are still recognized as lifesaving appliances by Coast Guard and SOLAS 74/83 even though no U.S. manufacturer has currently indicated their intent to produce this equipment.

Inflatable life rafts represent the state of the art in survival technology. Inflatable life rafts are the principal and most desirable lifesaving equipment for small vessels ranging from small yachts to large workboats and are used extensively on large vessels as well.

An inflatable life raft has a number of advantages and some disadvantages in comparison with other lifesaving appliances. Like a tire, it can strike against hard objects without permanent damage. Bumping against the side of a ship or a seaplane, or landing on rocks usually will not damage it unless it strikes a sharp point and tears its fabric. Even then it may be possible to patch it with material prepacked aboard the craft.

The air spaces in an inflatable life raft provide insulation against extremes of temperature. Such relative comfort is not available on buoyant apparatus, rigid life rafts, or even in large open lifeboats.

Once the raft is waterborne you must exercise suitable care in boarding it. Some manufacturers have bow ramps installed for this purpose. Once everyone is aboard the raft, you need to keep its interior dry by using the bailer and cellulose sponge provided. This will help ensure as much personal comfort as possible.

Life rafts can be launched either manually, as in figure 3-14, or by davit, as in figure 3-15. Try to board the life raft dry from the lowest position on the vessel.

The lightness of inflatable life rafts allows them to drift rapidly unless a sea anchor is used. Never let go of the operating cord (or painter) until the raft is boarded. Where the position of the vessel has been sent by radio prior to the use of life rafts, drift should be kept as small as possible to make rescue easier. Where several rafts are used, it is wise to use their painters to prevent drifting apart.

Once in the life raft follow the procedures outlined in the next chapter while staying in the immediate area. Search for survivors away from the ship and among the wreckage. Use the rescue line and quoit over an arm while swimming to persons in the water. Stream the sea anchor or drogue and, where possible, tie rafts together, towing bridle to towing bridle, allowing about 50 feet of rope between each to avoid separation; a group is more easily detected, and in any event this provides mutual incouragement.

### GETTING OFF THE SHIP ON YOUR OWN

If you cannot go over the side in a lifeboat or dry-shod into a life raft it will be necessary to find another method. Ensure your life jacket is properly secured, preferably with crotch straps. Then go over the side by lowering yourself, not jumping. Go over the side via:

Cargo net
Jacob's ladder
Pilot ladder
Accommodation ladder
Attached fire hose
Lifeline or monkey line
Any line attached after securing it to the vessel.

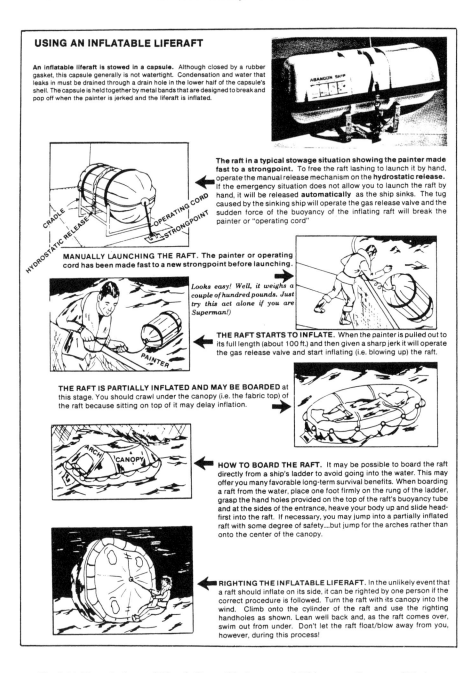

## USING AN INFLATABLE LIFERAFT

**An inflatable liferaft is stowed in a capsule.** Although closed by a rubber gasket, this capsule generally is not watertight. Condensation and water that leaks in must be drained through a drain hole in the lower half of the capsule's shell. The capsule is held together by metal bands that are designed to break and pop off when the painter is jerked and the liferaft is inflated.

**The raft in a typical stowage situation showing the painter made fast to a strongpoint.** To free the raft lashing to launch it by hand, operate the manual release mechanism on the **hydrostatic release.** If the emergency situation does not allow you to launch the raft by hand, it will be released **automatically** as the ship sinks. The tug caused by the sinking ship will operate the gas release valve and the sudden force of the buoyancy of the inflating raft will break the painter or "operating cord"

**MANUALLY LAUNCHING THE RAFT.** The painter or operating cord has been made fast to a new strongpoint before launching.

*Looks easy! Well, it weighs a couple of hundred pounds. Just try this act alone if you are Superman!)*

**THE RAFT STARTS TO INFLATE.** When the painter is pulled out to its full length (about 100 ft.) and then given a sharp jerk it will operate the gas release valve and start inflating (i.e. blowing up) the raft.

**THE RAFT IS PARTIALLY INFLATED AND MAY BE BOARDED** at this stage. You should crawl under the canopy (i.e. the fabric top) of the raft because sitting on top of it may delay inflation.

**HOW TO BOARD THE RAFT.** It may be possible to board the raft directly from a ship's ladder to avoid going into the water. This may offer you many favorable long-term survival benefits. When boarding a raft from the water, place one foot firmly on the rung of the ladder, grasp the hand holes provided on the top of the raft's buoyancy tube and at the sides of the entrance, heave your body up and slide head-first into the raft. If necessary, you may jump into a partially inflated raft with some degree of safety....but jump for the arches rather than onto the center of the canopy.

**RIGHTING THE INFLATABLE LIFERAFT.** In the unlikely event that a raft should inflate on its side, it can be righted by one person if the correct procedure is followed. Turn the raft with its canopy into the wind. Climb onto the cylinder of the raft and use the righting handholes as shown. Lean well back and, as the raft comes over, swim out from under. Don't let the raft float/blow away from you, however, during this process!

Fig. 3-14. Manual release of life raft. From *Able Seaman and Lifeboatman*. Courtesy of Marine Education Textbooks, Houma, LA.

Fig. 3-15. Davit launch of life raft. Courtesy of Viking, Denmark.

Jump as a last resort. Go on the weather side near the bow or stern (the stern is lower and better if the propeller is stopped). *Do not* go over the lee side where you could get trapped against the ship or among loose cargo in the water. Keep your shoes on.

After finding the best position on the vessel, you are ready to jump directly into the water. In this eventuality:

1. Do not jump from a height greater than 15 to 20 feet.
2. Do remove eyeglasses, contact lenses, neck chains, false teeth, or any sharp objects in your pockets.
3. Ensure that your life jacket is correctly secured.
4. Check for obstructions in the water.
5. Hold your life jacket down with one hand and block off your nose and mouth with the other hand (figure 3-16).
6. Keep your feet together; you may cross them when jumping.
7. Jump feet-first near a survival craft, floating debris, or near the painter of a life raft.

Fig. 3-16. Hand position for jumping overboard. Courtesy of U.S. Coast Guard.

8. Do not jump into the boat or on top of the life raft canopy so as not to injure yourself or people in the craft.
9. Jump as far out as possible sideways so you can fend off the side of the vessel if necessary.
10. Once in the water, clear the vessel.

There is a legend that every vessel has a tremendous suction that draws everything down within a radius of a hundred yards, like some terrifying miniature maelstrom. This is definitely an exaggeration. It is true that if a ship is really sinking it's a good idea to get perhaps 30 feet from it. But there is more danger from too great a hurry and panic in getting away than from suction.

There was a case in which a ship sank under several men in seven minutes and not one of them was dragged under. Naturally, if you are near some large opening like a main hatch or a funnel the water will rush in, dragging everything afloat—including you—with it. But even so, unless you get trapped, you will float out before you drown, or may even be pushed out by the escaping air.

If you are some distance from hatches and funnels, the chances are that you can almost certainly *walk* off safely, if you have to stay that long to do your job right. Once away from these dangers, slow down and swim toward your goal. You have more chance of being seen and picked up in a group.

Flash your life jacket light on and off quickly so that at least some of the flashes occur when you are at the crest of a wave. Also remember to blow your whistle.

If you have no life jacket or suit, any floating debris will help you stay up. You can sometimes get a better grip if you jab your knife into the wood. You can tread water, take off your pants or jacket, tie a knot in the legs or sleeves, button them up and swing them through the air so that the arms or legs fill with air. Then twist the open ends so that the air stays in and you have a life preserver. Lie on your back and float.

Don't thrash about or swim uselessly. Slow, relaxed strokes made with the arms moving like the oars of a boat when being rowed, and a slow kick help keep a man up if he has no life jacket. Every seafarer should know how to swim.

If you see sharks, make a commotion in the water to scare them and have your knife ready. If, as a last resort, you must go over the side into an oil slick or flames, you must take off your life jacket in order to swim underwater. Swimming in oil is like swimming through mud. Wait for a clear spot, gauge the distance, be sure you are facing windward, and then jump feet-first. Swim underwater. On coming up for air, turn so as to face the wind and push water away from you with short strokes. Breathe, submerge, and swim again to windward.

Once aboard the lifeboat or life raft, you must follow the procedures covered in the next chapter.

# CHAPTER FOUR

# In the Lifeboat or Life Raft

To abandon a vessel is only 50 percent of the complete survival problem. Survival at sea will be the subject of chapter 5. At this point it is pertinent to indicate what should be done for LIFE in our survival craft as it pertains to:

> Leadership and morale
> Immediate action
> First aid
> Equipment and navigation

## "L" IS FOR LEADERSHIP AND MORALE

As the survival craft commander, you must lead by:

1. Taking charge and assigning everyone aboard to duties according to their capabilities, however small. Place the sick or weak survivors next to you.
2. Enforcing discipline, vigorously, if necessary.
3. Exemplifying the will to survive.
4. Maintaining a calm frame of mind which is contagious.
5. Starting discussions, no matter how trivial, to divert the mind and keep up spirits.

Morale is kept high by making the persons aboard as comfortable as possible—trying to overcome the fact that a survival craft is not designed for comfort but to save lives. Signaling equipment should be ready, and used only when rescue vessels or aircraft are sighted or known to be in the vicinity. If possible, hoist metal reflectors for radar detection as high as they can be hoisted to assist radar-equipped rescue ships and aircraft in locating your survival craft. Maintaining the will to survive is contagious and will keep up the morale of all on board. Good morale will stem from good leadership, and whoever assumes leadership on the craft must assume threefold responsibility: physical, mental, and spiritual. The leader must translate this responsibility into wise discipline and humane comfort.

Confidence will be inspired and maintained by the craft itself and its equipment, which survivors can see for themselves. The allocation of routine chores, the encouragement of ingenuity in collecting water and seafood, the assured belief in imminent rescue—anything that stimulates and occupies the minds of the survivors will help to keep their spirits and morale high.

Fear, in many forms, can be a real and active danger (fear of the unknown, fear of personal weakness, fear of discomfort), and everything possible must be done to prevent it from ever gaining the upper hand. Uncontrolled, fear can give a person characteristics wholly alien to his or her nature, and can produce effects harmful to everyone within communicable distance. It is a sober fact that many people, because of fear, have lost faith in their own fortitude and ability and have fared badly in circumstances less dangerous than the fear of them.

Fear is natural, but it can be controlled and overcome. The duty of keeping it out of the craft is quite clearly the leader's, and he or she will find the craft a material help in doing so. Here, plainly visible to the survivors, are shelter, safe flotation, food, water, communication with rescue sources, and companionship.

### "I" IS FOR IMMEDIATE ACTION

### Lifeboats

#### *Checklist*

1. Clear the sinking vessel in case of explosion or surface fire.
2. Check with other lifeboats and then search for possible survivors. Stay in the general area, and deploy the sea anchor to reduce drift if seas are rough.
3. Take seasickness pills. If in cold weather, those most in need should put on an immersion suit or thermal protective aids.
4. Salvage any floating equipment which may be useful; stow and secure all items.
5. Ensure that the lifeboat is dry; make sure drain plug(s) is properly secured; bail out boat if necessary.
6. Check the physical condition of all aboard. Give first aid if necessary (see next section). If oil or gasoline is on someone's clothing or skin, have them wash it off.

7. Have all signaling equipment ready—smoke, dye, flares, mirrors, emergency radio, VHF radio. Lash EPIRB to the side of the vessel and in the water. Operate signaling equipment as necessary.

8. If there is more than one boat, keep close together to expedite rescue operations. Lash together, if possible, bow to stern with the full length of the painter. Make yourselves bigger, brighter, and/or better able to be seen.

9. Make a calm estimate of your situation and plan your course of action carefully.

10. Ration water and food; give *nothing* for the first 24 hours.

11. Assign duties to all on board and set up watches. The essential duties are (a) lookout; (b) medical; (c) boat integrity; (d) rations; and (e) navigation. Someone must be on the lookout at all times for rescue aircraft or ships. Rotate lookout duties frequently, especially in cold weather or in rough seas. It would be advisable to assign two lookouts. One can scan the sea while the other looks for aircraft. During the daytime sunglasses, if available, should be provided to the lookout. In hot weather, ensure that lookouts are protected from sunburn.

12. Don't row or operate your engine unless absolutely necessary. Conserve your strength or fuel until needed.

13. Keep a log. Record time of entry into water, names and physical condition of survivors, ration schedule, winds, weather, direction of swells, time of sunrise and sunset, and other navigational data. Inventory all equipment.

14. All survivors should read any survival manual provided. The effective use of the contents of the manual may be the key to survival and eventual rescue of all aboard. Have someone read aloud the important points.

15. Do not allow smoking since it creates thirst. If you must give in to smokers' demands, check the boat and surrounding water for fire hazards.

## Life Rafts

### *Checklist*

1. Get clear of the sinking vessel in case of explosion or surface fire. It may be necessary to use the paddles and bring in the sea anchor in order to clear the area fast.

2. Search for any possible survivors.
3. Salvage any floating equipment which may be useful; stow and secure all items. Deploy drogue or sea anchor to remain in the area of search and rescue operations.
4. Check the raft for proper inflation, leaks, and points of possible chafing. Bail out any water that may have entered the raft. Be careful not to snag the raft with shoes or sharp objects.
5. In cold oceans, inflate the floor immediately. Put on your immersion suit, if available. Rig the entrance cover. If you are with others, huddle together for warmth.
6. Check the physical condition of all aboard. Give first aid if necessary (see next section). Take seasickness pills. Wash oil or gasoline off of yourself and others.
7. Have all signalling equipment ready—smoke, dye, flares, mirrors, VHF radio, and EPIRB. Lash EPIRB to the side of the raft and in the water. Operate signalling equipment as necessary.
8. If there is more than one raft, keep close together to expedite rescue operations. Rafts should be tied together if possible about 50 feet apart from towing bridle to towing bridle. Make yourselves bigger, brighter, and/or better able to be seen. Unscrew bulbs during daytime hours.
9. Make a calm estimate of your situation and plan your course of action carefully.
10. Ration water and food; assign duties to the survivors. *No* food or water should be given for the first 24 hours.
11. Assign duties to all on board; set up watches. Someone must be on the lookout at all times for rescue aircraft or ships. Rotate lookout duties frequently, especially in cold weather or in rough seas. Organize watches in pairs, one outside, one inside—the outside watch to look for ships, aircraft, survivors, useful wreckage, and to flash the signalling mirror during sunny days; the inside watch to maintain the life raft, attend to the injured, and look after equipment.
12. Keep a log. Record time of entry into water, names and physical condition of survivors, ration schedule, winds, weather, direction of swells, times of sunrise and sunset, and other navigation data. Inventory all equipment.
13. The survival manual should be carefully read by all survivors. The effective use of the contents of this manual may be the key

to your survival and eventual rescue. If possible, have someone read aloud the important points. It would be best to read the manual before leaving the vessel but this may not be feasible or possible.

14. Do not become alarmed if air is heard escaping from a recently inflated raft. This is normal. Safety valves allow excess pressure to escape so the raft will not damage itself by overinflation. However, if air continues to escape and the raft starts to get soft, caps are provided so you can seal the safety valves and stop further air loss.

15. Do not allow smoking since it creates thirst. If you must give into smokers' demands check the surrounding water for fire hazards. Someone should watch the smoking individual(s) to ensure no fire is started or damage done, particularly in a life raft. The comfort of all must be considered when permission to smoke is granted.

Keep the interior of the raft well ventilated. A heavy concentration of leaking carbon dioxide gas (from the cylinders that inflated the raft) and exhaled breath is dangerous and has no odor.

In both lifeboats and life rafts, survivors should stay out of the sun to reduce loss of body fluids. After 24 hours one can of water per person is allotted (one third in the morning, one third at noon, and one third in the evening).

## "F" IS FOR FIRST AID

The following procedures were extracted from the "Instructions and Survival Manual for Inflatable Life Raft" by Switlik Parachute Company, Inc., and can also apply to first aid aboard lifeboats.

A first aid kit is contained in a waterproof case in the emergency pack. The contents are limited and care should be taken to see they are used effectively. Whenever the kit is opened, remove only those items which are needed for immediate use and return the remainder to the waterproof package. Common contents of a first aid kit can be found in table 4-1. An example of directions for the use of a first aid kit in a life raft can be seen in figure 4-1. What follows table 4-1 is a brief synopsis of the most common injuries one would encounter in survival situations.

**TABLE 4-1**

First Aid Kit Contents

| Item | Number per Package | Size of Package | Number of Packages |
|---|---|---|---|
| Bandage compress – 4 inches | 1 | Single | 1 |
| Bandage compress – 2 inches | 4 | Single | 1 |
| Waterproof adhesive compress – 1 inch | 16 | Single | 1 |
| Eye dressing packet: ⅛ ounce opthalmic ointment, adhesive strips, cotton pads | 3 | Single | 1 |
| Bandage, gauze, compressed 2 inches × 6 yards | 2 | Single | 1 |
| Tourniquet, forceps, scissors, safety pins | 1, 1, 1, 12 | Double | 1 |
| Wire splint | 1 | Single | 1 |
| Ammonia inhalers | 10 | Single | 1 |
| Iodine applicators (½ ml swab type) | 10 | Single | 1 |
| Aspirin, phenacetin, and caffeine compound (APC) 6½ gr. tablets, vials of 20 | 2 | Single | 1 |
| Sterile petrolatum gauze, 3 inches × 18 inches | 4 | Single | 1 |
| Instructions | | | |

## Rescue Breathing

Artificial respiration is not easy to accomplish in an inflatable life raft or lifeboat, especially in heavy weather. The most practical method is the mouth-to-mouth method.

1. Open the victim's mouth and remove any foreign objects, including false teeth, and ensure the victim's tongue is forward.
2. When the victim's mouth is clear, place him or her on his or her back, tilting the head backwards until the front of the neck is stretched tightly and the jaw is jutting out.
   (a) If the victim is an adult and his or her mouth can be opened readily, approach the victim's head from the side and lift the jaw with your thumb between the teeth.
   (b) If the victim is an infant, or if the mouth cannot be opened readily, raise the lower jaw by lifting it upward on both sides from the jaw hinge beneath the earlobes. *Note:* It is important to hold the jaw up throughout the rescue breathing.

## DIRECTIONS FOR THE USE OF THE FIRST-AID KIT

| ITEM TITLE | REMARKS |
|---|---|
| **Ammonia Inhalants** | Break one and inhale for faintness, fainting, or collapse. |
| **Aspirin, Phenacetin, Caffeine Tablets** | Chew up and swallow 2 tablets every three hours for headache, colds, minor aches, pains and fever. Maximum of 8 in twenty-four hours. |
| **Bandage compress, 4" and 2"** | Apply as dressing over wound. DON'T touch part that comes in contact with wound. |
| **Bandage, gauze, compressed, 2"** | For securing splints, dressings, etc. |
| **Burn Dressing** | The petrolatum gauze bandage is applied in at least two layers over the burned surface and an area extending 2" beyond it. The first dressing should be allowed to remain in place, changing only the outer, dry bandage as needed, for at least 10 days unless signs of infection develop after several days, in which case the dressing should be removed and the burn treated as an infected wound. Watch for blueness or coldness of the skin beyond the dressing and loosen the dressing if they appear. |
| **Compress, Adhesive, 1"** | Apply as dressing over small wounds. DON'T touch part that comes in contact with wound. |
| **Eye Patch** | Apply as dressing over inflamed or injured eye. |
| **Forceps** | Use to remove splinters or foreign bodies. Don't dig. |
| **Ophthalmic Ointment** | Apply in space formed by pulling lower eyelid down, once daily for inflamed or injured eyes. Don't touch eyeball with tube. |
| **Splint, wire** | Pad with gauze and mold to member to immobilize broken bones. Hold in place with bandage. Do not attempt to set the bone. |
| **Tincture of iodine, mild** | Remove protective sleeve, crush tube and apply with swab end. DON'T use in or around eyes. |
| **Tourniquet** | For control of hemorrhage. Loosen for a few seconds every 15 minutes. |

Fig. 4-1. Directions for the use of the first aid kit in a life raft. Courtesy of Revere Survival Products, New York, NY.

3. Take a deep breath.
4. Cover the victim's nose as follows:
   (a) If you are lifting the lower jaw with your thumb between the jaws, pinch the nose with your other hand.
   (b) If you are lifting the lower jaw with both hands and the victim is not an infant, seal the nose by resting your cheek against it. For an infant, cover both the nose and mouth with your mouth.
5. Seal your mouth tightly over the victim's open mouth, or in the case of an infant, over the mouth and nose.
6. Blow into the victim's mouth. (For an infant, only a small amount, as the lungs are delicate and must not be damaged.)
7. While blowing, watch the victim's chest. When the chest rises, stop blowing and remove your mouth from the victim's.

8. Let the victim exhale without assistance.
9. Repeat blowing 12 to 20 times per minute until the victim breathes for him- or herself.

Examine the injured person. Ask what hurts. Do not just take care of the wound that you see. Notice if he or she is pale or faint. The victim may be hurt inside or be bleeding from some spot that you did not see at first. Handle him or her gently.

### Bleeding

If possible, clean the wound thoroughly with water and apply a sterile pad directly to the wound, applying firm pressure either by hand or by bandaging. If practicable, elevate the limb until the bleeding has stopped. If the bleeding is severe, endeavor to control it by finger pressure. *Only use a tourniquet as a last resort.* Arteries are easily found and gentle pressure with the fingers will find the best position to control bleeding. Figure 4-2 shows the location of main arteries and pressure control points.

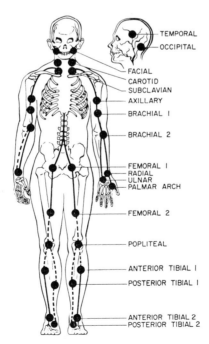

Fig. 4-2. Arteries and pressure points. Courtesy of Switlik Parachute Company, Inc., Trenton, NJ.

A tourniquet should only be used as a last resort when the bleeding cannot be controlled by hand or dressing. Apply the tourniquet above the wound and release for several seconds every 15 minutes. Should the extremity become cold and bluish in color, release the tourniquet more frequently. In extreme cold, the tourniquet should be released at more frequent intervals and every effort should be made to keep the treatment area as warm as possible.

## Shock

In case of shipwreck or abandonment for any cause, all survivors will suffer from shock in one degree or another. It is therefore important that survivors are kept as warm as possible, but not overheated. Except in the tropics, the entrances should be closed and the temperature in the craft raised as quickly as possible. Some will suffer more than others and may have pale, cold skin. They may sweat, breathe rapidly, and have a weak pulse. They may also be confused or unconscious. For survivors in this condition, lay them flat with feet raised and keep them as warm as possible. If the case is a bad one, another survivor whose body is relatively warm should lie on top of the shock victim, the two being covered with any additional clothing or blankets which may be available. Body warmth is the quickest and surest way of assisting survivors suffering from shock.

### *Treat and Prevent Shock*

1. Stop the bleeding, if present.
2. Remove wet clothing, under covers if possible. Wrap the person in blankets to keep in the body heat. Remember that more blankets are needed under the body than over it.
3. Raise the legs so that they are about a foot above the body and put rolled-up blankets or clothes under the body so that it also is higher than the head, unless the head is injured. In this case put the folded blanket or coat under the head and shoulders. The patient should not sit up. Keep him or her as quiet as possible.
4. Apply heating pads, found in the abandon ship kits, to the belly and groin. Great care should be taken not to burn the skin, especially of a person who has fainted. Wrap the pad in a piece of clothing to prevent overheating the skin. Too much heat is just as harmful as cold.

5. Pass aromatic spirits of ammonia under the nose of the patient if he or she has passed out. Try it on yourself first. If the patient is conscious, give him or her a teaspoonful in a half glass of water and repeat every half hour until he or she feels stronger. If you can get hot drinks, give hot water, tea, or coffee, one teaspoon at a time, so that the patient has a total of one cup once every hour. *Never pour liquids into the mouth of a person who has passed out.*

6. Pain makes shock worse. If there is severe pain, give one-half grain of morphine, if available. To give morphine, take off the transparent cover of the morphine Syrette. Take hold of the wire loop and push the wire in so that it makes a hole in the inner seal. Pull out the wire and throw it away. Be careful not to let fingers or anything else come in contact with the needle. Hold the loose skin on the forearm, leg, or belly between the fingers, thrust in the needle to half its length, and slowly squeeze the tube from the end. It takes 20 to 30 minutes to get the total effect. An additional dose may be given in three hours if necessary. Do not give morphine in a head injury case or to a person who has fainted.

7. Rub the patient's arms and legs briskly in an upwards direction under the covers to increase circulation and help warm him or her.

8. The patient may vomit as he or she starts to recover. Do not let the patient get up but raise the head slightly and turn it to one side.

## Burns

Apply a petrolatum gauze bandage in at least two layers over the burned surface and extending about two inches beyond it. The first dressing should be allowed to remain in place, changing only the outer dry bandage as needed for at least 10 days, unless signs of infection develop after several days. If infection does develop, the dressing should be removed and the burn treated as an infected wound. Watch for blueness and coldness of the skin beyond the dressing, and loosen the dressing if this occurs. APC (an aspirin, phenacetin, and caffeine combination) tablets taken every three hours will help relieve the pain. Keep the burned part at rest. If it is necessary to open a blister because of pain, size, or pressure, use a sterile needle to pierce the blister at the edge near healthy skin and obtain drainage by this method.

## Sprains

Bandage the sprain and immobilize the area. Application of a cold compress may prevent swelling. Elevate the injured extremity. Six to eight hours after the swelling has decreased, the application of heat to the local area will ease the pain. If it is necessary to use the sprained limb, immobilize the injured area as much as possible with a splint or heavy wrapping. If no broken bones are involved, a sprained limb can be used to certain limits.

### Fractured Bones

Handle the injured person with care to avoid causing additional injury. Do not attempt to remove clothing from a broken limb. If a wound exists, cut away clothing (most easily cut at the seams) and treat the wound. A wire splint is provided in the first aid kit and additional splints may be improvised by the use of sections of the boat's paddles (see figure 4-3). Pad the paddles with soft materials. The splint should be long enough to support the joints both above and below the fracture. Do not attempt to reset any broken bones. Give the victim APC tablets to reduce the pain and keep him or her quiet.

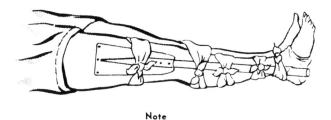

**Note**

If paddles are not available, use sound leg.

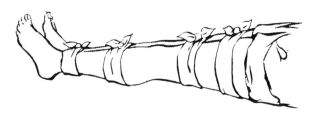

Fig. 4-3. Splinting with paddles. Courtesy of Switlik Parachute Company, Inc., Trenton, NJ.

## Dislocations

If there is no one who knows how to put a dislocated shoulder back in place, put the arm in a sling and tie the upper arm to the body with a broad bandage so that it can't move.

## Chest Wounds

Open chest wounds through which air can be heard passing should be covered with a large dressing. Air entering the wound will collapse the lungs. Consequently, the patch should be firmly applied at the moment of maximum exhalation, just before more air is inhaled. The patch should be firm enough to seal the wound but not tight enough to restrict chest movements.

## Eye Injury

Clean the eye as thoroughly as possible by rinsing it with clean water. A foreign body not stuck in the eye may be removed by filling the eye with boric acid ointment which will bring the particle to the edge of the eye where it can be removed. Do not attempt to remove foreign bodies embedded in the eye. Fill the eye with eye ointment and cover with a dressing. Give APC tablet for pain.

## Sore Eyes

Glare from sky and water may cause eyes to become bloodshot, inflamed, and painful. Improvise an eye shield from cloth, and bandage the eyes lightly if they hurt. Moisten a piece of gauze or cotton with seawater and lay it over the eyes before bandaging.

## Saltwater Sores

Do not open or squeeze them. Keep them as dry as possible. Apply antiseptic, if available.

## Infection Prevention

Cut away clothing to get to the wound. Do not touch the wound with fingers or dirty objects, if possible. Wash the wound as thoroughly as possible with clean water and apply a sterile bandage. Secure the dressing so as not to restrict the flow of blood. Iodine may be used to sterilize the skin surrounding the wound, but should not be poured directly into an open wound. Let the iodine dry in the air before a bandage is applied. Keep the wounded part at rest.

## Treatment of Wounds

If serious, *stop the bleeding*, then *treat shock,* then *prevent infection.*

1. Lay the patient flat, if possible.
2. Get at the wound by cutting the clothing, if absolutely necessary, and cut away as little as possible so that the patient won't be cold.
3. If the wound has stopped bleeding do not wash away the clot or scab unless it is crusted with dirt, as it may start bleeding again. Fuel oil on the clot will not do any harm.
4. Sprinkle sulfanilamide powder, if available, on the wound and surrounding skin, or if that is not available, apply antiseptic. Do not try to remove pieces of clothing, metal, or bone from the wound unless they are loose, as the bleeding may start again or increase. If necessary, wash the wound with seawater.
5. Do not touch the wound with your fingers. Take large compresses—without touching the side to be put next to the wound— cover the injury, and hold in place firmly with a bandage. Do not disturb the dressing unless it becomes painful; then loosen it but do not remove it. If blood soaks through, put another large compress on top and hold it in place firmly with another bandage. The compresses are made up of many square layers of gauze and are in the first aid kit.
6. Stop any bleeding. Usually the compress and bandage do the trick.
   (a) If an arm or leg is bleeding, raise it high. Bleeding can often be stopped by putting the hands tightly around the arm or leg.
   (b) If the blood is dark red and flowing smoothly, it is from a vein. A large compress over the wound, held firmly in place with the hand, is put on first. Try to get a firm pressure with the hand down to the bone—this will stop almost all bleeding. Then put on a firm but not tight bandage. If bleeding continues, put pressure with the fingers on the nearest pressure point on the side of the wound away from the heart.
   (c) If the blood is bright red and flows in spurts, it is from an artery. Raise the leg or arm, and put pressure with the fingers on the nearest pressure point between the heart and the wound.
   (d) If the bleeding continues and everything else fails, apply a tourniquet about a hand's breadth below the groin in the case

of a leg wound. Never apply it anywhere else. Apply the tourniquet over clothing or several layers of bandage. Use any piece of cloth at least two inches wide. Take two turns and tie a square knot. If this does not stop the bleeding, insert a stick and twist it to tighten the tourniquet, until the bleeding just stops, and no tighter. *Loosen every fifteen minutes and do not tighten again if the bleeding has stopped.* Always indicate by tag or mark whether a tourniquet is in use. Leave it in place in case bleeding starts again, but keep it loose in the meantime. It is rarely necessary to use a tourniquet.

    (e) Treat the wound as described under (3) and (4).

7. Keep the patient warm.
8. If the pain is very great, give morphine to stop the pain and help prevent shock. Do not give morphine if you think the patient has a concussion or a fractured skull.
9. Bleeding from head or face wounds can almost always be stopped with a pad placed firmly over the wound.
10. Never give liquid if there is severe bleeding or a belly wound or if the patient coughs blood. It makes the bleeding worse or starts it up afresh.
11. If a wound becomes infected, soak it in hot water for an hour and repeat in six hours if necessary. In a lifeboat use seawater, or use compresses or clothes soaked in seawater.
12. Each wounded or burned patient should be given eight sulfadiazine tablets at one time. No more should be given.

## Urine and Constipation

A dark color to the urine and difficulty in passing it is normal. Do not get worried. Lack of bowel movement is normal also. Do not be disturbed about it. Do not take a laxative, even if available. Exercise as much as possible.

## Frostbite

Frostbite is the freezing of some part of the body. It is a constant hazard in subzero temperatures, especially when the wind is strong. As a rule, the first sensation of frostbite is numbness rather than pain. You can see the effects of frostbite—a grayish or yellow-white spot on the skin—before you can feel it.

Use the buddy system. Watch your buddy's face to see if any frozen spots show and have him or her watch yours.

Warm the frozen part rapidly. Frozen parts should be thawed in water until soft, even though the treatment is painful. This treatment is most effective when the water is exactly 107°F, but water either cooler or warmer can be used. If warm water is not available, wrap the frozen part in blankets or clothing and apply improvised heat packs.

Use body heat to aid in thawing. Hold a bare, warm palm against frostbitten ears or parts of the face. Grasp a frostbitten wrist with a warm, bare hand. Hold frostbitten hands against the chest, under the armpits, or between the legs at the groin. Hold a frostbitten foot against a companion's stomach or between his or her thighs.

When frostbite is accompanied by breaks in the skin, apply a sterile dressing. Do not use strong antiseptics such as tincture of iodine. Do not use powdered sulfa drugs on the wound.

Never forcibly remove frozen-on shoes or mittens. Place them in lukewarm water until soft and then remove gently.

Never rub frostbite. You may tear frozen tissue and cause further tissue damage. Never apply snow or ice; that just increases the cold injury. For the same reason, never soak frozen limbs in kerosene or oil.

Do not try to thaw a frozen part by exercising. Exercise of frozen parts will increase tissue damage and is likely to break the skin. Do not stand or walk on frozen feet. You will only cause tissue damage.

## Immersion Foot (Trench Foot)

Immersion foot is a cold injury resulting from prolonged exposure to temperatures just above freezing. In the early stages of immersion foot, your feet and toes are pale and feel cold, numb, and stiff. Walking becomes difficult. If you do not take preventive action at this stage, your feet will swell and become very painful. In extreme cases of immersion foot, the flesh dies, and amputation of the foot or the leg may be necessary.

Because the early stages are not very painful, you must be constantly alert to prevent the development of immersion foot. To prevent this condition:

1. Keep your feet dry by wearing waterproof footgear and keeping your raft dry.
2. Clean and dry your socks and shoes at every opportunity.
3. Dry your feet as soon as possible after getting them wet.

4. Warm the feet with your hands, apply foot powder, and put on dry socks.
5. When you must wear wet socks and shoes, exercise your feet continually by wiggling your toes and bending your ankles. When sleeping in a sitting position, warm your feet, put on dry socks, and elevate your legs as high as possible. Do not wear tight shoes.
6. Treat immersion foot by keeping the affected part dry and warm. If possible, keep the foot and leg in a horizontal position to increase circulation.

## Sunburn

Keep the face, head, and body covered if possible. The salve for burns or the eye ointment in the first aid kit will give relief. If blisters form don't open them. If they break, dust them lightly with sulfanilamide powder, cover with gauze, and bandage lightly. If you have no sulfa powder, cover with a wet bandage or rag. Don't use massage oil.

## Heat Exhaustion and Sunstroke

These are not the same thing and are different in symptoms and in treatment. In heat exhaustion the victim is dizzy, weak, often has nausea, cramps in the muscles, and is only partly conscious. The face is pale, the skin cool and perspiring. The pulse is weak and breathing is shallow. Loosen the clothing and protect the victim from the sun if possible. Keep him or her warm and perfectly quiet. If the patient can be aroused, give aromatic spirits of ammonia, one-half teaspoon to one-half glass of water, and drinking water if there is some.

In sunstroke the victim is dizzy, irritable, and has a headache. The face is flushed, very hot, and dry to the touch. He or she may suddenly fall unconscious. His or her pulse is strong and he or she breathes heavily. Shade the head and body if at all possible. Cool the victim off by putting his or her wrists in the sea.

## "E" IS FOR EQUIPMENT AND NAVIGATION

## Lifeboats

A description of the equipment found in the lifeboat is given in appendix A. For review purposes the equipment is listed under the following generalized areas:

## Handling Equipment

Boat and sea painters
Storm oil
Heaving line
Boat hooks
Sea anchor
Hatchets

## Survival Equipment

Bailer
Bilge pump
Buckets
Protective cover
Fishing kit
First aid kit
Provisions
Water
Desalting kit
Drinking cup
Jackknife

## Lighting Equipment

Flashlight
Lantern
Illuminating oil
Matches

## Specialized Equipment

Gunwale ladder
Ditty bag
Fire extinguishers
Tool kit

## Rescue Equipment

Life preservers
Table of lifesaving signals
Floating orange distress
signals
Red rocket parachute flares
Red hand-held distress signals
Signalling mirror
Compass

Read the instructions that come with each item and thoroughly comply with them. Have someone read the instructions aloud so all aboard may know the capabilities and limitations of each item.

## Sea Anchor

A sea anchor (figure 4-4) is worth its weight in gold. Every lifeboat is required to have one. It acts as a drag just as a parachute does but it lies horizontally in the water. It keeps the boat end-on to the seas.

With a sea anchor at the bow a well-found lifeboat will ride out a whole gale. The seas may sweep the boat, but it will stay right side up. But let the boat get broadside to and a relatively small comber will roll it over like a cardboard box in the wind.

Any piece of canvas stretched so that it will catch in the water will do for a sea anchor in a pinch. You can use your sail and spars, but have them securely lashed. If you haven't got anything better, put a bucket overboard on as long and heavy a line as you've got. Wrap the rope with canvas to prevent chafing over the gunwale.

On a well-constructed sea anchor, the towing beckets should go completely around the anchor, with the sides of the canvas cone sewn to the ropes. It is essential to provide the anchor with a towing swivel at each end, otherwise it will kink up the towing rope so badly that it will become useless in a very short time.

The tripping line is made fast at the point of the cone, preferably to a strop sewn completely around the sea anchor.

Directly above the flat base of the oil cone, the canvas in the anchor should be doubled, and four to six number 4 brass grommets set in to reduce the water pressure on the anchor.

## Use of Sea Anchor

When hove to, the sea anchor is let out over the bow with sufficient drag-line to place it as near as possible in the far end of the sea trough when the boat is on the crest of the wave. Consequently, a boat traveling with the moving wave crest with the sea anchor lying in slack water may even be drawn in the opposite direction. This would be due to the undertow of the next wave—but the dragline would tighten up and so keep the boat head to the sea.

Never pay the dragline out to the bitter end. Make the bitter end fast to the forward thwart. The method of using a sea anchor may be different in a covered or partially enclosed lifeboat. Always keep enough slack to allow for a round turn around the thwart and a couple of fathoms to spare. Then when the full force of the wave hits the boat, the strain on the drag line is eased off. Otherwise, the line will break.

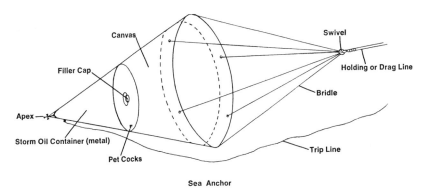

Sea Anchor

Fig. 4-4. Lifeboat sea anchor. Courtesy of U.S. Coast Guard.

When the crest of the wave has been passed, the boat is running downhill, and the sea anchor is in the wash of the next wave, the drag-line will slacken up and afford an opportunity to haul back in the slack just paid out. You are then ready for the next wave.

A sea anchor should not be used, as a rule, over the stern of the boat. At times, however, for some reason—as in sailing before the wind—it may be found necessary to have some steadying agent besides the steering oar or rudder out over the stern. The anchor may be towed point first by means of the tripping line, thereby offering less resistance most of the time, and only turned to full pull when at the crest of a wave.

If, in a fair wind and following sea, it is desired to provide a sea-smoothing oil slick, the anchor can be towed point first all of the time.

The uses of a sea anchor can be remembered with the word HOLD:

H for *Head*—into the sea
O for *Oil*—to distribute oil
L for *Landing*—to assist in landing
D for *Drift*—to prevent drifting

### Using the Oars in a Gale

If you don't have a sea anchor, you'll have to keep the boat end-on with the oars by keeping the blade held vertical. This is not easy, but it may be necessary for continued existence. You may decide to keep the nose into the sea. You may have to because of the boat's design.

With the double-ender whaleboat type you'll probably find it easier to take the seas over the stern. With stern to sea and enough motion from the oars to give steerageway, you have an ideal situation under the circumstances. Or at least as ideal a situation as one could have riding out a gale in midocean in a lifeboat.

The boat will be taking the seas end-on—or nearly so. It's moving, so the seas do not smack it very hard. The boat's not moving fast enough to dive into a trough (and maybe pitchpole) or teeter on the crest of a wave, completely out of control.

Always use a steering oar in heavy weather. It's hard work, but your rudder's liable to be hoisted clean out of water just when you need it, and there will be many times when it won't give you the leverage you need. Keep the boat on an even keel or slightly stern-heavy.

If you're heading into a sea be sure that the bow isn't too light or it may be picked up by a sea and, before you know it, swung broadside-to, which is a setup for the next roller.

## Oil on Seas

Oil on seas that are breaking has a calming effect that is little short of miraculous, and it doesn't take much. Your gallon or so may have to last a long while, so contrive some means of having it ooze out slowly.

It is useful to have a canvas bag filled with an absorbent material, such as oakum or waste, soaked in oil. Prepare this on the ship. Puncture the bag with a heavy sail needle before using. Make no more holes than necessary, in order to save oil.

The important thing is to spread a blanket of oil over that area to windward through which breaking seas are sweeping at you. Conditions will determine where your bags should be put—maybe in the sea anchor—although if you're yawing badly it may not spread out enough.

It may be sufficient to drop a single bag over the windward end of the boat, or you may need three small ones—one to windward and one on either side. Watch how the slick forms and change the bags as necessary.

## Navigating a Lifeboat

Before any lengthy voyages are undertaken, all the facts and circumstances should be considered. Today with EPIRBs and communication capabilities it would probably be wisest to stay in the general area and deploy your sea anchor. An attempt to travel a great distance might be unnecessary, and could expose the survivors to unnecessary risk. Engines for lifeboats are required to have only sufficient fuel to operate for 24 hours. Lifeboats are not fitted with deep keels or centerboards and have only small sail area, so it is unwise to try to sail in a direction from which prevailing winds blow. The rowing of lifeboats for a long distance is a tough job. Except under wartime emergencies, most of the great lifeboat passages of history, such as that of Captain Bligh of *Bounty* fame, were made in warm weather in the direction toward which the steady trade winds were blowing. These men used boats made to be sailed in an era when radio, aircraft, and speedy rescue vessels were unknown.

The wise lifeboat commander becomes thoroughly familiar with the theory of navigation: the celestial triangle, the circle of equal altitude, and the other basic principles involved. He or she should be able to identify the most useful stars, and know how to solve sights by any widely used method, because his or her favorite method may not be available. The lifeboat commander should be able to construct a plotting sheet with a protractor. Familiarity with the coordinates (latitude and longitude) of land points in the area of operations, ability to interpret wind and weather signs, knowledge of the ocean currents, and skill in handling a small boat are parts of the practical navigator's basic education which assume their greatest importance in an emergency. For the navigator prepared with such knowledge, and a determination to succeed, the situation is never hopeless. Some method of navigation is always available.

### Emergency Navigation Kit

If practicable, full navigational equipment should be provided. As many as possible of the items in the following list should be included. All of these, except a timepiece, and possibly a sextant and radio, can be kept in the emergency navigation kit.

1. *Notebook* suitable for use as a deck log and for performing computations.

2. *Charts and other plotting materials.* A pilot chart is most suitable for lifeboat use, both for plotting and as a source of information on variation of the compass, shipping lanes, currents, winds, and weather. During World War II, pilot charts were printed on waterproof material suitable for use in a lifeboat. Plotting sheets are useful but not essential if charts are available. The plotting sheets should cover the latitudes in which the ship operates. Universal plotting sheets may be preferred, particularly if the latitude coverage is large. Several maneuvering boards and several sheets of graph paper (preferably with 10 squares per inch) should be included, as these have many uses.

3. *Plotting equipment.* Pencils, erasers, straightedge, protractor, dividers, and compasses (not essential, but useful), and a knife or pencil sharpener should be included.

4. *Timepiece.* A good watch is needed if longitude is to be determined astronomically. This watch should be waterproof or kept in a waterproof container. The watch should be wound regularly and a record kept of its error and rate of change. Even if one or more such watches are available, the possibility of taking along the chronometers from the ship should not be overlooked.

5. *Sextant.* A marine sextant should be taken along if possible. A lifeboat sextant can be made of wood or other rigid material, two small mirrors, and a pivot. The graduations of the arc should be double those of a compass rose (an angle of 5° should be labeled 10°, etc.). It is not necessary to provide a vernier, or

means of adjusting the sextant, since accuracy of 0.1° is satisfactory for lifeboat use.

6. *Almanac.* A nautical almanac for the current year is desirable. In an emergency an almanac for another year can be used.

7. *Tables.* Some form of table will be needed for reducing celestial observations. Traverse tables are useful.

8. *Compass.* Each lifeboat is required to carry a magnetic compass. A deviation table for each compass should be made while in port, with magnetic material in its normal place.

9. *Flashlight.* A flashlight is required to be carried in each lifeboat. The batteries should be replaced from time to time, as necessary. Extra batteries and bulbs might well be carried.

10. *Portable radio.* If a portable radio is available, be sure it is included. Do not overlook it, as it may be used as a radio direction finder.

As soon as possible in the lifeboat, plot your position carefully on the charts. Pilot charts give the figures on prevailing winds and currents in the various parts of the ocean, and other valuable information. Keep them clean and dry.

*The compass is your most precious possession.* Be sure that it is lashed. Mount it accurately in a fore and aft line, in the centerline if possible, where the helmsman can see the card. Arrange for enough illumination at night so that he can see the lettering. Arrange the light, however, so that the compass will not be deflected by it. A large flashlight held close to the compass can pull your needle around till you can't tell east from west.

Always assume that your compass has a large error (and in a steel lifeboat you'll probably be right). Find out what the error is as soon as you can. Your best check is the North Star, always within a couple of degrees of true north for observers between the equator and latitude 60°N.

There are two causes of error in a compass, *variation* and *deviation.* The chart tells you what the variation in that locality is. The deviation, which is due to the iron in the boat, you will find out for yourself. Forget about it until you've set your course. To find out what the deviation is, take a bearing of the North Star. It should bear 000°. You find it bearing 030°. If the variation is 20° west, your deviation must be 10° west. Or if the star bears 010° it means that the westerly variation has been partly offset by a deviation of 10° east. The same procedure can be utilized with the sun at noon when it is on the meridian.

Remember this deviation and always figure on it as long as you're anywhere near that course. But if you make a considerable course change, check it again, because it will probably be different.

The course you will decide to take will be based on the proximity of other vessels, of land, on whether or not you have a sail, the present wind, and the direction of the prevailing winds and currents in that area as indicated on the chart. Whether you stay where the ship went down depends on all these factors.

There are two schools of thought here also. One advises staying put under all but the most favorable circumstances. Another assumes that you will not be picked up, and advises not to waste time heading for what you think might be a busy shipping lane. Head for the beach, and pick out something big to steer for, like a continent—something you can't miss. Don't waste time hunting for small islands, unless they're a great deal closer than the continent. Columbus found a continent with only a compass and a chart.

In the absence of reliable longitude information it is better to head for a point at the latitude of destination and then head east or west, since most large land masses of the earth are oriented in a general north-south direction.

If there are several lifeboats, keep them together since the benefits of accurate navigation in any one boat may be shared. A close check should be kept on the direction and distance made good taking into account wind and current. Long voyages have been successfully completed by such dead reckoning and landfalls have been made with surprising accuracy.

If a compass is not available, any celestial body can be used to steer by, if its diurnal apparent motion is considered. A reasonably straight course can be steered by noting the direction of the wind, the movement of the clouds, the direction of the waves, or by watching the wake of the boat. A line can be secured to the side of the boat at a point amidships or forward. The line should tend parallel to the centerline of the boat if on a straight course. The angle between the centerline and the wake is an indication of the amount of leeway. The accuracy of the towed-object or wake method is affected adversely by a cross sea.

A body having a declination the same as the latitude of the destination is over the destination once each day, at the time when its hour angle is the same as the longitude, measured westward through 360°. At this time it should be dead ahead if the boat is following the great circle leading directly through the destination.

*Motive power.* A lifeboat is equipped with one or more of the following means of locomotion: oars, hand-operated propeller, motor, or sail. Of these, only sail offers a practical means of travel over an extended period of time. People living in an open boat, perhaps on reduced rations, should not attempt to expend their strength on oar locomotion, except for short periods. Likewise, the comparatively small fuel supply in a motorboat should be hoarded jealously. It may be desperately needed later, in landing through a surf, preventing the boat from drifting onto a rocky coast, or making the land when a strong current is carrying the boat past an island.

A sail should be rigged, for in it lies the best hope of reaching distant land. If the standard lifeboat sail is not available, a substitute can usually be devised, using the boat cover, or even clothing, and oars.

*Distance* can be determined directly between accurate fixes, but generally it is found by means of speed and elapsed time. A loaded lifeboat will not travel fast, under normal conditions. With a fair wind and weather it may make good a speed of about two to four knots through the water. Hence the importance of wind and current. The navigator used to observing the sea from a high bridge usually overestimates his or her speed in a lifeboat, where he or she is only a few feet from the water. With practice, the navigator's ability should improve.

*Speed* may be determined by using a form of chip log. Attach a long line to a heavy, floating object. Put one knot in the line twelve or fifteen fathoms from the object, and another just ten fathoms (or any convenient distance) from the first. Stream the device over the side and let the line run out freely, noting the elapsed time between passage of the two knots through the hand. A variation of this is the Dutchman's log. A floating object is thrown overboard at the bow, and the elapsed time required for a known length along the centerline to pass it is noted. If a line is attached to the object, it may be used many times. With either variation, it is important to tie the bitter end of the line to the boat, to minimize danger of losing the whole device overboard.

With either the chip or Dutchman's log, the speed is determined by the formula:

$$S = \frac{60 \text{ seconds per minute} \times 60 \text{ minutes per hour} \times \text{feet between marks}}{6,000 \text{ feet per mile} \times \text{seconds of elapsed time}}$$

This is equal to:

$$S = \frac{3{,}600 \times \text{feet between marks}}{6{,}000 \times \text{seconds of elapsed time}} = \frac{0.6 \text{ feet between marks}}{\text{seconds of elapsed time}}$$

Since the feet between marks is constant, a convenient number can be selected. Thus, if the length is $16\frac{2}{3}$ feet, the formula becomes

$$S = \frac{10}{\text{seconds of elapsed time}}$$

If the elapsed time is ten seconds, the boat is traveling at one knot; if five seconds, at two knots; if eight seconds, at $1\frac{1}{4}$ knots, etc.

It is not always possible to head directly along the course to the destination, because of adverse winds. It is better to make good progress in the general direction desired than none at all, and much better for morale. However, at times, conditions may be so adverse that it will be best to drop sail until the wind shifts or abates. At such a time a sea anchor should be streamed to minimize loss of precious mileage, and, in severe conditions, to keep the boat headed into the sea.

### *Position by Dead Reckoning*

Plotting can be done directly on a pilot chart or plotting sheet. If this proves too difficult, or if an independent check is desired, some form of mathematical reckoning may be useful. Table 4-2, a simplified traverse table, can be used for this purpose. This is a critical-type table, various factors being given for limiting values of certain angles. To find the difference or change of latitude, in minutes, enter the table with course angle, reckoned from north or south toward the east or west. Multiply the distance run, in miles, by the factor. To find the departure, in miles, enter the table with the *complement* of the course angle. Multiply the distance run, in miles, by the factor. To convert departure to difference of longitude, in minutes, enter the table with mid-latitude. Divide the departure by the factor.

Example: A lifeboat travels 26 miles on course 205°, from L 41° 44′N, λ 56°21′W.

Required: Latitude and longitude of the point of arrival.

Solution: The course angle is 205° − 180° = S25°W, and the complement is 90° − 25° = 65°. The factors corresponding to these angles are 0.9 and 0.4, respectively. The difference of latitude is 26 × 0.9 = 23′ (to the nearest minute) and the departure is 26 × 0.4 = 10 mi. Since the course is in the southwestern quadrant, in the northern hemisphere, the latitude of the point of arrival is 41°44′N − 23′ = 41°21′N. The factor corresponding to the mid-latitude 41°32′N is 0.7. The difference of longitude is 10 − 0.7 = 14′. The longitude of the point of arrival is 56° 21′W + 14′ = 56°35′W.

    Answer: L41°21′N, λ 56°35′W.

**TABLE 4-1**

Simplified Traverse Table

| Angle | Factor |
|---|---|
| 0° | |
| | 1.0 |
| 18° | |
| | 0.9 |
| 31° | |
| | 0.8 |
| 41° | |
| | 0.7 |
| 49° | |
| | 0.6 |
| 56° | |
| | 0.5 |
| 63° | |
| | 0.4 |
| 69° | |
| | 0.3 |
| 75° | |
| | 0.2 |
| 81° | |
| | 0.1 |
| 87° | |
| | 0.0 |
| 90° | |

    This decision about whether to stay or leave may be the most important one of the entire experience. Until comparatively recent times there was no problem. Because there was virtually no hope of assistance, the lifeboat crew had to rely upon itself. Since the development of modern communication and rescue facilities, however, it is often wiser to remain than to complicate the rescue problem by increasing the area to be searched.

    The decision should not be made until careful consideration has been given to all factors, nor should it be delayed longer than necessary. Considerations vary with the circumstances, but certainly the following should be included.

    Was a distress message sent before the ship was abandoned? Did it include the correct position of the ship? How accurate was the position?

Is there any reasonable doubt that the message was received? If no message was sent, how soon will the ship be missed? What rescue facilities are available? How far away are they and how long will it be before help arrives? How conspicuous is the lifeboat? What facilities are available for attracting attention, either visually or by radar? How proficient is the crew in using such equipment? Is a radio transmitter available? What is the probable running time to the nearest land in several directions, considering the prevailing winds and currents, the motive power available, and the ability of the crew to use it? How long will the fresh water and rations last, and will they be sufficient to sustain the crew in the physical exertion required?

If the decision is to stay, how will the crew occupy its time, remembering the increased morale problem with an idle crew? How will position be maintained, or regained if the boat drifts? Would it be practical to wait two or three days, perhaps, in the hope of rescue, and then to set out for land if help does not come?

If the decision is to leave, where should the boat head? How soon can a well-traveled shipping lane be reached? In time of war, where is the enemy and where are friends? How large and conspicuous is the land in each direction, considering the low height of eye in a lifeboat? It may be better to head for conspicuous land 500 miles away than for a small, low island 200 miles away, particularly if the latter is in a direction of unfavorable winds or currents, or takes the boat farther away from shipping lanes.

Avoid, if possible, a hasty decision that will later be recognized as unwise. Discuss the matter thoroughly with the crew, and when the decision is made, inform them of the reason for it. Do this in a manner that will invite their confidence and support. Inform them of the best estimate of the situation.

### *Distance Off*

At sea in a lifeboat the navigator is handicapped by his or her limited range of visibility. Distance to the horizon, in nautical miles, is given approximately by the formula $1.15\sqrt{h}$, h being the height of eye in feet. Thus, distance in miles is approximately $1\frac{1}{7}$ times the square root of the height in feet. At an eye height of nine feet, the horizon is about $3\frac{1}{2}$ miles away. A ship, whose mast height is about 81 feet above the waterline, could be seen $1.15 \times \sqrt{81} = 10.35$ miles by an observer at zero height of eye. At a height of eye of nine feet the top of the mast should break the horizon when the ship is about 13.8 miles off.

If the height of an object above the horizon, or the distance between points on it, is known, a simple proportion can be solved to determine the distance off by use of the cross-staff or a similar device. To do this, align the two ends of the crosspiece with top and bottom, or two ends, of the object. The ratio of the length of the crosspiece to the length from this piece to the eye is the same as the ratio of the height (or length) of the object to its distance from the observer (figure 4-5). Thus, if the crosspiece is 18 inches and the intercepted length of the long piece is 31 inches, the distance to an island 1½ miles wide in the line of sight is found from the proportion

$$\frac{18}{31} = \frac{1.5}{D}, \text{ or } \frac{D}{1.5} = \frac{31}{18}$$

$$D = \frac{1.5 \times 31}{18} = 2.6 \text{ miles}$$

In this proportion the two parts of either fraction must be expressed in the same units if results are to be obtained without a conversion factor. Thus, both 18 and 31 are expressed in inches, and both 1.5 and 2.6 are in miles. For small or distant objects the crosspiece may be too long. In this case replace it with a shorter one, or use half or less of it, or substitute some other device such as a rule held at arm's length. In the case of a height, only the visible part of the object is used if the horizon is between the observer and the object.

A variation of this method can produce approximate results rather quickly. Hold a pencil, stick, or finger vertical at arm's length. Close one eye and align the vertical member with one end of an object such as an

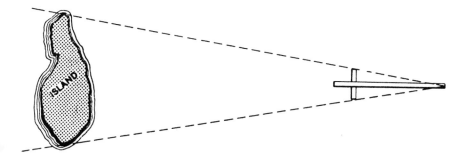

Fig. 4-5. Using the cross-staff to measure distance. From *American Practical Navigator* by Nathaniel Bowditch.

island. Open the closed eye and close the other one. Estimate the distance the vertical member appears to move against the background. The distance of the background object is ten times the amount of apparent movement, in the same units. The actual ratio varies somewhat among individuals and can be determined by comparing the length of the outstretched arm with the distance between eyes—or by practice on objects of known size at known distances. For vertical objects, hold the extended member horizontal and bend the head until it, also, is horizontal.

Our navigation should get us in the vicinity of shipping lanes or land. For signs of land, see chapter 6.

## Life Rafts

A description of the equipment found in the life raft can be found in figures 2-17a–d, pages 43–46. For review purposes the following equipment is listed under generalized areas.

*Operational Equipment*
   Inflating pump or bellows
   Repair kit
   Sea anchors
   Paddles
   Bailers
   Sponges
*Survival equipment*
   Floating sheath knife
   Can openers
   Provisions
   Water
   Drinking vessel
   First aid kit
   Seasickness pills
   Fishing kit
   Survival instructions
*Rescue Equipment*
   Survival manual
   Red parachute flares
   Hand-held distress flares
   Signaling mirror and whistle
   Flashlight

Read the instructions that come with each item and thoroughly comply with them. Have someone read the instructions aloud so that all aboard may know the capabilities and limitations of each item.

The raft should be kept clean and dry at all times. It will be found that any moisture in the raft will drain into the bilges around the periphery of the inflatable floor. Large quantities of water should be removed with the bailing buckets provided and dampness or moisture should be dried with the compressed sponges. A dry raft is essential for the survivors' comfort. Keep the raft clean. Unless there are sharks or other dangerous fish in the vicinity, ditch all rubbish over the side. Take every opportunity to dry and air clothing. In cold climates, watch for condensation in the life raft and wipe it off with the compressed sponge. The inflation-deflation pump may be used for pumping the bilges, especially in areas where it is difficult to use the bailing bucket. Follow the instructions for use of the pump.

## Inflation
Be sure that the raft is kept properly inflated. During the day, if the temperature rises, the gases in the buoyancy chambers will expand and any excess will be relieved to atmosphere through the pressure relief valves. At night as the temperature falls, the gases will contract and the raft will become soft. This condition should be corrected by use of the manual inflation pump. There is one manual inflation valve for the lower buoyancy chamber, one for the upper chamber and arches, and one for each floor section. Rig the pump for inflation and insert the nozzle into the manual inflation valve and pump until the chamber feels hard. Remember that you cannot overinflate the life raft since any excess will be relieved by the safety valves. The arch tube system is fed through the nonreturn valves from the upper buoyancy chamber on the raft and, therefore, will be inflated at the same time. The floor should be kept inflated at all times except in the tropics where it may be desirable to obtain the cooling effect of the sea. Inflate through the manual inflation valve provided, and if necessary, deflate through the deflation plug by removing the plug. However, if this is done, care should be taken not to lose the plug since the floor may require reinflation at a later date. The floor may be removable and can be used for rescue operations by utilizing it as a surfboard or platform.

## Raft Damage
Do not have any loose objects rolling around in the bottom of the raft. Remember that fishhooks, knives, ration tins, and other sharp objects can

damage the fabric. While it is desirable for the survivors to continue wearing their shoes, carefully examine them to make sure there are no protruding nails or sharp edges. No leaks will occur in the properly treated raft, but if they do, they may be controlled by the proper application of repair clamps or patches. Follow the instructions for their use closely.

Sometimes a valve will leak because of dirt getting under the seating, in which case the valve should be blanked off with the plug provided.

If the leak cannot be controlled with the means available, remember that one chamber is sufficient to support the entire complement of the life raft.

### Sea Anchor

The sea anchor is one of the most important pieces of life raft equipment. Properly used, it holds the craft headed into the wind, checks drifts, and provides the best available means of steadying the raft in a heavy sea. If the painter line is cut or parted by the sinking vessel, it should be checked at the earliest possible moment to assure that it is free of any entanglements. If through any cause the original sea anchor is lost, a spare one is provided in the emergency pack. This spare sea anchor should be bent onto the wire strap attached to the forward boarding ladder by means of a bowline knot.

Remember, if at any time it is necessary to maneuver the raft, the sea anchor should be recovered and streamed again when the maneuver is complete.

### Ventilation

If the weather is fine and the occupants are warm, both entrances should be kept open to allow free passage of air through the raft. With the sea anchor streamed, the raft will head into whatever wind is available and the cooling effect will reduce perspiration and loss of body fluids. Other than posting lookouts at each entrance to watch for rescuers, keep the entrances clear to allow maximum circulation of air. If the sea is rough and the weather is not good, the entrance on the weather side can be closed and that on the lee side left open. If the weather is really bad, both entrances may be closed, although it is recommended that at all times the lee entrance be adjustable to allow for a lookout. If this is not done, a lookout should be posted to open the canopy at least every 15 minutes and sweep the horizon for rescue vessels.

## Rescue Line Outfit

It is anticipated that the rescue line outfit will not be required for its original purpose once the survivors are aboard the raft. Therefore, a quoit and line should be detached from its position at the aft end of the raft on the outer canopy and secured on the inside. The line may be used for a variety of purposes such as fishing lines, bird snares, etc.

## *Maneuvering the Life Raft*

The raft is provided with two four-foot sectional paddles which may be used to maneuver the life raft over short distances. To do this, make sure the sea anchor is not streamed and then paddle through the entrance of the life raft.

If paddles have been lost or if the paddlers need assistance, the best method is for those who have sufficient energy and can swim to enter the water and swim with one hand attached to the outer lifeline. A method requiring less energy is for the swimmer to lie on his or her back and kick with his or her feet.

Someone may suggest that the sea anchor be used for maneuvering the raft by throwing it ahead and pulling the raft through the water. This is exhausting labor and very little progress can be achieved by this method.

## *Navigating a Life Raft*

Usually the position of a casualty is known, and rescue forces will take into account the drift due to the natural elements of wind and ocean currents. The best way of aiding these rescuers is to keep the sea anchor streamed and maintain a good lookout.

The normal method for search procedures is to take the last known position and make box searches in the direction the raft will take, allowing for the action of the ocean currents and winds. If survivors attempt to navigate the raft, this increases the difficulties which the rescue teams have to overcome in order to find survivors. The rate of drift for an inflatable life raft is fairly constant. This is known to your rescue coordinators who will direct the search accordingly. If land is sighted, attempts should be made to reach it, but remember that paddling or towing a raft by swimming is exhausting work, and one should make as much use as possible of the natural elements. Maneuvering a life raft is difficult due to its construction and shallow draft. Propulsion is limited to using paddles, as rafts are not equipped with mast and sail.

Usually the land heats up much faster than water, particularly in the early morning. There will be a tendency for the hot air over the land to rise and the cold air from the sea coming in to replace it. This will cause a wind blowing towards the land. This process will be reversed in the evening. Advantage may be taken of this by keeping the sea anchor out of the water during the sunlight hours and returning it to water at night.

Islands frequently deflect the direction of currents, and survivors counting on an early landing often find themselves paralleling the coastline instead of drawing closer, and have difficulty in staying within sight of the land. Do not exhaust yourselves if you find you are making no headway against the currents.

Birds fly far from land and cannot be taken as an indication that land is near. Generally speaking, winged insects are normally found not far from shore. Certain indicators other than birds and insects may help survivors in their approach to land. One indicator is fixed cumulus clouds in an otherwise clear sky or in a sky where all other clouds are moving. This type often hovers over or slightly downwind of an island. Shallow water indicating the approach of land will have a light color. Deep water is dark green or dark blue.

Sometimes the reflection in the sky, such as the greenish tint from a tropical island, or light-colored reflection in the clouds in the Arctic from ice fields or snow-covered land may be seen. Mirages frequently occur in tropical areas, especially during the middle of the day.

If visibility is bad, one may often approach sufficiently near to shore to detect land by odors and sounds. The smell of burning wood will carry a long way. The roar of surf is heard long before the surf can be seen. The smell of swamps and mud flats, and the cry of seabirds from one direction indicate the roosting place is on nearby soil.

## Attracting Attention

Know exactly how to use your signals before you need them. They should be in the charge of a responsible person. Their number is limited, so use them only when they will be effective—not too soon. You can see an airplane or a ship long before it can see you. Wait until you are reasonably sure that your signal can be seen.

The duties of the lookout are to look and listen continuously, first of all for other survivors, then for land, rescue ships, or aircraft, and for likely hazards such as rocks. While there is a chance of other survivors being picked up, listen for calls or whistles, watch for lights, and listen and look for any sound or sign of life. At night, use the torch to search the water. The craft can be maneuvered to pick up survivors, but before the paddles or oars are used, the sea anchor should always be hauled in.

On routine watch, keep a continuous lookout in all directions in daylight and in darkness. Watch for the smoke of ships, listen for the sound of aircraft, and remember that cumulus clouds indicate land. In darkness, watch for the lights of ships or aircraft, or lights that may indicate land is near.

The lookout must be kept conscientiously for 24 hours a day. Lookout duties should be carried out in watches, preferably with two on watch at the same time for periods of about one hour. The bright color of the craft helps it to be seen, but in rough weather a solitary craft may be difficult to see or, even if seen, may be difficult to keep in sight from an aircraft or ship. The person who is responsible for lookout duties must, therefore, use every device at his or her command to make and keep contact with searchers.

## *Flares*

In no circumstances must flare distress signals be discharged without the express instructions from the captain of the craft.

Distress signals are supplied in the emergency pack and can be seen for about 25 miles under clear conditions by surface vessels and for greater distances by aircraft. These signals should be kept at hand so that no opportunity to catch the attention of rescuing vessels is lost, but the distress signals must also not be wasted. It is important to remember that they are visible for a relatively short time and it is better to wait until there is a good chance of the signal being seen, rather than to discharge it at random. Be careful to fire the signals downwind so that no burning particles are likely to fall on the craft.

Two types of flares are provided: parachute distress rockets and hand-held signal distress flares. The quantity is limited and flares should only be used on instruction from the raft captain. Thoroughly familiarize yourself with the flares and with the instructions printed on them so that their use at night becomes automatic. Be very careful of firing parachute rockets in the vicinity of helicopters.

By following the procedures for LIFE aboard your survival craft your chances for rescue within 48 hours are just about certain today. When a rescue aircraft or vessel is in the vicinity there are various methods of attracting attention.

**Mirror**
Your craft is equipped with two signaling mirrors and to supplement
these, any ordinary pocket mirror or any bright piece of metal may be
used. With metal, punch a hole in the center of the metal piece for
sighting. On hazy days an aircraft can see a flash from the mirror before
survivors can see the aircraft. So flash the mirror in the direction of the
sound of the aircraft. Keep signaling and never neglect any means of
attracting attention or keeping it once an aircraft has been sighted. To use
the mirror, hold it a few inches from your face and sight at the airplane
through the hole. A spot of light through the hole will fall on your face,
hand, or shirt. Adjust the angle of the mirror until the reflection of the
light spot in the rear of the mirror disappears through the hole while you
are sighting an airplane through the hole. Do not continue to flash the
mirror in the direction of the plane after receipt of the signal has been
acknowledged.

When the sun and rescuer are separated by a great angle, the hand
nearest the sun may have to be moved to turn it to the required slant. For
best results, use all mirrors available to signal. Practice sweeping the
horizon at all times even though no rescuer is visible. Signals can be
clearly seen for 10 miles.

**Signaling**
A signaling flashlight will be found in the equipment container together
with spare batteries and bulb. Make sure that the flashlight is working
correctly and have it available at all times. Familiarize yourself with
Morse code, particularly the distress signal SOS—three dots, three
dashes, three dots. Use a flashlight at night whenever a vessel or aircraft
is sighted.

*Caution!* Your signaling aids will deteriorate if allowed to become
saturated with salt water. Keep items ready at hand, but always in their
waterproof containers so they will function readily when required.

**Additional Aids**
Other ways of attracting attention include tying material to an oar or
paddle and waving it as a flag; tying an empty tin or other metallic article
to a paddle handle and holding it as high as possible. This can give a
radar echo which might be picked up even though visibility is bad.

When a searching aircraft or ship is following an established search
pattern, it may not at first appear to have recognized distress signals, or
to have sighted the craft. Do not be unduly alarmed if it seems to be going

away. By keeping to the routine lines of the pattern it will return within a given period.

## Aircraft Acknowledgments
The standard acknowledgments for messages received and understood is for the aircraft to rock from side to side. At night the aircraft will make green flashes with a signal lamp. If the message is received but not understood, the aircraft will indicate this by making a complete circle in a clockwise direction, and at night by making red flashes with a signal lamp.

## Ship or Plane?
It is very common for people to imagine that they see ships or planes when none is actually there. Instruct the survivors to whisper word of anything seen to the person on watch. He or she should then ask the others what they see. If one person says a plane and another a ship, you will know that it is imagination.

If you ask the survivors if they see a ship, they will almost always imagine that they do see it. But if you ask them what they see and they all say a ship and their descriptions are alike, it is probably there. This procedure will prevent many heartbreaking disappointments.

## One Last Caution
When you survive getting off the ship and the perils of the lifeboat or life raft, there is still one more precaution to take. Remember, no one is a survivor until they have been rescued.

If you lose your head when the rescue ship comes alongside, you're lost. Deplorable loss of life and injury have occurred in the scramble to board the rescue ship.

Survivors who have reposed in safety in a craft for hours or days have, understandably, rushed from it as if it were plague-ridden. Some have only broken a leg, but some were crushed between the hulls of the ship and boat. Once again—take it on the slow bell!

If, alas, all the efforts to rescue your craft fail, you have no other recourse except to survive at sea, which is the subject of discussion in the next chapter.

# CHAPTER FIVE

# Survival at Sea

You are in your survival craft and the prospect of immediate rescue is dim. The objectives now are protection, location, water, and food—in that order. Whether you stay in the immediate area or decide to head for the shipping lanes or nearest land you must now survive at sea. The four survival problems are:

1. Exposure
2. Water
3. Sharks
4. Starvation

Your survival depends upon knowledge, self-control, and training. For each of these survival problems this chapter will attempt to provide the knowledge required.

## EXPOSURE

The number one cause of death is exposure. In cold waters the cold will kill. Water can conduct heat 25 or more times faster than air. That means when you're in the water you can lose body heat very quickly. If you are in the water and the water's temperature and weather conditions are severe enough, you may find the length of time you can survive greatly reduced. Survival depends on your knowledge of hypothermia, how to prevent it, symptoms that indicate hypothermia is taking place, and first aid for hypothermia victims.

Hypothermia is the loss of body heat. If body temperature becomes lower than the normal 98.6°F you become a hypothermia victim. There are two types of hypothermia.

### Chronic or Long Onset Hypothermia

Chronic or long onset hypothermia usually occurs if you are exposed to cold weather from a few hours to several days. It happens because you have not prepared for cold weather or because you think you can handle the cold weather when you really can't. Chronic hypothermia usually develops when the air temperature is between 30° and 50°F. When such low temperatures are combined with wind the possibility of chronic hypothermia taking place increases. This happens because of windchill, which is the effect of the wind on temperatures. Windchill makes low temperatures much more severe as illustrated in figure 5-1. Often, chronic hypothermia victims do not realize how dangerous it is to be wet in such temperatures. Victims become wet from sweating, being out in the rain or snow, or by being splashed/sprayed by waves. Survivors from a maritime disaster who have spent some time in a survival craft can easily become chronic hypothermia victims.

## Acute or Rapid Onset Hypothermia

Acute or rapid onset hypothermia occurs if you are immersed in cold water (figure 5-2). Acute hypothermia may begin to develop in as little as 10 to 15 minutes or it may take several hours. It takes place because an average person cannot generate enough heat to keep up with the heat that is lost to the water when the water temperature is 72°F or lower. Thin people cool off more quickly than heavy people and men cool off more quickly than women of the same body size.

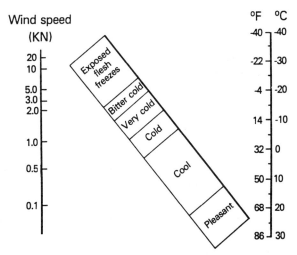

Fig. 5-1. Windchill factor. The subjective feeling of exposed flesh (such as face or hand) can be estimated with a straightedge. Line up the wind speed and the temperature. The intersection with the solid line in the center indicates the subjective feeling. For example, a temperature of 32°F (0°C) with a wind speed of 20 knots will be experienced as "very cold." From *Dr. Cohen's Healthy Sailor Book.* Courtesy of International Marine Publishing Co., Camden, ME, and TAB Books, Blue Ridge Summit, PA.

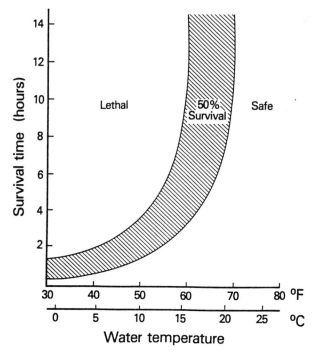

Fig. 5-2. Predicted survival in cold water. From *Dr. Cohen's Healthy Sailor Book.* Courtesy of International Marine Publishing Co., Camden, ME, and TAB Books, Blue Ridge Summit, PA.

In order to prevent hypothermia you must be able to keep warm on the water and in the water.

In order to keep warm on the water:

1. Reduce heat loss by providing good insulation. The best insulation is layers of clothing worn loosely at ¼ inch thickness. Each layer traps warm air. The best clothing materials are wool and synthetic fabrics.
2. Remember that maximum heat loss occurs from the head, sides of the neck, armpits, sides of the chest, and the groin. Ensure these areas are covered.
3. Use "foxhole" exercises—isometrically tense and relax muscles.
4. Wear a windbreaker to diminish the effect of the windchill factor (see windchill diagram, figure 5-1).
5. Keep clothing dry. Avoid sweating, which causes heat loss. Clothing should have a means of ventilation.
6. Ingest hot foods and do not drink alcohol, since the effect is to delay the rise in the body core temperature.

In order to keep warm in the water:

1. Dress warmly with a life jacket or wear a survival suit.
2. Enter the water gradually to avoid the possibility of hyperventilation.
3. Keep your head out of the water.
4. Do not swim or exercise. Both cause loss of body heat. Do not swim towards land unless you are sure you will make it. (Rule of 50s: 50 yards in 50°F = 50:50 chance of survival.)
5. If alone, adopt the heat escape lessening posture (HELP) (figure 3-2, page 59).
6. If with other survivors, adopt the HUDDLE position (figure 3-3, page 59).

To keep warm and prevent yourself from becoming cold, comply with the following:

C—Keep clothing *clean* so that it does not cling, become matted or greasy, and impair insulation.

O—Keep clothing *open* to avoid *overheating*.

L—Clothing should be worn *loosely* and *layered*.

D—Keep clothing *dry*.

Hypothermia may not always be easy to spot (see figure 5-3). Usual and/or obvious symptoms are:

1. Violent shivering
2. Blue-gray coloration and bluish lips
3. Slow and/or difficult breathing
4. Stiff and/or uncoordinated body movements
   (a) loss of ability to use hands and feet
   (b) muscle spasms (jerks)
   (c) drunk or drugged appearance
5. Mental confusion
   (a) forgetfulness
   (b) change in personality
   (c) loss of ability to make decisions
   (d) wrong decisions
6. Loss of consciousness
7. Appearing to be dead

It is very important to know which type of hypothermia a victim is experiencing. The treatment for each type is different. Victims of acute or rapid onset hypothermia should be rewarmed quickly. Their bodies

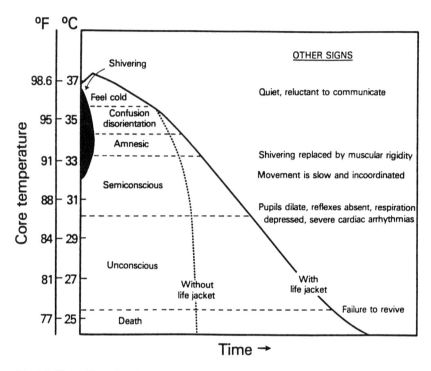

Fig. 5-3. Signs of hypothermia. From *Dr. Cohen's Healthy Sailor Book*. Courtesy of International Marine Publishing Co., Camden, ME, and TAB Books, Blue Ridge Summit, PA.

probably did not have time to undergo dangerous biochemical or fluid changes.

Victims of chronic or slow onset hypothermia may have had plenty of time for their bodies to undergo dangerous biochemical or fluid changes. The cooling of their bodies took place over several hours or many days. *The rewarming and treatment of these victims should be left up to a doctor or paramedic.* If you stay in the immediate area such assistance should soon be provided by rescue units.

### First Aid for Either Type of Hypothermia Victim

For either type of hypothermia victim it is important to:

1. Prevent further heat loss from occurring.
2. Handle the victim as little as possible.
3. Handle the victim as gently as possible.

*First Aid for an Acute Hypothermia Victim*

1. Gently move the victim to shelter and warmth as rapidly as possible.
2. Gently remove all of the victim's wet clothing.
3. Apply heat to the central core of the body (head, neck, sides, and groin). Use one of the following methods. *Not all are feasible in a lifeboat or life raft.*
   (a) Place the victim flat on his or her back on a hard surface with the head low and the feet elevated. Wrap warm, moist towels, or other materials, around neck, shoulders, sides, and groin. As these packs cool, rewarm them by adding warm water (approximately 110°F). Check the temperature of the water by testing it with the elbow; it should be warm, but must not burn. Placing the victim on a hard, flat surface will permit someone to administer CPR (cardiopulmonary resuscitation) if it becomes necessary.
   (b) Wrap a warm, heated blanket around the victim's trunk and head. A method of heating the blanket is to pour warm water over it. As the blanket cools, it can be rewarmed by adding more warm water. Hot water bottles inside the blanket with the victim also work well.
   (c) You may rewarm a victim suffering from mild hypothermia by placing him or her in a tub filled with water of about 105° to 115°F temperature. Keep the arms and legs out of the water, and keep the water circulating. This method should not be used on unconscious hypothermia victims.
   (d) Set the victim in a shower of warm spray directed at his or her trunk.
   (e) A time-tested field method of rewarming a hypothermia victim is for one or more rescuers to use their naked bodies to warm the victim's naked body. Use a sleeping bag or blanket.
   (f) Use mouth-to-mouth resuscitation. Your breath is warm and can be used to help rewarm the victim. This can be used even when the victim is breathing on his or her own. You must be careful to breath with the victim, not against him or her. You can use this method at the same time you are using one of the others.
   (g) Wrap the victim's head in a loose scarf or other covering. This will reduce the heat loss, and will also trap some of the

heat in the victim's exhaled breath. That heat will be used to prewarm the next breath.

(h) Use a warm, moist oxygen inhalation rewarming unit. This method requires special equipment that is not always available.

4. Get the victim to a hospital or other medical facility as soon as possible.

### First Aid for a Chronic Hypothermia Victim

Only a qualified doctor or paramedic should treat a chronic hypothermia victim. You may take the following steps while you are waiting for qualified help to arrive.

1. Gently move the victim to shelter and warmth as soon as possible.
2. Prevent further heat loss.
3. Prevent shock.

A hypothermia victim may become unconscious and even appear dead but still be alive. A hypothermia victim should only be declared dead by a doctor after the victim has been rewarmed. This rule should also be followed with victims drowning in cold water, especially when the victim is a child. A number of people have been revived after being underwater.

### Do Not!

1. *Do not* give the victim any form of alcoholic beverage.
2. *Do not* rub the body of a hypothermia victim, especially with snow.
3. *Do not* give liquid to a hypothermia victim.
4. *Do not* wrap a chronic hypothermia victim in a blanket without a source of heat in the blanket with him or her. Only use a blanket to protect a chronic hypothermia victim from further heat loss caused by exposure to wind or other cold.

### Helicopter Evacuation

If a hypothermia victim is to be evacuated by helicopter, he or she should be protected from the rotor blast. Anything that will protect the victim from the rotor blast should be used. It is especially important to *always* protect the head.

In all cases, hypothermia victims should be taken to some medical facility where a qualified medical person can decide when treatment should be stopped.

In summary, in cold climates you must:

1. Keep warm and dry.
2. Close canopy curtains as much as possible.
3. Huddle together for warmth.
4. Do simple exercises to help stay warm:
   (a) Open and clench your fists.
   (b) Stretch your arms and legs.
   (c) Wiggle your toes, ankles, fingers, and wrists. These movements will keep your blood circulating, but will not waste energy.
5. Avoid exposure. Rotate the lookout often.

The dangers from exposure to cold are obvious, but don't forget the sun, wind, rain, and sea.

A life raft comes with a built-in canopy to protect you. Modern covered lifeboats are excellent for protecting you from exposure to the sun and weather.

Open lifeboats, however, offer you no protection from exposure. When you abandon ship, remember to take the boat cover with you. You can use it to cover yourselves. It will prevent overexposure from the hot sun, wind, rain, sea, and cold. You can also use it to collect rainwater.

Don't cook yourself in the sun! Serious burns and loss of valuable body fluids could result from a sunburn. Wear light clothing, or stay under the cover.

For hot climates you must:

1. If possible, keep a breeze blowing through the survival craft. Sometimes you can change the position of the sea anchor to increase ventilation.
2. Avoid sunburn.
3. Reduce need for water by avoiding any extra exertion. If you exert yourself, you will sweat and use a lot of fluids.
4. Keep the outside of the raft wet.
5. Wet your clothing during the day with seawater.

Finally, in moderate seas, when there is no danger of the raft capsizing, you should take your life jacket off and sit on it. The rubber raft constantly moving under you tends to wear your skin until soreness occurs. Keep in mind that a life raft rides better in a rough sea when it is soft.

## WATER

SOLAS Regulation III/41.8.9 requires every lifeboat to have watertight receptacles containing a total of three liters of fresh water for each person the lifeboat is permitted to accommodate, one liter of which may be replaced by a desalting apparatus. This desalting apparatus must be capable of producing an equal amount of fresh water in two days. The U.S. Coast Guard requires every lifeboat to carry plastic packages in lockers which total up to three quarts for each person of the lifeboat's authorized complement. These packages must be replaced at least every five years.

For life rafts, SOLAS Regulation III 38.5.19 requires watertight receptacles containing a total of 1.5 liters of fresh water for each person the life raft is permitted to accommodate, of which 0.5 liters per person may be replaced by a desalting apparatus. This apparatus must be capable of producing an equal amount of fresh water in two days. The U.S. Coast Guard requires one quart of water be provided for each person the life raft is supposed to carry. This quart of water is contained in plastic packages which must be replaced every five years.

Next to exposure, the drinking of seawater is believed to be the most common cause of death in oceanic survival episodes. Once a man has succumbed to the temptation to quench his thirst from the sea, he seldom lasts much longer.

Unless you are close to land, no water should be given for the first 24 hours. This saves water and the body does not need it. Then give 18 ounces to each person every 24 hours, six ounces three times a day. This amount is enough to keep a person healthy so that he or she should be able to live another ten days after the water is exhausted. Without water, survivors may become delirious in four days and may die in 8 to 12 days.

Water is one of the most important factors in survival. Food is of secondary importance, for the body can survive on water alone for short periods. If you have no water, do not eat; but if your water ration can be supplemented to allow two quarts of water or more a day, you can eat any additional food you may catch, such as birds, fish, shrimp, crabs, etc.

The average normal healthy body contains 80 pints of water. The minimum with which it can survive is 40 pints. Evaporation loss from the action of sunlight in an open boat in the tropics is approximately five pints per day if the body is resting. In the inflatable life raft with its double-skinned canopy this evaporation loss can be cut to approximately one pint per day. It is, therefore, important that survivors remain under the canopy and avoid direct sunlight. Rest as much as possible and leave the entrances open and the raft lying to its sea anchor to obtain the maximum amount of air movement in the raft.

When drinking water, get all the pleasure you can out of each mouthful. Keep it in your mouth for some time, gargle with it, and then swallow it. Drink all the rainwater you can hold. When it rains, wake all hands to collect as much rainwater as possible. The body can store a certain amount of water.

While rescues are normally effected very quickly, there is no certainty as to the amount of time you may have to spend in the lifeboat or life raft. Therefore, every effort should be made to conserve the water supplies and to collect as much rainwater as possible. The canopy of the life raft is fitted with rainwater catchment areas, and tubes will lead this water into storage bags on the inside of the raft. A spray may have dried on the canopy and certain amounts of salt will be washed in with the collected rainwater. However, a small amount of seawater mixed with rain will hardly be noticeable and will not cause any harmful physiological reaction. In rough seas it may be difficult to obtain uncontaminated fresh water. Rainwater lacks minerals and is very tasteless and one can drink a considerable quantity and still not feel satisfied. Whenever it rains, fill the water storage bags and the emergency pack and equipment containers if possible. Then if further water is available, drink as much as the body can hold.

In arctic waters it may be possible to obtain old sea ice for water. This ice is bluish and has rounded corners and splinters easily. It is almost free from salt. New ice can be identified as gray in color, milky, hard, and salty. Water obtained from icebergs will be fresh, but icebergs are dangerous to approach and if possible survivors would do well to keep clear of them. Ice and snow will tend to chill your stomach and reduce your body temperature. If someone is on the verge of hypothermia no ice or snow should be eaten.

## Other Fluids

### *Fish Juices*

Fish fluids are recommended as a water substitute by many individuals with more enthusiasm than knowledge. It is true that all flesh contains water, but this water occurs only in muscle cells and cannot be extracted by any method available under life raft survival conditions.

*Urine*

Drinking urine cannot improve a survivor's chances. The kidneys are already doing the best they can. The only use to which urine can be put is to cool clothing by evaporation, thereby cutting down on water loss in sweat.

*Seawater*

*Never drink saltwater:* it increases thirst and may cause death.

Although survival craft generally carry a limited quantity of potable water, they may be equipped with desalting kits or a solar still. A solar still is a sun-powered device that can remove salt from seawater and thereby provide additional drinking water. Each desalting kit provides about one pint of safe drinking water. Although the water is likely to be acrid and discolored, it is safe when prepared according to the instructions on the kit. The capacity of a solar still is limited to about eight pints of water per day in temperate climates with sufficient sunlight. Yet this distilled water looks and smells better than the water produced by desalination.

If the temperature is freezing at night, seawater can be collected in a can. The salt collects in the center, forming a slush which is surrounded with ice, containing very little salt. This ice can then be melted when there is sun.

Chewing a piece of gum or cloth, or holding a button in the mouth reduces thirst.

## Methods of Conserving Water

This is as important in the tropics as a generous supply of drinking water. The body loses water by evaporation of sweat—as much as 1½ quarts a day in a calm on a raft in a tropical sea. To conserve water:

1. Keep clothing wet.
2. Rig an awning, if possible, so as to shade the body without cutting off the breeze.
3. Get the benefit of any breeze that is blowing. The body should be cool enough to feel slightly uncomfortable but not chilly. In this way a person with no drinking water can keep him- or herself in better physical condition than a person with a quart of water a day who does not carry out any of these directions.
4. Use one of the sponges provided in a life raft to soak up water that condenses on the inside of the raft. Squeeze the water into a cup and drink or store it. Keep the sponge clean and away from saltwater.

Finally, preserve your body fluids by avoiding seasickness. Life rafts are very uncomfortable to ride in. Your raft will be in constant motion even on a calm sea. Every time someone moves inside, or the water moves underneath, the raft will wiggle. You will be confined in a cramped and stuffy space. Even the most experienced seafarers tend to get seasick in a raft. Seasickness must be avoided if at all possible. It is a very miserable illness and can affect your will to survive.

If you have seasickness pills aboard ship, take one before you abandon ship if you can. If you can't, take the seasickness pills provided in the raft's supply kit as soon as all of your shipmates have been helped into the raft. The pills will keep you from vomiting, which empties your stomach of valuable fluids. You must keep those body fluids. If you lose them, they will be difficult or even impossible to replace as long as you're in the raft. Remember how cramped your survival conditions may be. If one person vomits, others will probably do the same.

### SHARKS

The possibility of being attacked by a shark is greatly exaggerated by some people. Probably the most important thing for you to remember about sharks is that they are unpredictable.

The curiosity of some large fish may present a hazard to the life raft and its survivors. These can normally be chased away by splashing water with the flat blade of the paddle, but sharks present a special problem and every endeavor should be made to avoid attracting them and to avoid annoying them. Sharks are scavengers and continuously on the move for food. Be careful about any refuse that is thrown outside the life raft. Don't fish from the craft if sharks are in the vicinity, and always abandon the hooked fish if a shark approaches. Sharks have a habit of lurking in the shadow underneath the life raft and a careful check should be made before any survivor goes into the water.

Blood in the water attracts and excites them. If you or other survivors are bleeding, stop the flow of blood as quickly as you can. Also be very careful if you clean fish at the edge of the survival craft. Don't trail your hands or feet in the water when sharks are nearby.

Stay with your shipmates. Sharks are less likely to attack groups than a person who is alone. Remain still and quiet if in the water. Clothing, especially if it is a dark color, is good protection. Light-colored objects seem to attract sharks.

In 1956, a U.S. vessel went down off the east coast of the United States. Of 44 crew members only four survived. The remainder were killed by sharks. Sharks are a definite threat and are therefore the third cause of death in oceanic survival episodes.

## STARVATION

SOLAS Regulation III/41.8.12 requires a lifeboat to have a food ration totalling not less than 10,000 kJ (a measurable unit of work/energy) for each person the lifeboat is permitted to accommodate; these rations shall be kept in airtight packaging and be stowed in a watertight container. The U.S. Coast Guard requires every lifeboat to provide one pound of condensed milk for each person the lifeboat is authorized to carry. This condensed milk must be stowed in the boat's lockers. In addition, two pounds of provisions for each person must be provided on the lifeboat for each authorized person to be carried. These provisions are to be stowed in the boat's lockers.

SOLAS Regulation III/38.5.18 requires a life raft to carry a food ration totaling not less than 10,000 kJ for each person the life raft is permitted to accommodate; these rations shall be kept in airtight packaging and be stowed in a watertight container. The U.S. Coast Guard requires two pounds of provisions be provided for each person the life raft is authorized to carry.

Food is much less necessary than water, as long, continued fasts have shown. A person in good physical condition can live 20 to 30 days without food.

If you have solid food but no water, you will survive longer if you do not eat at all. You will need considerably more water if you eat chocolate, pemmican, bully beef, or bouillon cubes found in some survival kits. If you can stand it and there is little chance of being picked up soon, it is better not to eat anything for the first three or four days.

The emergency pack in your survival craft may contain a biscuit-type ration. It has a high carbohydrate content which provides energy and helps retain body fluids. These biscuits are hard and should be nibbled. Do not soak the biscuits in liquid. They have a distinctive smell and taste. However, they do not taste bad, and will satisfy your hunger. Each survivor should be allowed ½ tin per day. If you are in a survival craft for a long period of time, wait until the fourth day before you reduce the daily ration of food. Reduce it only if it's absolutely necessary. Do not reduce it by more than one half.

The lack of space in life rafts limits the amount of emergency food that can be carried. Therefore, every endeavor should be made to supplement the rations in the raft. If you can gather two or more quarts of extra water a day, you can eat any additional food you catch, such as birds, fish, shrimp, crabs, etc.

## Birds

One of the greatest contributions made to a successful life craft existence was the observation that the sea is rarely without birds. They have a tendency to roost on the rafts, usually in the early morning and late evening. They have little fear of man and once survivors learn to take advantage of their habits, they can be a more dependable source of food than fish.

Birds are curious and can be caught in many ways. They are all potential food and will assist materially in the struggle for survival. They may be caught with hooks, or small pieces of metal or wood. To catch those that settle on the raft, be sure that you can reach the bird in one movement, and wait to grasp them after they have folded their wings and settled.

The birds illustrated in figure 5-4 are seabirds. If other birds are sighted, there is a possibility land is nearby.

COMMON TERN    SHEARWATER    FULMAR

COMMON TERN    SHEARWATER    FULMAR

STORM PETREL    STORM PETREL

Fig. 5-4. Sea birds. Courtesy of Switlik Parachute Company, Inc., Trenton, NJ.

## Fish

Most fish caught in the open sea are edible, but do not, under any circumstances, have any contact with jellyfish. A fishing kit is provided in the emergency pack. Fishing is not only useful for supplementing the rations, but it also keeps the survivors from becoming bored. The deadliest enemy of survival can often be overcome by occupying the mind.

Most of the information concerning fish poisoning is not based on scientific study and there are no steadfast rules to go by. It may safely be stated that the danger is greatly exaggerated, but you should nevertheless take precautions.

The principle symptoms of fish poisoning are nausea, vomiting, diarrhea, itching, cramps, paralysis, and a metallic taste in one's mouth. The symptoms appear suddenly, from one to six hours after eating. No antidote is known and the poison is not destroyed by cooking. Such sickness is not to be confused with the far more common fish poisoning caused by bacterial decomposition which may be destroyed by cooking. In either of the above cases, as soon as the symptoms appear, drink seawater and force yourself to vomit.

Poisonous fish (figure 5-5) are seldom if ever found in the open sea, but shore forms such as puffer fish, porcupine fish, trigger fish, and parrot fish possess toxic substances in their flesh. All of these fish can be found around rocky or coral reefs and muddy or sandy shores. *Do not eat any of the puffer or porcupine fish, as practically all are poisonous.* These fish do not have true scales. Their bodies are covered with smooth skin or by a rough shagreen-like texture (a kind of untanned leather with a granular surface), or bristles or spines. The gill openings are short oblique or vertical slits. By inflating themselves with air they become balloonlike, hence the name puffer or balloon fish.

Many of the trigger fishes are brilliantly colored. All have a sharp dorsal spine, scales that do not overlap, and the eyes set very far back. They can be caught easily but none are desirable as food. The striped trigger fish is common in the southwest Pacific.

In certain seasons of the year in localized areas the red snapper and parrot fish around tropical islands are said to be poisonous, and these should be eaten sparingly until proven to be nontoxic. It is thought that these fish become poisonous by eating poisonous marine organisms or plantlike growths around these islands. Parrot fish have true scales and their mouth is formed of long plates resembling the beak of a parrot.

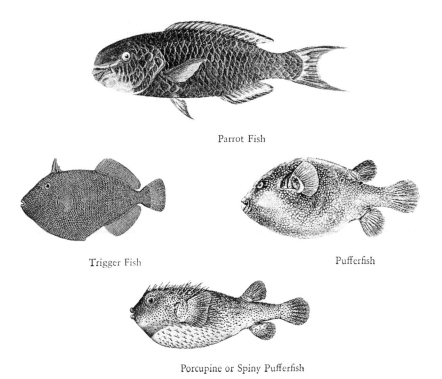

Parrot Fish

Trigger Fish

Pufferfish

Porcupine or Spiny Pufferfish

Fig. 5-5. Inedible fish. Courtesy of Switlik Parachute Company, Inc., Trenton, NJ.

There are many ways of improvising fishhooks; some methods are shown in figure 5-6. Hooks can also be improvised from pins, pencil clips, shoe nails, fish spines, bones, and in many other ways. For lines, the rescue line outfit on the outside of the canopy can be used together with shoelaces, or even thread from clothes. It will be noticed that small fish usually gather underneath the shadow of the raft. Try to catch these first and use them for bait with heavier hooks and lines for dolphin or other large fish. Sometimes large fish will be attracted to the shadow of your raft. Make a spear by attaching a knife to the paddles or shape the metal paddle blade into a spear. Remember to see that there is good bob or the fish may be lost. The spare sea anchor may also be used for fishing, treating it as a net to scoop up the small fish and possibly even crabs or shrimp. A dip net can easily be fashioned by the use of a paddle and light clothing.

Fish are attracted by light on the water, and at night the flashlight may be used, or the signaling mirrors used to reflect moonlight. Some fish, especially flying fish, may actually land in the craft.

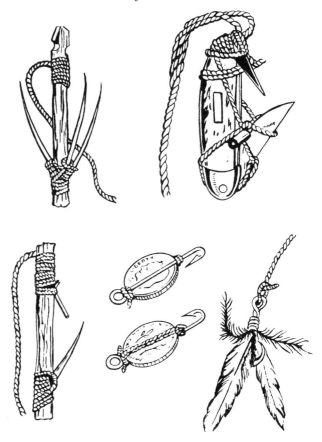

Fig. 5-6. Improvised fish hooks. Courtesy of Switlik Parachute Company, Inc., Trenton, NJ.

Be careful that fishing lines are not made fast either to the raft or to the person fishing. Fish or bright objects dangling in the water by the raft may attract large and dangerous fish. Keep a good lookout posted at all times and take care that if large fish are caught, the raft is not damaged in bringing the fish aboard. The best method is to stun the fish in the water by use of a paddle and then, unless sharks are present, have one person go over the side and help lift the fish aboard. A fish should be cleaned and gutted immediately after being caught. That which is not eaten immediately should be preserved by cutting it into thin strips and drying thoroughly in the sun. On no account should the liver be eaten. Reject fish with unpleasant odor, slimy gills, sunken eyes, flabby skin, or flesh that stays dented when pressed.

Do not fish where sharks are as they may cut your lines. Shark meat and liver are salty, so don't eat them unless you have plenty of water. If you do harpoon a small shark or other fish, keep the line taut so that the fish won't roll over and sever it.

All sea snakes are poisonous and have scales. Eels have no scales and are good to eat.

## Seaweed

Seaweed is good to eat, but shake out the jellyfish and crabs. The crabs may be chewed for juice and the shells spat out. In addition, the question of hand grabbing fish should not be ignored. A crew of four who drifted 33 days reported catching about 30 pounds of fish by hand grabbing.

The fishing kit is for emergency use. Guard it carefully. It may well save your life. If you have had enough to eat you can chew the fish for its water content and spit out the solid part.

## Miscellaneous Foods

Survivors are sometimes able to salvage food from the sea, such as coconuts, which may be available in warmer waters.

It will be noted there are many ways of increasing the survivor's rations and, in doing so, the survivor will be helping him- or herself physically and mentally, especially in relieving boredom and creating the will to survive. Every effort should be made by the raft leader to encourage survivors to take an active part in supplementing their rations.

Other items of concern in survival at sea include exposure to sun and weather, care of the feet, bathing, sleep, and elimination.

### ADDITIONAL SURVIVAL CONCERNS

## Sun and Weather

Keep the body, and particularly the head and the nape of the neck, covered. Thin clothes are better than none—those that keep off all of the sun's rays are best to prevent sunstroke. If there is not enough protection for all, give it to the redheads and the fair-skinned people who freckle easily. They can stand the least exposure.

You can burn in cloudy weather as well as in the sun. You can cut off some of the sun's glare by tying a piece of cloth over your nose up to your eyes so that when you look straight forward you do not see the horizon. Strip the clothing from those who die and distribute it. Also, in hot weather, do any necessary work after sundown.

Fuel oil and grease are no protection against sun and do more harm than good. Massage oil is useless for protecting against sunburn.

## Care of the Feet

If your socks and shoes are wet, take them off if it is possible to dry them quickly. If not, leave them on as protection against sunburn as well as cold. If there is no way of keeping the feet dry and they begin to swell, keep the socks or shoes on. Uncovered feet will swell worse and be more painful.

Rub massage oil, if available, on feet, legs, and buttocks as soon as you can after getting on the boat but do not rub the feet if they swell or if sores appear.

## Bathing

If the weather is warm, go in swimming, but not more than once or twice a day. Be careful that there are no sharks, barracudas, bluefish, or stinging jellyfish around.

Go over the side slowly to keep the saltwater out of your mouth. Don't dive. Remember that in the tropics you can get sunburned underwater.

You can have another person make a line fast under your armpits and, holding one end of the rope, put you over the side for a moment and then haul you in. If you have boils, keep yourself as dry as possible.

## Sleep

Regular sleep helps prevent exhaustion and keeps up morale, but it is possible to live for long periods without it. Oars placed on the bottom boards forward make a sleeping platform for those off watch.

## Elimination

Because of the small amount of food, it is unlikely that there will be a bowel movement. This will do you no harm. Do not take a laxative.

You will pass less water than usual and it will be dark in color. This is natural because of the small liquid intake and is not harmful.

If you did not urinate within a few hours before boarding the survival craft, you should do so within two hours in order to maintain elimination functions as long as possible.

The traumatic effects of a disaster at sea may make urination difficult. You could damage your bladder if you do not pass urine. Here are two methods that might help you urinate: (1) have someone pour seawater slowly back and forth from cup to cup in front of you; and, (2) hang over the side with the water waist high; the cool water should help.

## SOME FINAL SUGGESTIONS TO HELP YOU SURVIVE AT SEA

You must keep a positive attitude after abandoning ship. Never allow thoughts about giving up or not being rescued to creep into your mind. Believe you are going to be rescued! Do everything you have learned to do to keep alive! Many people have died before their time because they gave up the will to fight for their lives.

If you are in charge, it is very important for you to tell the other survivors what you are doing and what you will be doing. When you do something or tell someone else to do something, explain to everyone why it's being done. This may help prevent the other survivors from worrying or having doubts. Be a cheerful but firm leader. Keep things organized and maintain positive discipline.

As time passes on a survival craft awaiting rescue, the group's morale may weaken seriously. Keeping survivors active is a very important factor. An assignment to various tasks—nursing care, supply tally, or rescue watch, among other activities—will help to divert and occupy the mind and may help to keep hopes high. A lone survivor should make every effort to conserve his or her energy and resources. Survivors may imagine that they hear voices, or see things which are not really there. Keeping the mind active with mental exercises may help to prevent this state.

Recognition and treatment of mental disturbances is the duty of all survivors, but the ultimate responsibility rests with the captain of the survival craft. Anxiety is contagious and can well destroy chances for survival on the open sea. Immediately after rescue, bewilderment and disbelief are natural reactions, and some victims will be hysterical and agitated.

The best treatment for anxiety is to reassure victims and assign small tasks to keep them occupied. Acute agitation should be treated promptly, as the situation demands. For some victims forcible restraint may need to be applied.

Preexisting medical problems often call for a change in management on the survival craft. Unless withdrawal of prescribed medications is life-threatening, such medicines should not be taken while awaiting rescue.

Prescribed medications which should be continued are digitalis preparations, medicines for the control of epilepsy, cortisonelike drugs, and nitroglycerin. Other medicines should be withheld unless there is danger of an immediate and serious medical problem.

## Conclusion

In conclusion, your survival depends upon your knowledge, self-control, and training. Although the inflatable life raft is on survival equipment's leading technological edge, the real weak link in the system often can be the people who must use the equipment rather than the equipment itself. This could mean you—especially if you have never received any formal hands-on inflatable life raft training. Consider this point carefully and take every opportunity to participate in such training if offered.

Just knowing that this fine piece of lifesaving gear is aboard and ready to spring into service tends to give crew members a false sense of security. Although all crew members know where to find the life raft, few have benefited from the hands-on experience of using it, although some may have seen a helpful videotape of an inflatable life raft in use.

It takes a background of small boat seamanship to appreciate the problems a life raft faces as it bounces off a ship's shell plating, scrapes against barnacles, and snags on fittings in the water next to a large vessel. In addition, inexperience or lack of clear thinking can lead you to drop the painter and lose the raft in an emergency. Even a strong swimmer may not catch and board an untethered inflatable life raft caught in a strong wind gust!

Swimming around in the sea adds a new dimension that may not have been included in a classroom training program or even in a placid swimming pool. Reading about a life raft is no substitute for actually getting in the water and learning how to right it and use it properly.

Ask yourself these questions and seek your own realistic answers.

1. Can I really right an overturned life raft alone (figure 5-7)?
2. How do I help survivors aboard (figure 5-8)?
3. What can I do if half of the raft fails to stay inflated?
4. Do I know what to do if, for instance, somebody sits on the can opener and pokes a hole in the fabric, or some other careless act damages the raft?

Fig. 5-7. Righting an overturned life raft: When you are on the raft, hold onto the righting strap. *Stand on the CO$_2$ tank.* Pull the righting strap toward your head, and fall over backwards into the water. If you move the righting strap through your hands, your head should be clear of the raft as it hits the water.

Do not turn over when you are righting the raft so the raft lands on your back. It will hang up on your life jacket and may cause problems in getting free. Land face up on your back. (Courtesy of U.S. Coast Guard.)

5. Can I make effective use of each item of equipment in an inflatable life raft to secure my own survival?

6. Can I as the leader not only save myself but others as well by my superior knowledge of this equipment? Or will somebody have to save me?

7. Are the inflatable life rafts on my vessel being properly maintained by the crew and serviced ashore?

8. Are the inflatable life rafts properly installed so they can function in an emergency? (Appearances can be deceiving!)

9. Can I make reasonable repairs to the raft in an emergency?

10. Will my performance coupled with good equipment design and good leadership lead to my own and my crew's survival?

If your vessel is equipped with inflatable life rafts, you owe it to yourself to think of these matters and seek some good, substantial answers. Your life is on the line!

Fig. 5-8. Helping injured survivors board survival craft. One of your shipmates may be injured and unable to help himself aboard the survival craft. Two people can help an injured person board an inflatable life raft using these steps:

1. Placing their outboard knees on the top of the buoyancy tube.
2. Turning the injured man with his back toward them.
3. Grabbing of the injured person's life jacket with their inboard hands.
4. With their outboard hands, grabbing the injured man's upper arms.
5. Pushing the injured man slightly down into the water and using his buoyancy to help them, springing him up and over into the life rate, back first.

To help a person aboard a lifeboat, the position of the injured person should be reversed to avoid injury to his back. The gunwale is hard and would cause back injuries. (Courtesy of U.S. Coast Guard.)

CHAPTER SIX

# Survival on Land

In order to survive on land we must look for signs of land, beach the craft through the surf at the right time, and get ashore. Once ashore we will utilize different procedures in order to survive.

## SIGNS OF LAND

There are a number of signs which may indicate that the lifeboat is approaching land.

The sky will sometimes indicate a break in the open sea. A small, fixed cloud, when surrounding ones are in motion or absent, will usually be over or close to land. At high latitudes, a light-colored reflection in the sky might be over an ice area; a light green reflection in the tropical sky might indicate a shallow lagoon. Such indications may be even more apparent on the underside of a uniform cloud layer.

Birds most often fly away from land at dawn and toward it at dusk. A large number of birds may indicate the nearness of land.

Swell, properly interpreted, may be used as a guide to land. Consecutive swells travel parallel until they reach an island and then "bend" around it. Eddies are formed where the distorted swell meets beyond the island. This eddy line may be used as a bearing to land, sometimes at a considerable distance.

The color of the sea may act as a guide in finding land, as the open sea generally appears dark blue or dark green, and a lighter shade indicates shallow water, which may be near land.

The sound of the surf is often heard while still a considerable distance from land. Other sounds may also be heard at great distances. Odors, as from burning wood, sometimes carry a long way out to sea. Sounds and odors may be particularly helpful in periods of reduced visibility.

Large, fleecy, white clouds (cumulus), as a rule, indicate land; so do some seabirds.

If you are drifting near shore, you are more likely to get an onshore wind (pushing you toward the beach) after the sun rises.

In the daytime, the sun heats the air over the land. Over water, the air temperature remains almost the same. As the air over the land is warmed relative to the air over the water, the heavier air over the water moves toward the shore to replace the heated, lighter air.

In this way sea breezes are created (figure 6-1). Sea breezes sometimes blow over 15 knots and can be much stronger when they are in the same direction as the normal wind. The normal wind is caused by the existing atmospheric pressure over the area.

## BEACHING A LIFEBOAT

The beaching of a lifeboat may be one of the most dangerous parts of the entire experience. The approach to an island should be made on the lee side, if possible, and every effort should be made to attract the attention of any inhabitants so that advice on the best place to land, and perhaps assistance, may be obtained. If no help is available, sail parallel to the coast to study the terrain and determine the safest place to beach the boat. A lagoon or other sheltered area may be available. It may be necessary to delay the landing overnight to make a complete study of the terrain and to beach the boat by daylight. Surf appears less rough from the sea than from land. High spray indicates a rough surf.

Landing through surf, unless absolutely necessary, is best avoided. The Coast Guard and lifesaving organizations of foreign nations, whose duties require the launching and beaching of boats through surf, have crews familiar with local conditions, boats designed for this operation, and men trained and physically conditioned. These conditions are un-

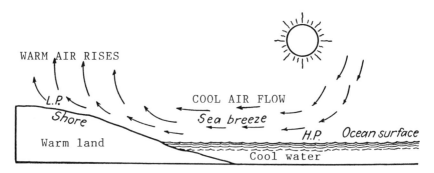

Fig. 6-1. Formation of a sea breeze.

likely to exist for a merchant vessel lifeboat, particularly when women, children, and elderly persons may be among those to be landed. Should you have reason to believe that an inhabited shore is close, signal and wait for rescuers to come and pick you up.

If it is necessary to beach a pulling boat (a boat powered by rowing), the method recommended is to keep the boat's head to sea and row to meet breaking waves; i.e., beach the boat stern-first. The sea anchor can be used to assist in keeping the boat from broaching (beaching from the side). The oars may be backed as sea conditions allow. Even in a power-driven boat, it may be best to use the oars. Everyone should put on their life jackets before entering the surf line.

If a steering oar is available, the rudder should be unshipped before the boat is brought in, as the steering oar will provide better control in the surf zone. Storm oil should be used, if available, to reduce the roughness of the surf. It is possible that the course can be altered somewhat while heading into the beach, to take advantage of a better opening, but care should be taken to avoid broaching.

In order to land through a surf with oars (figure 6-2) it is necessary to remain outside the breakers for a long enough time to study the surf carefully. (If it becomes necessary to head seaward, follow the steps in figure 6-3.)

The large seas come in a more or less regular sequence, usually three or four in a series. A period of smaller seas then follows during which there is another build-up. It is during this time that the entrance into the line of breakers must be made. The boat must be kept headed directly into the seas by having first one side and then the other give way as necessary. As each wave passes, it is necessary to "stern all." With each overtaking wave, the boat will be carried shoreward a considerable distance, even though the oarsmen are pulling against it.

Broaching is most apt to occur when the seaward end of the boat is lifted by an onrushing wave. A great amount of power is necessary to overcome the forces that tend to cause broaching.

Oarsmen should use a short, fast, powerful stroke so that they may back-water with as little delay as possible as each wave passes.

When a sea anchor is used in a boat landing through a surf, it must be carefully tended by those seated in the bow so that there is always a strain on the towing line when a wave overtakes the boat. When the wave passes, it is desirable to "stern all," and haul the tripping line taut so that the sea anchor passes easily through the water. The coxswain and those tending the sea anchor must be alert to slack the tripping line well in

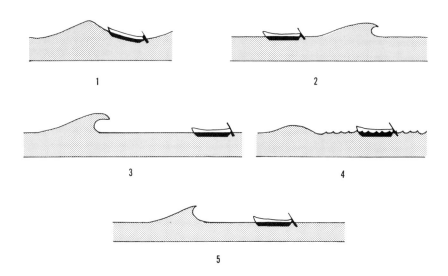

(1) Boat seaward of first line of breakers approaching wave about to
break astern of boat—GIVE WAY
(2) Wave breaking astern—BACK WATER
(3) Wave breaking at safe distance ahead—CONTINUE BACKING
(4) Wave breaks at safe distance ahead but surf is overtaking boat:
In heavy surf—GIVE WAY
In moderate surf—HOLD WATER
In light surf—CONTINUE BACKING
(5) Wave about to break in dangerous position—GIVE WAY

Fig. 6-2. Going shoreward through the surf in a lifeboat under oars.

advance of the arrival of the next wave in order to allow it to fill with
water and keep the bow pointed seaward.

The procedure for beaching in a surf will necessarily differ with
the conditions prevailing. In light surf with only small waves breaking
close inshore, as will often occur at or near the time of low water, the
boat can be beached more deliberately than in a heavy surf at high water
when there may be only one line of breakers of dangerous proportions
where the boat must be beached and hauled clear of the breakers as
quickly as possible. The two different procedures follow.

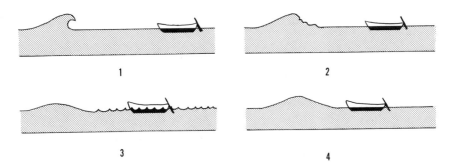

(1) Wave about to break safe distance ahead—HOLD WATER
(2) Wave breaking at safe distance ahead—GIVE WAY
(3) Wave broken, boat in advancing surf—CONTINUE PULLING
(4) Approaching wave about to break astern of boat—CONTINUE
     PULLING

Fig. 6-3. Going seaward through the surf in a lifeboat under oars.

### In Light Surf on a Gradually Shelving Shore

On reaching shallow water the coxswain boats the steering oar, and he
or she and two stroke oarsmen jump out and hold the boat stern-on to the
beach while the remainder of the crew continue backing and keep the
boat bow-on to the waves. As the boat grounds, the coxswain orders the
crew to get out smartly, in pairs from aft forward, the bowmen being the
last to leave (the crew leave in this order because the forward oarsmen
are required to keep the boat bow-on to the surf until the last possible
moment); then, seizing the gunwale abreast their respective thwarts, the
crew haul the boat smartly up the beach clear of the water.

### In Heavy Surf when the Beach Is Steep-to

Under these conditions the line of breakers must be crossed and the boat
beached in the shortest possible time, not only to avoid the breaking
waves but also to avoid the strong undertow. As before, the coxswain
should turn the boat stern to shore. When a favorable opportunity occurs,
the boat must be backed smartly inshore, and on the coxswain's orders
the whole crew must jump out and haul the boat clear of the water as

quickly as possible. If the boat is not hauled up before the next wave breaks there is a chance that the boat and crew will be dragged into it by the undertow.

## Landing Through a Surf with Power

Beaching under power (figure 6-4) is very much like landing with an oar-propelled vessel. The major difference is that the propellers and rudder must be protected, and therefore the vessel must be brought in bow first. The coxswain should make the approach at a low speed. As the last big wave of a pattern runs in lifting the forebody, full ahead throttle must be applied to bring the boat riding in just behind the breaking wave. The throttle is used to control the position on the wave and the tendency to override. Broaching is a problem due to very little speed through the water and this tendency must be counteracted. Do not get the boat's center of gravity forward of the wave's crest, as you stand a chance of being pooped or broached by the wave.

The sketch below illustrates how waves of the open sea, encountering shallow water on bars at the entrance to inlets, may form breakers which must be avoided at all cost by the boatman running an inlet. At A and B, at the crests, the velocity is the highest—in this case, 22 knots for waves that are advancing with a speed, at C and D, of 15 knots. At E a swell is shown starting to peak up as it feels the effect of the beach declivity, G. At F, the direction of currents of recession and the undertow is reversed, with a speed of 2 to 3 knots. The boat is shown with drogue set, the tow line attached to a bridle at the large end. The trip line is attached to the smaller aft and is slack, and if the boat must gain speed to escape a breaker astern, the trip line will be hauled in to upset the drogue.

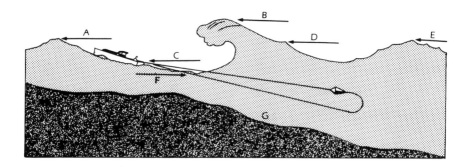

Fig. 6-4. Landing through a surf with power.

## BEACHING A LIFE RAFT

You must use great caution when beaching a raft in surf and rocks. This should not be attempted at night unless it's necessary. The life raft commander will probably decide to stream the sea anchor and wait until daybreak to paddle the raft ashore. If an inhabited shore is close, signal and wait for rescuers to come and pick you up.

The raft may be punctured by sharp rocks and coral found near a beach. You and the other people may be spilled into the water. The depth of the water, its temperature, the physical condition of the survivors, and the distance to shore must be taken into consideration.

Do not leave your life raft when land is sighted. Take it ashore with you for use as a shelter. Life rafts are extremely tough and have gone through lava reefs and landed on crusted lava without damage, whereas people have deserted their rafts and been severely injured.

When going ashore in the raft, keep seated with your clothes and shoes on. Do not stand up in the entrances since any sudden or abrupt movement of the raft may throw you out.

If you have to go through surf to reach the shore, keep the sea anchor streamed and assist the raft wherever possible by the use of the paddles. Have a spare sea anchor to stream immediately if the original anchor should be cut or damaged on underwater obstacles.

Remember to put your life jacket back on before entering the surf line!

It is better to go through a break in the reef, at the mouth of a stream, or wherever you see a depression or valley in the shoreline. Openings in reefs may also be discovered by the action of breakers. Waves that do not break on the reef, but continue their run toward shore, mean a channel or area generally clear of rock and coral.

Because the surf will always appear smoother when viewed from a survival craft, extreme caution must be used before entering the surf. You should take some time to study the pattern of the waves before trying to beach the life raft.

Open both canopy curtains of the raft to reduce wind resistance.


## ASHORE

Once ashore, carry your raft up so there is no chance of it being washed back to sea. The raft and equipment may be vital for your survival until help can reach you. Now find the best possible area to make camp. Carry your raft to it and make it secure so it will not blow away in a sudden storm. It will then be the responsibility of the craft commander to see that camp is properly organized. Use the raft as shelter. Make a clearing a short distance from the raft to keep it safe from the sparks of a campfire or signal fires.

The first decision will be whether to stay or travel, and this can usually be best decided upon if the following points are carefully borne in mind. To travel, you must be fit and able to reach habitation without assistance from outside sources. You should be certain of your position and know that you can reach shelter, food, and help with the equipment available. It may be advisable to travel if you are convinced that rescue is not coming.

By staying with your camp you will have your equipment available and you can lay out signals that can be seen by searching aircraft. You can also light at least three fires and lay out ground signals. A single fire may indicate an isolated group of campers whereas three fires would indicate need of assistance. If you decide to travel, be sure to leave markers all along your route so your trail can be followed.

Once you have rested, see that the camp is properly organized. The first requirement for life raft survivors will be an adequate supply of fresh water, and this should be located with the least possible delay. If fuel is available, an adequate supply should be collected for the purpose of providing warmth and cooking food. See what food can be obtained, either edible plants, or animals or birds caught by setting traps. Lay out signals so that you can be readily located by searching aircraft. Remember your signals must be bigger, brighter, and better able to be seen.

The action taken will vary according to the type of climate and the region in which survivors have made their landfall. Desert and arctic areas will bring their own particular problems but, as in the survival craft, the will to live is important. Activities, as far as the strength of the survivors will allow, should be encouraged in order to build morale and provide strength for the ultimate rescue.

The problem remains of leading the survivors to civilization. Perhaps the land will be heavily populated and the craft met by local people, or the way to safety may be indicated by a road or trail. But the craft may be beached at a deserted place where there are no signs of life.

The choice of an initial course is almost as important in this case as it is at sea. Generally, it is good practice to follow the coast, but if the shore is obviously unsuitable for craft activity, a port is not likely to be nearby. The jungle should be avoided for travel, but it may be a plentiful source of food if nonpoisonous plants can be recognized. Often a stream can be followed to an inhabited place. In an arid region, distant vegetation may be an indication of habitation.

Many of the methods used to determine position at sea may also be used ashore, and usually with greater accuracy due to the absence of motion. A distinctive method of determining the meridian while ashore is a variation of the equal altitude method. Place a stick or rod upright on a level area, using a plumb bob to establish the perpendicularity of the stick. About an hour before noon mark the point where the tip of the stick's shadow falls, and draw a circle through this point, with the base of the stick as its center. At noon mark the point where the tip again falls exactly on the perimeter of the circle. Midway between the two points lies the meridian of the observer.

The compass from the lifeboat/raft along with the charts would aid greatly in determining what course of action to take.

## WATER AND FOOD

If you land in the tropics you can probably get food and water without much difficulty.

*Water.* Dig a hole at low tide just below the high water mark. The water which runs in may be salty and brownish in color, but it can be used.

If there is a salt marsh or pond beyond the beach, dig near the foot of the slope which runs to it. You may find fresh water from three to five feet down. Go no deeper because lower down it may be salty.

In jungles, good water may be found at the base of the leaves of air plants growing in the trees. Strain out bugs and wigglers.

Good drinking fluid will often flow from the cut stem of bamboo, palms, and the larger rattan vines. Cut the stem off and catch the water as it drips.

Running water is usually safe if there are no people living near it.

Standing fresh water anywhere in the tropics is dangerous. Boil it, if you can, before drinking. You can boil water in a section of bamboo before the fire burns through. Or heat stones in the fire, pick them up with branches bent like tongs, and throw them in the water container. Begin with a little water, then add more water and hot stones.

*Food.* Turtles come ashore, mostly at night, to lay their eggs. Find them by following the trail the turtle makes across the sand to where the eggs are buried. Eat the eggs cooked or raw.

All of the turtle can be eaten except the shell, stomach, and kidneys. The liver should be eaten and the blood drunk as soon as the turtle is killed. While cutting off the head, the jaws and claws can do damage. Catch turtles by the shell near a hind leg and turn them on their backs.

Tropical fruits are almost all good to eat. But eat nothing that has a bitter taste, unless you are sure of what it is and know that it is safe. Avoid all plants with a milky sap. Anything that you see monkeys eat is all right. If you think that you have been poisoned, drink saltwater and stick your finger down your throat to make yourself vomit.

Rattans are long, slender vines with sharp, curved thorns. At the top of many palm trees and rattans is a large tender bud or cabbage. Cut it out and eat it raw or cooked. Bamboo sprouts grow up to a foot high and can be eaten raw or boiled. Young leaf-shoots of bamboo and the young curled-over shoots of ferns can also be eaten.

Coconuts contain a delicious and nutritious fluid and good white meat. Strip off the husk and break the nut.

Papayas grow in clusters like coconuts and can be eaten raw or cooked.

Breadfruit is oval, about six inches across, with a warty surface. To roast it, put it in a hole in the ground, cover it with leaves, lay hot stones around it, and cover the hole with dirt.

Wild yams and sweet potatoes are common in the tropics and can be dug up and cooked. The vine has a leaf shaped like a maple and a flower shaped like a morning glory.

The durian, a large fruit with great spines, smells horrible but tastes like custard. Eat it raw.

Freshwater fish of any kind, freshwater snails, crabs, shrimp, and crawfish are all unsafe to eat unless thoroughly cooked. Drop them in boiling water or roast them. They often hang on branches that dip in the water, and can be lifted out.

Only two kinds of shellfish are dangerous. They are found in the Indian Ocean and in tropical parts of the Pacific. Each has a shell that is in a single piece and has poison in the teeth. One is shaped like a sharp spindle. The other is thicker, rounder, and shaped like a short, flat cone at one end.

Fish are found in pools on reefs, in shallow water, or among rocks at high or low tide. Use your harpoon or block the opening of a pool at high tide so the fish cannot get out. Poisonous puffers sometimes go into fresh water. The flesh of other fish in fresh water is never poisonous. Cook them like breadfruit.

In parts of New Guinea there are great spiders whose webs are useful. Make a flat net by bending a branch and passing it back and forth through a number of webs. Then bait it with a bug and set it where small fish can see it. They will get tangled in the web.

All animals are safe to eat: monkeys, bats, lizards, land turtles, frogs, and even snakes, including poisonous snakes. They taste like the white meat of chicken.

All birds are good to eat, cooked or raw. Their blood and livers are edible. Birds will sometimes light on your back or head. Catch every bird you can. Save the feathers and use them to make fishing jigs or stuff them inside your shirt to keep you warm.

Birds follow schools of fish, thus showing you where the fish are. When feeding on a school, birds sometimes get so excited that you can get right up to them and harpoon them.

Large birds will often take a bait of fish on a hook trolled or dragged on top of the water. If nearby, they will often come after chum or a piece of fish tossed into the air.

Protect yourself from mosquitoes as well as you can, especially in inhabited islands. They carry diseases and can infect you with their bite.

### CONCLUSION

Survival on land requires the same type of leadership as exhibited on water. Your priorities become shelter, water, food, and rescue with the equipment available to you. After setting up camp, action will be taken according to the type of climate and the region where landfall was made. Activities, as far as the strength of the survivors will allow, should be encouraged in order to build morale and provide for the ultimate rescue. Travel only if you are convinced that rescue is not coming. Maintain the will to live. Survivors never give up.

# CHAPTER SEVEN

# Search and Rescue

The intent of this chapter is to describe the development of the emergency position-indicating radio beacon (EPIRB), the Global Maritime Distress and Safety System (GMDSS), the U.S. Coast Guard's compliance with the 1988 amendments to SOLAS 1974, and search and rescue (SAR) procedures, including what can be done by the crew of the survival craft to assist in their own rescue.

## EPIRB DEVELOPMENT

In the 1960s the only possible means of rescue in an emergency was another ship. EPIRBs then operated on 2182 khz, with a low frequency, low power, poor range, and the product was large and cumbersome.

In about 1965 distress identification was supplemented by 121.5 MHz and 243 MHz, the civil and military aeronautical watch channels equivalent to channel 16 (156.8 MHz) on a shipboard VHF radio-telephone. Although you could be heard, you could not be easily located unless the aircraft was a SAR (search and rescue) helicopter or Nimrod aircraft incorporating a direction finder. The standard radio frequencies and key words were as follows:

### RADIO FREQUENCIES

| | | |
|---|---|---|
| *Lifeboat Radio* (Lifeboat radio could send and receive manually on both frequencies.) | 500 kHz | Trip auto alarm in radio room by sending 12 four-second dashes per minute (CW) and three SOS groups (automatic signal). |
| | 8364 kHz | Send three SOS groups and a 30-second dash (CW) (automatic signal). |
| *VHF ch 16* | 156.8 MHz | Distress, safety, and call-up frequency (voice). |
| *Sideband* | 2182 kHz | International distress frequency (voice). |

**KEY WORDS**

| | |
|---|---|
| *MAYDAY* | Distress—vessel in grave danger, request immediate assistance. |
| *PAN* | Urgency—urgent message about safety of a vessel. |
| *SECURITE* | Safety—message about safety of navigation. |

Very high frequency (VHF) channels and frequencies that can be utilized for various types of communication including search and rescue (SAR) can be found in Table 7-1.

**TABLE 7-1**

VHF–FM Channel Usage in the United States

| Channel Number | Frequency (MHz) | *Intended Use* |
|---|---|---|
| 6 | 156.300 | *Intership safety.* Required for all VHF–FM equipped vessels for intership safety purposes and search and rescue (SAR) communications with ships and aircraft of the U.S. Coast Guard. Must not be used for non-safety communication. |
| 9 | 156.450 | *Commercial and noncommercial (intership and ship-to-coast).* Some examples of use are communications with commercial marinas and public docks to obtain supplies, to schedule repairs, and contacting commercial vessels about matters of common concern. |
| 12 | 156.600 | *Port operations (intership and ship-to-coast).* Available to all vessels. This is a traffic advisory channel for use by agencies directing the movement of vessels in or near ports, locks, or waterways. Messages are restricted to the operational handling, movement and safety to ships and, in emergency, to the safety of persons. It should be noted, however, in the Ports of New York and New Orleans channels 11, 12, and 14 are to be used exclusively for the Vessel Traffic System being developed by the United States Coast Guard. |
| 13 | 156.650 | *Navigational—(ship's) bridge to (ship's) bridge.* this channel is available to all vessels and is required on large passenger and commercial vessels (including many tugs). Use is limited to navigational communication such as in meeting and passing situations. Abbreviated short operating procedures and one watt maximum power (except in certain special instances) are used on this channel for both calling and working. For recreational |

*(Continued on next page)*

**TABLE 7-1**—*Continued*

| Channel Number | Frequency (MHz) | Intended Use |
|---|---|---|
| 13 | 156.650 | vessels, this channel should be used for *listening* to determine the intentions of large vessels. This is also the primary channel used at locks and bridges operated by the U.S. Army Corps of Engineers. |
| 14 | 156.700 | *Port operations (intership and ship-to-coast).* Same as channel 12. |
| 15 | 156.750 | *Environmental (receive only).* A receive only channel used to broadcast environmental information to ships such as weather, sea conditions, time signals for navigation, notices to mariners, etc. Most of this information is also broadcast on the weather (WX) channels. |
| 16 | 156.800 | *Distress, safety and calling (intership and ship-to-coast).* Required channel for all VHF-FM equipped vessels. Must be monitored at all times station is in operation (except when actually communicating on another channel). This channel is monitored also by the Coast Guard, public coast stations, and many limited coast stations. Calls to other vessels are normally initiated on this channel. Then, except in an emergency, you must switch to a working channel. For additional information see the sections on operating procedures. |
| 17 | 156.850 | *State control.* Available to all vessels to communicate with ships and coast stations operated by state or local governments. Messages are restricted to regulation and control, or rendering assistance. Use of low power (one watt) setting is required by international treaty. |
| 20 | 157.000 (161.600) | *Port operations (ship-to-coast).* Available to all vessels. This is a traffic advisory channel for use by agencies directing the movement of vessels in or near ports, locks, or waterways. Messages are restricted to the operational handling, movement, and safety to ships and, in emergency, to the safety of persons. |
| 21A | 157.050 | *U.S. government only.* |
| 22A | 157.100 | *Coast Guard liaison.* This channel is used for communications with U.S. Coast Guard ship, coast, and aircraft stations after first establishing communications on channel 16. *It is strongly recommended that every VHF radiotelephone include this channel.* |
| 23A | 157.150 | *U.S. government only.* |

*(Continued on next page)*

**TABLE 7-1**—*Continued*

| Channel Number | Frequency (MHz) | Intended Use |
|---|---|---|
| 24 | 157.200 (161.800) | *Public correspondence (ship-to-coast).* Available to all vessels to communicate with public coast stations operated by telephone companies. Channels 26 and 28 are the primary public correspondence channels and therefore become the first choice for the cruising vessel having limited channel capacity. |
| 25 | 157.250 | *Public correspondence (ship-to-coast).* Same as channel 24. |
| 26 | 157.300 | *Public correspondence (ship-to-coast).* Same as channel 24. |
| 27 | 157.350 | *Public correspondence (ship-to-coast).* Same as channel 24. |
| 28 | | *Public correspondence (ship-to-coast).* Same as channel 24. |
| 65A | 156.275 | *Port operations (intership and ship-to-coast).* Same as channel 12. |
| 66A | 156.325 | *Port operations (intership and ship-to-coast).* Same as channel 12. |
| 68 | | *Noncommercial* |
| 69 | | *Noncommercial* |
| 70 | | *Noncommercial* |
| 71 | | *Noncommercial* |
| 72 | | *Noncommercial* |
| WX1 | 162.55 | *Receive only for NOAA weather radio* |
| WX2 | 162.40 | *Receive only for NOAA weather radio* |

By 1982 COSPAS-SARSAT satellites, a joint venture of the United States and the Soviet Union, were in orbit receiving on the following frequencies:

121.5 MHz for regional coverage mode position fix—homing and alerting

406 MHz for worldwide coverage mode position fix—alerting

By June 1991 six satellites were in orbit and 17 local user terminals (LUTs) and 9 mission control centers (MCCs) were in operation. Of the six satellites three are Russian and three are U.S. Two of the three U.S. satellites can also receive on 243 MHz. Additional satellites, LUTs, and MCCs are planned.

This system (figure 7-1) can receive EPIRB signals operating on 121.5 and the 406 MHz band. As the satellite passes over an activated emergency beacon, it perceives a doppler shift and computes the location to within two to five miles from the 406 MHz EPIRB signal (figure 7-2) or to within 20 miles from a 121.5 MHz signal.

Due to the rotation of the earth relative to the satellites and the careful location of them, all signals received are in "earshot" of a LUT station.

The function of the LUT is to:

1. Receive distress signals and data from satellites.
2. Process signals/data.
3. Compute EPIRB position and generate alert data.

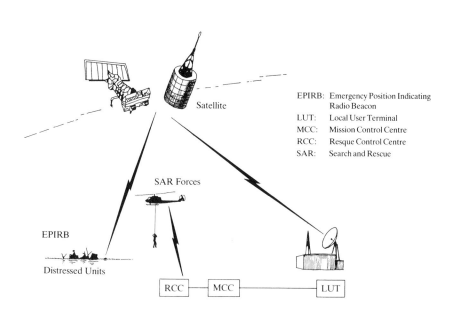

Fig. 7-1. COSPAS/SARSAT System. Courtesy of Jotron Electronics A.S., Norway.

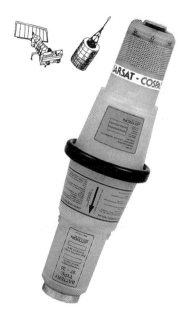

Fig. 7-2. 406 MHz EPIRB. Courtesy of Jotron Electronics, A.S., Norway.

The function of the MCC is to:

1. Receive alert data from one or more LUTs.
2. Receive alert messages from other MCCs.
3. Forward alert messages to national rescue coordination centers (RCCs), other countries' SAR point of contacts (SPOC), and to other MCCs.

On 406 MHz EPIRB transmission, the beacon's precoded information gives vital information to make the task of sending the correct rescue service easier. In addition, the 406 EPIRB is the most powerful, generating five watts versus the average of 0.1 watts for other EPIRBs. Correct information about the ship in distress is important to communicate to the SAR teams, because there are so many different types of ships. For example, sending one helicopter if a passenger vessel is in distress is meaningless.

The 406 MHz EPIRB transmission can be relayed immediately or held in memory. In addition, a 121.5 MHz homing signal is transmitted along with activation of a strobe light for visual identification. The 121.5 MHz transmission *cannot* be held in satellite memory. To be successful on a 121.5 MHz transmission, the satellite must be in simultaneous view of the EPIRB and the LUT.

From September 1982 through the end of June 1990, the COSPAS-SARSAT system provided assistance in rescuing 1,664 people in 616 SAR events. Of these events, 203 were maritime distress situations.

Two examples of the system's effectiveness involved a Norwegian fishing vessel and a demasted yacht.

The Norwegian fishing vessel *Falbakk* went down and the crew's distress call was heard by an RAF Hercules aircraft and a Lufthansa jet. Within 48 minutes the life raft was located and 50 minutes later three survivors were winched aboard a Sea King helicopter scrambled from Norway.

The single-handed yacht *Jester* lost its mast in a storm en route from Halifax, Nova Scotia, to Plymouth, England. EPIRB signals from the vessel, picked up by the Soviet satellite and passed to an RAF Nimrod, guided a freighter to the location. The same Nimrod received a second EPIRB signal and was able to direct a second merchant vessel to the location of the Scottish-registered yacht *Clarinda* some 150 miles away. All were rescued.

### GLOBAL MARITIME DISTRESS AND SAFETY SYSTEM (GMDSS)

The 1988 SOLAS amendments establish internally agreed-upon require-ments for the Global Maritime Distress and Safety System (GMDSS), which is a worldwide marine radio communication system imple-mented on 1 February 1992. It is based on satellite communications, digital data transfer, and other modern communications technology. The basis of the system is that rescue authorities ashore, as well as shipping in the immediate vicinity of any ship in distress, be informed of the distress incident and be able to assist in a coordinated rescue operation.

Operationally, the oceans of the world have been divided into four areas based on the coverage of maritime communications satellites. Required equipment is based on the areas of operation. The designated sea areas are:

Area A1—up to 20-30 miles from the coast
Area A2—approximately 75-150 miles from the coast
            outside of area A1

Area A3—within the coverage area of INMARSAT satellites (excluding areas A1 and A2)

Area A4—the remaining sea areas outside areas A1, A2, and A3 (primarily the polar regions)

Depending upon in which of the four areas a vessel operates, and based on the miles from shore, compliance for existing as well as new vessels will require the installation of various equipment. This includes radio-telephones, survival-craft radar transponders, and satellite-compatible emergency position-indicating radio beacons (EPIRBs).

The system will be coordinated by a designated RCC which will be informed of any alert, either through the INMARSAT and the COSPAS-SARSAT maritime communications satellite systems, or from coastal radio stations. A number of amendments to the 1974 International Convention for the Safety of Life at Sea have been adopted relating to GMDSS. Among these amendments is the revision of all SOLAS certificates.

Owners of existing cargo ships of 300 gross tons or more have until 1 February 1999 to comply with all applicable requirements of this safety system, and every ship constructed on or after 1 February 1995 must comply with all applicable requirements.

The 1988 SOLAS amendments require SOLAS ships to be equipped with two 9 GHz radar transponders: search and rescue transponders (SART), one mounted on each side of the ship, in a position ready to be taken to one of the survival craft. (Cargo ships of 300 gross tons and over, but less than 500 gross tons, are required to carry only one 9 GHz radar transponder.) The 9 GHz radar transponder requirement replaces the requirement for 121.5 MHz class S survival craft EPIRBs that was in the 1983 SOLAS amendments.

Recent tests of 9 GHz radar transponders have shown that they do not have the 10-mile operational radius that was expected when the 1988 SOLAS amendments were developed. However, 121.5 MHz class S survival craft EPIRBs, as well as the 121.5 MHz homing beacon required on all 406 MHz satellite EPIRBs, do have an operational range which exceeds 10 miles. This frequency can be monitored by virtually any aircraft, and most aircraft and ships equipped for search and rescue can home on this signal. Consequently, the United States is exploring ways, in the appropriate international forums, to have 121.5 MHz homing beacons for lifeboats and life rafts. These beacons would be in addition to or in place of the radar transponders. In the meantime, vessel operators are urged to carry either class S Epirbs or 406 MHz satellite Epirbs in lifeboats and life rafts.

In addition to the 406 MHz satellite Epirbs, the 1988 SOLAS Amendments provide for two other types of Epirbs to become operational. One is the L-band EPIRB. This EPIRB would operate with geostationary satellites of the INMARSAT system. Unlike an alert from the 406 MHz system, which is delayed until a polar-orbiting satellite passes over the EPIRB's location, the L-band EPIRB would provide an instantaneous alert of a casualty. The system would not work in areas where there is no geostationary satellite coverage, such as polar areas, and it relies on an interface with the ship's navigation system for updates on the ship's position. Once the EPIRB has floated free, it transmits the last position of the ship, and the position of the EPIRB cannot be updated through the satellite after that. The second system is the VHF channel 70 digital selective calling (DSC) EPIRB. This EPIRB must have a 9 GHz SART attached. The EPIRB would operate through coast stations only in near-coastal areas where a DSC system is in operation. Personal locator beacons (similar to "mini Bs") are available and can transmit on 121.5 MHz and 406 MHz. Table 7-2 compares distress alerting systems pre- and post-GMDSS. Another important part of the GMDSS is the dissemination of marine safety information (MSI). Navigational and meteorological warnings and urgent information to shipping will be automatically broadcast to vessels at sea. Table 7-3 indicates the various elements of the GMDSS and their intended functions.

TABLE 7-2

Pre- and Post-GMDSS Distress Alerting Systems

| *Pre-GMDSS* | *Post-GMDSS* |
| --- | --- |
| Ship-to-ship system | Primarily a ship-to-shore system |
| Radio equipment determined by size of ship | Equipment requirements determined by Sea Area of ship operation |
| Normal communications range of approximately 150-200 miles | World wide communications range |
| Propagation conditions determined quality of communications | Use of satellites and data transmissions significantly improves quality |
| Combination of manual and semi-automatic watch on distress frequencies | Automatic watch on distress frequencies |

Courtesy of Chevron Shipping Company, Safety Bulletin of April 1992.

**TABLE 7-3**

Various Elements of the GMDSS and Their Intended Functions

| Shipboard radio equipment | Function |
|---|---|
| 406 MHz satellite EPIRB | Ship-to-shore alerts via satellite to a Rescue Coordinating Center |
| VHF radio (DSC and voice) | SAR communications: ship-to-ship and ship-to-shore |
| MF radio (DSC and voice) | Ship-to-ship distress alerts and communications |
| HF radio (DSC, NBDP and voice) | Ship-to-shore alerts and communications |
| INMARSAT ship earth station (SES) with EGC capability | Ship-to-shore alerts, communications, and Marine Safety Information |
| Navtex receiver | Marine Safety Information |
| 9 GHz radar transponder (SART) | SAR locating beacon for use on survival craft |
| Two-way VHF portable radios for survival craft | SAR communications for use on survival craft |
| 2182 kHz watch receiver/auto alarm | Receipt of radiotelephone alerts until 1999 |

Courtesy of Chevron Shipping Company, Safety Bulletin of April 1992.

## U.S. COAST GUARD COMPLIANCE

The U.S. Coast Guard conveyed compliance with the 1988 amendments to the 1974 SOLAS convention in their *Navigations and Vessel Inspection Circular* (NVIC) No. 9-91. The implementation of this circular states the following:

(a) Under the requirements of the 1988 SOLAS amendments, every ship certificated under SOLAS will be required to carry a satellite EPIRB, 9 GHz radar transponders, and two-way radiotelephone apparatus for survival craft. This equipment will have to be on board by various dates before 1 February 1995. These dates vary, depending upon the size of the vessel and the keel-laying date.

(b) Under FCC regulations, all class A EPIRBs manufactured before October 1, 1988, carried to meet a Coast Guard regulation, were to be replaced by August 1, 1991. The Coast Guard recommends replacement with a category 1 406 MHz satellite EPIRB.

(c)  The Coast Guard strongly encourages the installation of 406 MHz satellite EPIRBs on oceangoing and Great Lakes vessels. Coast Guard and FCC proposed regulations would eventually require 406 MHz satellite EPIRBs on oceangoing and Great Lakes commercial vessels. Until final rules are in effect, one FCC type accepted category 1 406 MHz satellite EPIRB will be accepted as equivalent to a class A EPIRB required by any regulation under Title 46 of the Code of Federal Regulations (46 CFR). One FCC type accepted 406 MHz category 1 satellite EPIRB will be accepted as equivalent to one or two class C EPIRBs required by regulations for Great Lakes vessels under 46 CFR. The 406 MHz satellite EPIRB must be installed in a manner so that it will automatically float free and activate in the event of a sinking.

(d)  These two-way survival craft VHF radios should meet FCC regulations and IMO recommendations. Eventually, these radios will be required to meet new FCC regulations and operate on 156.3 MHz (channel 6) and 156.8 MHz (channel 16). Other transceivers used on board the vessel when the requirement goes into effect, and which are compatible with the appropriate requirements of the FCC, are acceptable to meet this requirement for a limited time. Under the 1988 SOLAS amendments, lifeboats may be provided with permanently installed radios to meet this requirement.

(e)  The hand-cranked portable lifeboat radiotelegraph (and the lifeboat radio cabin-installed version on passenger ships) is not a required item for SOLAS ships under the GMDSS. This device is no longer required to be carried on ships equipped with a 406 MHz satellite EPIRB. Antenna mounting arrangements and trans-ceiver mounting brackets for this radio, in lifeboats and life rafts, do not have to be retained if the ship does not carry the portable lifeboat radio.

Enclosure 1 to this circular provides radio lifesaving equipment tables for implementation depending upon the size of the vessel and the keel-laying date.

### SEARCH AND RESCUE (SAR)

It is accepted as the normal practice of seamen, indeed there is an obligation upon masters, that they render every assistance within their power in cases where a person or persons are in distress at sea. These obligations are set out in regulation 10 of Chapter V of the International Convention for the Safety of Life at Sea (1974):

Distress Messages—Obligations and Procedures.

(a) The master of a ship at sea, on receiving a signal from any source that a ship or aircraft or survival craft thereof is in distress, is bound to proceed with all speed to the assistance of the persons in distress informing them if possible that he is doing so. If he is unable or, in the special circumstances of the case, considers it unreasonable or unnecessary to proceed to their assistance, he must enter in the logbook the reason for failing to proceed to the assistance of the persons in distress.

(b) The master of a ship in distress, after consultation, so far as may be possible, with the masters of the ships which answer his call for assistance, has the right to requisition such one or more of those ships as he considers best able to render assistance, and it shall be the duty of the master or masters of the ship or ships requisitioned to comply with the requisition by continuing to proceed with all speed to the assistance of persons in distress.

(c) The master of a ship shall be released from the obligation when he learns that one or more ships other than his own have been requisitioned and are complying with the requisition.

(d) The master of a ship shall be released from the obligation, and if his ship has been requisitioned, from its obligation if he is informed by the persons in distress or by the master of another ship which has reached such persons that assistance is no longer necessary.

(e) The provisions of this Regulation do not prejudice the International Convention for the unification of certain rules with regard to Assistance and Salvage at Sea, signed at Brussels on 23 September 1910, particularly the obligation to render assistance imposed by Article 11 of that Convention.

The International Convention on Maritime Search and Rescue, 1979, and Article 12(2) of the Convention on the High Seas, 1958, require that every coastal state promote the establishment and maintenance of an adequate and effective search and rescue service regarding safety on and over the sea and—where circumstances so require—by way of mutual regional arrangements to cooperate with neighboring states for this purpose. In accordance with the Safety of Life at Sea (SOLAS) Conventions governments are charged with the responsibility of ensuring that arrangements are made for the rescue of persons in distress at sea around their coast. Guidance for search and rescue can be found in the IMO publication *IMO Search and Rescue Manual (IMOSAR)*. The manual provides guidelines for a common maritime search and rescue policy, encouraging all coastal states to develop their organizations on similar lines and enabling adjacent states to cooperate and provide mutual assistance.

Taking into account that maritime and aeronautical search and rescue organizations are complementary, the manual has been aligned as closely as possible with the International Civil Aviation Organization (ICAO) search and rescue manual to ensure a common policy.

Guidance for ships is in the IMO publication *Merchant Ship Search and Rescue Manual (MERSAR)*. The manual provides guidance for those at sea who may require assistance from others or who may be able to render such assistance themselves. It is designed to aid the master of any vessel who might be called upon to conduct search and rescue (SAR) operations at sea for persons in distress. Guidance for SAR operations in the United States can be found in the *National SAR Manual U.S.C.G. Instruction (COMDTINST) M16120.SA / The Joint Chiefs of Staff Publication PUB 3-50*. Since the reporting of positions is so important in search and rescue it is strongly recommended that masters participate in such systems as AMVER.

The automated mutual-assistance vessel rescue (AMVER) system is operated by the U.S. Coast Guard. Over 60 states (other governments) provide radio stations for free relay of AMVER traffic. This computerized worldwide merchant vessel plotting program will maintain and provide information on vessels for use in search and rescue operations. In order to participate in the AMVER program, a vessel need only file its sail plan and periodic position reports. There is no enrollment required and no agreement to sign.

AMVER will plot ships anywhere in the world who send their sail plans and position reports to the center and such participation is free of cost.

Surface pictures are provided to any recognized search and rescue agency in the world for use in saving lives and/or property at sea.

Vessels participating in the AMVER program are under no greater obligation to render aid in emergency situations than are nonparticipants.

The AMVER system requires discipline from the users. Reports have to be given in time to avoid a SAR operation if not needed. In case of emergency, the plot will tell which ships are in the vicinity and best able to assist according to regulation 10, chapter V of the SOLAS Convention.

In an emergency a vessel will normally have time to send a distress message. There have been cases, however, of vessels disappearing on regular trade routes without a trace.

Apart from the lone yachtsman or pleasure yachts sailing outside normal shipping routes, who can only be left to themselves until and unless they require assistance, there are few ships at sea today whose position is not known by reason of modern communication systems.

Shipowners themselves have a good and regular check on the position of their fleets, and this, together with ship reporting systems, means that it is unlikely vessels will be lost for very long before it becomes known and emergency procedures are put into action.

In order for survival craft to assist in their own rescue the craft commander should be aware of SAR communication.

## SAR COMMUNICATIONS

Communications may be the most important, and often the weakest, link in the SAR system. SAR communications occur between the distressed unit and the SAR system, and between the components of the SAR system. Ensuring that the message sent is the message received is crucial to the success of SAR operations.

Personnel in distress have a variety of methods for alerting the SAR system. Daylight visual signals may include mirrors, fluorescent material, sea dye markers, and smoke signals. Night devices include strobes, incandescent or chemical lights, fires, star shells, or other pyrotechnics.

There are special electronic signals used to indicate distress although these are rarely used for incidents in near-coastal waters. These signals are radio alarms that are internationally recognized, such as the radiotelegraph alarm signal, the radiotelephone alarm signal, the all ships selective call signal, and the navigation warning signal. All Coast Guard radio stations are equipped to detect these distress signals.

### Emergency Frequencies

Several frequencies in different radio bands are assigned for distress, urgency, safety, or SAR signals and messages. The unit in distress, or a station that has been assigned controlling responsibility by the unit in distress, controls distress traffic. (For cases involving international civil aviation, the station addressed by the distress message controls distress traffic.) Of the following distress emergency frequencies, the ones of most interest are those in the VHF-FM band.

## Distress Frequencies

1. 500 kHz—international CW/MCW distress and calling.
2. 2182 kHz—international SSB voice distress, safety, and calling.
3. 4125 kHz—international SSB voice distress, safety, and calling (backup frequency not presently guarded by the Coast Guard).
4. 6215.5 kHz—international SSB voice distress, safety, and calling (backup frequency not presently guarded by the Coast Guard).
5. 8364 kHz—international CW/MCW lifeboat, life raft, and survival craft.
6. 121.5 MHz—international VHF voice aeronautical emergency, ELT (emergency locator transmitter), and EPIRB.
7. 156.8 MHz—(channel 16)—international VHF-FM voice distress, safety, and calling.
8. 243.0 MHz—joint/combined VHF military voice aeronautical emergency, international survival craft, and ELT beacon.
9. 27.065 MHz (citizens band channel 9)—monitored by many public service organizations and, to a limited extent, by Coast Guard stations.

## SAR Dedicated Frequencies

In addition to those frequencies listed, each SAR coordinator may assign additional government frequencies for SAR operations.

1. 3023.0 kHz—international SSB on-scene voice/CW (for communications with aircraft).
2. 5680 kHz—international SSB on-scene voice/CW (for communications with aircraft).
3. 123.1 MHz—international VHF on-scene voice SAR used to communicate with aircraft.
4. 156.3 MHz (channel 6)—VHF-FM merchant ship and Coast Guard SAR on-scene communication between vessels.
5. 282.8 MHz—joint/combined VHF on-scene and DF.
6. 40.5 MHz (FM)—U.S. military joint common VHF frequency (this is primarily an army distress frequency).
7. 8364 kHz—U.S. Navy SSB frequency for navy maritime patrol aircraft operations in support of fleet units (aircraft may monitor this, but it is used mainly by survival craft).

## IFF Equipment

Identification friend or foe (IFF) equipment consists of a radar interrogator and a transponder. The interrogator, incorporated into air search radar, transmits an electronic challenge. Any transponder within range replies with a user-identified code and, in most transponders, altitude. Transponder replies may be detected at greater range than the radar return of the craft itself. The user can dial codes into the transponder to signal a message to the interrogator operator. Code 7700 indicates a distress, Code 7600 a communications failure, and Code 7500 an unlawful interference with the aircraft. When no other code is assigned, Air Force and Coast Guard aircraft are authorized to use Mode 3, Code 1277 in domestic airspace, on official SAR missions, and en route to or within a search area.

## EPIRB and ELT

The emergency position-indicating radio beacon (EPIRB) and the emergency locator transmitter (ELT) are small emergency radios that may be fully automatic, semiautomatic, or hand activated. They may be transmitters only, transceivers, beacons only, or a combination. No EPIRBs have receiver capability.

### *EPIRBs*

Class A—automatically activated on 121.5 and 243 MHz and designed to be detected by aircraft. Required on all vessels inspected for ocean and coastal trade more than 20 miles from a harbor of safe refuge.

Class B—manually activated on 121.5 and 243 MHz. Their use is voluntary for uninspected vessels. Mini Bs are appropriate for attachment to immersion suits.

Class C—transmits on 1.5-second alarm on VHF-FM channel 16 followed by a 15-second homing signal on channel 15. Both signals are repeated periodically.

Category I—automatically activated on 406 MHz. This device is coded with vessel information, when activated, the information is transmitted via the COSPAS-SARSAT satellite system to the appropriate RCC. Required for all commercial fishing vessels, SOLAS, and other classes of vessels.

Category II—manually activated on 406 MHz. Vessels are encouraged to replace aging class B EPIRBs with these.

*ELTs*

Also referred to as crash position indicators, ELTs emit a distress signal on 121.5 and/or 243 MHz when activated manually or subjected to extreme G-forces, such as a crash. 406 MHz ELTs are better and are coming into broader use internationally. ELTs are required on most aircraft.

## AIRCRAFT/MARINE CHANNELS

*Aircraft* normally communicate on voice channels only, and usually guard at least one channel. Both military and civilian aircraft use HF (AM/SSB) for long-range. Civil aircraft use VHF (AM) for short-range, and military aircraft use UHF (AM) or VHF for short-range. If the ground aeronautical radio station that is working the aircraft is known, contact may be established through it. Military aircraft flights normally maintain communications guard with a military ground aeronautical radio station. Civil commercial aircraft on both long-range and short-range flights normally maintain communications with Aeronautical Radio Incorporated (ARINC) radio stations. Military aircraft not on instrument flight rules (IFR) flight plans normally maintain communications guard with a parent activity's radio station, usually "home base." All aircraft on IFR flight plans maintain a communications guard with an air traffic control (ATC) facility and may be contacted through the nearest air route traffic control center (ARTCC).

*Merchant vessels* normally communicate on MF or HF telegraph or voice frequencies. INMARSAT provides satellite voice and telex services to vessels equipped with an INMARSAT terminal. The NAVTEX system can also be used to contact vessels equipped with NAVTEX receivers.

When attempting to establish contact with a merchant vessel, a call should be made first on 500 kHz (CW), 2182 kHz voice, or 156.8 MHz voice. Use of 500 kHz will be phased out when GMDSS is implemented. Since some merchant ships do not keep a continuous guard on these frequencies, if a distress occurs the auto alarm signal should also be transmitted prior to any distress message. After contact is made, a shift to a working frequency should be made.

Commercial marine radio stations such as Mackay, RCA, and ITT World Communications handle most communications for merchant ships worldwide. Certain stations broadcast a "traffic list" every two hours and are copied by many merchant ships. If a maritime SAR coordinator or SAR mission coordinator (SMC) is unable to contact a ship directly, assistance from a commercial station may be obtained by notifying either New York or San Francisco rescue coordination center (RCCs). That RCC can contact the commercial radio station and request that the ship's call sign be included in the next traffic list. If the ship does not establish contact after two traffic list broadcasts, the SAR coordinator should begin the process again.

Ships equipped with INMARSAT terminals may be contacted immediately by voice or telex. If desired, INMARSAT can alert all ships in an area simultaneously.

Merchant ships under way in U.S. harbors and waterways monitor bridge-to-bridge or vessel traffic system frequencies.

*Small craft*, such as fishing vessels and pleasure craft, normally communicate on MF voice and VHF-FM voice. Only commercial boats carrying passengers for hire are required to guard 2182 kHz continuously. If initial attempts to contact fishing boats or pleasure craft on 2182 kHz or 156.8 MHz (channel 16 FM) are unsuccessful, the following voice frequencies may be used:

1. 2003 kHz, Great Lakes.
2. 2635 kHz, all areas.
3. 2638 kHz, all areas.
4. 2738 kHz, all areas except Great Lakes and Gulf of Mexico.
5. 2830 kHz, Gulf of Mexico.
6. 156.3 MHz (channel 6), all areas.
7. 156.45 MHz (VHF-FM channel 9).

### ALERTING SHIPS AT SEA AND EN ROUTE AIRCRAFT

Frequently the most immediate help available to a distressed ship or aircraft is provided by ships or aircraft already in the vicinity.

*Ships* can best be alerted by a maritime coastal radio station (CRS). Normally, the RCC originates a message to all ships and sends it to a CRS for broadcast. The RCC should include instructions on whether to use the alarm signal, and whether to issue the broadcast as a distress broadcast or as an urgent marine broadcast. The CRS should then use the procedures in international radio regulations.

An urgent broadcast should be used during the alert phase.

A distress broadcast should be used during the distress phase when the distressed unit may not be able to transmit an alert, or when a distressed unit has sent an alert not acknowledged by assisting units. The alarm signal should be used before an initial distress broadcast and, judiciously, for subsequent distress traffic.

When the incident is in waters usually traversed by oceangoing merchant ships, 500 kHz should be used for emergency broadcasts; 2182 kHz should be used when the incident is within 300 miles of shore; and 156.8 MHz (channel 16) when the incident is within 30 miles of shore. Incidents within 300 miles of shore may require broadcasts on all three frequencies.

In exceptional circumstances, the SAR mission coordinator (SMC) may direct an additional broadcast on another frequency (e.g., 2638 kHz or 2738 kHz) after broadcasts on 500 kHz, 2182 kHz, or 156.8 MHz. Local factors, such as ship-to-ship and ship-to-shore frequencies in use by fishing or pleasure craft in the area of the incident, determine additional frequencies to be used.

The SAR coordinator may alert small craft listening to the above frequencies by contacting marine operators, commercial radio broadcast stations, and the National Weather Service (NWS). They should be asked to include the missing craft information in their regular marine news or weather broadcasts, asking anyone who has information to contact the controlling RCC.

If a need exists to alert surface craft for an extended time, a notice to mariners should be issued in a coastal area and a navy hydro message for ocean areas.

*En route aircraft* on IFR flight plans can be informed of emergency situations in their vicinity by air route traffic control center (ARTCC), which is aware of and able to communicate with aircraft available to assist. Under some circumstances en route aircraft might be alerted by aircraft towers or approach control facilities, usually when incidents occur in the vicinity of these facilities. Alerting of aircraft should be done during the alert or distress phases, when en route aircraft may intercept and escort distressed craft, locate survivors transmitting on aeronautical emergency frequencies, or sight the incident. SAR coordinators should consult with aeronautical authorities in advance to determine the best method of alerting en route aircraft in their area.

## MEDICO MESSAGES

Maritime and overseas SAR coordinators often become involved with medical emergencies at sea. Medico messages request or transmit medical advice from and to a ship.

Each medico message is a potential SAR mission. Medico messages may be addressed to SAR coordinators from ships at sea. Replies to such messages must indicate the medical facility which provided the advice, to avoid the impression that the SAR coordinator is prescribing medical treatment.

Medico messages should be prefixed "DHMEDICO" to tell communications personnel to handle them as medico messages. However, fishing vessels and small craft will probably not know about this procedure. Personnel who might be involved with such traffic should be alert for incoming medico messages that can be identified as medico only by the text.

Further information on radio medical advice to ships at sea is contained in Defense Mapping Agency Hydrographic/Topographic Center publication 117, *Radio Navigational Aids.*

### SAR MISSION MESSAGES

Situation reports (SITREPS) are used by the on scene commander (OSC) to keep the SAR mission coordinator (SMC) informed of on scene mission progress and conditions. The SMC uses the SITREPS to keep interested agencies informed of mission progress. The OSC addresses the SITREPS only to the SMC unless otherwise directed, and the SMC may address SITREPS to as many agencies as necessary. Often a short SITREP is used to provide the earliest notice of a casualty or to pass urgent details when requesting assistance. A more complete SITREP is used to pass amplifying information during SAR operations, or to pass information to the agency SAR authorities or the craft in distress. Initial SITREPS should be transmitted as soon as details of an incident become clear enough to indicate SAR involvement, and are not to be delayed unnecessarily for confirmation of all details.

SITREP format is established by agency directive. In the case of near-coastal SAR, for which the U.S. Coast Guard is responsible, each district has defined the format to be used for SITREPS although the Coast Guard expects to standardize the SITREP format in the future.

While details of format vary, all SITREP formats normally provide the following information:

1. *Identification*—The date/time group provides unambiguous identification, together with the subject line, the SITREP number, and a short description of the emergency and its phase. SITREPs

are numbered sequentially; when an OSC is relieved on scene, the new OSC continues the SITREP numbering sequence.

2. *Situation*—A description of the case, the conditions that affect the case including on-scene weather, and any amplifying information that would clarify the problem. After the first SITREP only changes to the original reported situation are included.

3. *Action taken*—A report of all action taken since the last report, including results of such action. When an unsuccessful search has been conducted, the report includes the areas searched, a measure of effort such as sorties flown or hours searched, and the coverage factor (c) or probability of detection (POD).

4. *Future plans*—A description of actions planned for future execution, including any recommendations and, if necessary, a request for additional assistance.

5. *Status of case*—This is used only on a final SITREP if the case is closed or the search is suspended pending further developments.

## SEARCH OPERATIONS

All preparations should be completed before the vessel enters the search area. Communications should be established with the OCS, SAR frequencies and homing equipment guarded, observers positioned, and rescue gear readied. Scanners should have binoculars and should be stationed as high as possible to increase sighting range. A 360° lookout should be maintained.

Vessels searching where no electronic or visual reference points exist should maintain a dead reckoning (DR) plot of the best-known position of the incident, their own position, and the position of other ships and aircraft in the vicinity. The plot should also show the date, time, possible drift of survivors, and areas searched.

To attract survivor attention, a vessel should periodically make heavy black smoke, rotate a searchlight beam around the horizon during nighttime, or turn on deck lights. Periodic sound signals can help when searching for survivors under raft canopies. Crew members should be alert for signals from survivors and other signs, such as floating wreckage or objects, indicating their presence. At night or when visibility is seriously restricted, the engines, if feasible, may be stopped periodically and a listening watch maintained for survivor signals.

SAR vessels will conduct searches according to various patterns. A pattern commonly utilized is the expanding square or sector pattern. In an expanding square or sector pattern, a worksheet is used to record the courses and turn times. Plotting these patterns on a chart adds to the clutter and consequent confusion. However, it is a good practice to draw the radius of the pattern on the chart to determine if the pattern runs into the shore! The search leg lengths and the search speeds have been preselected so that the leg times are all in even minutes, i.e., all turn times occur on an exact minute. This characteristic eliminates the navigator having to handle seconds in the computations.

Figure 7-3 illustrates use of the expanding square worksheet. In the illustration the track spacing has been assigned as 1 NM, eight legs of the pattern are to be run, and the vessel chooses to search at 10 kt. The ETA at Datum is 1523, and the vessel elects to commence search at 1530. The navigator notes the track spacing row, and circles the 10 kt column through the first eight legs. The numbers in the column circles are the number of minutes that leg takes, and are added to the clock times in the time column to determine the turn time at the end of each leg—which is also the start time for the next leg. The course information is corrected for deviation and variation; the helmsman needs compass course to steer. If the pattern is run adjusting for leeway, compass courses are calculated by the navigator to adjust for current and wind drift.

Figure 7-4 illustrates the use of the sector search worksheet. In this illustration the radius has been assigned as 2 NM, and the search is executed starting at Datum and finishing at Datum. The vessel elects to run at 12 kt, and deploys a datum marker before the start of the search. As in the previous example, the start is elected to be at 1530 to allow time between arrival at Datum and start of search to confirm position. The navigator notes the radius row, circles the 12 kt column and calculates the clock time for each leg start using the leg time in the marked column. He also calculates the clock time for passing through Datum (halfway between the third and fourth starts, and halfway between the fifth and sixth starts) so the helmsman can verify the track of the search pattern.

## CONCLUSION

By being familiar with SAR procedures and communications the life raft commander will be better able to facilitate the search. The commander

*Survival Guide for the Mariner*

will also be better able to keep up the morale of all aboard and maintain the will to survive until the ultimate rescue.

```
      SEARCH PATTERN WORKSHEET for EXPANDING SQUARE SEARCH
=================================================================
                    S=5 mi      |15k|20k|25k|30k| - | - | - | - | - |
                    --------------------------------------------------
                    S=4 mi      |12k|16k|20k|24k| - | - | - | - | - |
                    --------------------------------------------------
                    S=3 mi      | 9k|12k|15k|18k|30k| - | - | - | - |
                    --------------------------------------------------
                    S=2 mi      | 6k| 8k|10k|12k|20k|24k|30k| - | - |
                    --------------------------------------------------
            ---->   S=1 mi      | 3k| 4k| 5k| 6k|10k|12k|15k|20k|30k|
                    --------------------------------------------------
                    S=¹/₂ mi    | - | 2k|2.5| 3k| 5k| 6k|7.5|10k|15k|
=================================================================
   Start #1  15 30  000°T  35F  C  |20'|15'|12'|10'| 6'| 5'| 4'| 3'| 2'|
             -----------------------------------------------------------
   Start #2  15 36  090°T  076  C  |20'|15'|12'|10'| 6'| 5'| 4'| 3'| 2'|
             -----------------------------------------------------------
   Start #3  15 42  180°T  168  C  |40'|30'|24'|20'|12'|10'| 8'| 6'| 4'|
             -----------------------------------------------------------
   Start #4  15 54  270°T  256  C  |40'|30'|24'|20'|12'|10'| 8'| 6'| 4'|
             -----------------------------------------------------------
   Start #5  16 06  000°T  35F  C  |60'|45'|36'|30'|18'|15'|12'| 9'| 6'|
             -----------------------------------------------------------
   Start #6  16 24  090°T  076  C  |60'|45'|36'|30'|18'|15'|12'| 9'| 6'|
             -----------------------------------------------------------
   Start #7  16 42  180°T  168  C  |80'|60'|48'|40'|24'|20'|16'|12'| 8'|
             -----------------------------------------------------------
   Start #8  17 06  270°T  256  C  |80'|60'|48'|40'|24'|20'|16'|12'| 8'|
FIN Start #9 17 30  000°T  _____  C  |100|75'|60'|50'|30'|25'|20'|15'|10'|
             -----------------------------------------------------------
   Start 10  _____  090°T  _____  C  |100|75'|60'|50'|30'|25'|20'|15'|10'|
=================================================================
         1-  Select Track Spacing "S" in mi.

         2-  Select Speed in k.

         3-  Circle Corresponding Leg Time Column

         4-  Add leg time to Start time for next Start time
=================================================================
Reference Data:

         1-  Datum _____

         2-  ETA at Datum  15 23     3-  Vessel   RAGDOLL

         4-  Call Sign  VZ 2158      5-  Reg No _____
```

Fig. 7-3. Expanding square worksheet illustration. Courtesy of U.S. Coast Guard.

## SEARCH PATTERN WORKSHEET for SECTOR SEARCH

```
==============================================================
              R=5 mi        |15k|20k|25k|30k| - | - | - | - | - |
              --------------------------------------------------
              R=4 mi        |12k|16k|20k|24k| - | - | - | - | - |
              --------------------------------------------------
              R=3 mi        | 9k|12k|15k|18k|30k| - | - | - | - |
              --------------------------------------------------
     ──→  R=2 mi        | 6k| 8k|10k|(2k|20k|24k|30k| - | - |
              --------------------------------------------------
              R=1 mi        | 3k| 4k| 5k| 6k|10k|12k|15k|20k|30k|
              --------------------------------------------------
              R=¹/₂ mi      | - | 2k|2.5| 3k| 5k| 6k|7.5|10k|15k|
==============================================================
Start #1 /5 30  000°T  358   C  |20'|15'|12'|10'| 6'| 5'| 4'| 3'| 2'|
              --------------------------------------------------
Start #2 /5 40  120°T  107   C  |20'|15'|12'|10'| 6'| 5'| 4'| 3'| 2'|
              --------------------------------------------------
Start #3 /5 50  240°T  230   C  |40'|30'|24'|20'|12'|10'| 8'| 6'| 4'|
              --------------------------------------------------
         /6 00  Pass through Datum
              --------------------------------------------------
Start #4 /6 10  000°T  358   C  |20'|15'|12'|10'| 6'| 5'| 4'| 3'| 2'|
              --------------------------------------------------
Start #5 /6 20  120°T  107   C  |40'|30'|24'|20'|12'|10'| 8'| 6'| 4'|
              --------------------------------------------------
         /6 30  Pass through Datum
              --------------------------------------------------
Start #6 /6 40  240°T  230   C  |20'|15'|12'|10'| 6'| 5'| 4'| 3'| 2'|
              --------------------------------------------------
Start #7 /6 50  000°T  358   C  |20'|15'|12'|10'| 6'| 5'| 4'| 3'| 2'|
              --------------------------------------------------
         /7 00  Return to Datum
==============================================================
```

1- Select Pattern Radius "R" in mi.

2- Select Speed in k.

3- Circle Corresponding Leg Time Column

4- Add leg time to Start time for next Start time

```
==============================================================
```

Reference Data:

1- Datum _____

2- ETA at Datum __/5 23__   3- Vessel __RAGDOLL_____

4- Call Sign __VZ 2158__   5- Reg No _____

Fig. 7-4. Sector search worksheet illustration. Courtesy of U.S. Coast Guard.

# CHAPTER EIGHT

# Rescue, Reports, and Returning Home

Rescued at last. Once you have been spotted, the ordeal is not necessarily over. There are still problems to overcome. An aircraft may spot your survival craft and report your position to the Coast Guard or other similar SAR-type organizations. *Remember,* it may be some time before a helicopter or ship can get to you. You will need to continue to ration food and water. The rescue operation itself can be a hazardous experience. Great caution should be taken.

## RESCUE BY SHIP

Remain calm when the rescue ship comes alongside. Deplorable loss of life and injury have occurred in the scramble to board the rescue ship. Survivors who have reposed in the safety of a survival craft for hours or days tend to rush from it as if the craft were plague-ridden. The possibility of being crushed between the hulls of the rescue ship and lifeboat must be taken seriously.

The rescue ship will approach from the windward side of the survival craft unless the ship's rate of drift is greater than that of the craft. The approach, however, is at the discretion of the rescue ship's master or captain. Survivors should, after donning life jackets or immersion suits, step off the survival craft onto the rescue craft only when the survival craft is on the crest or top of a swell. This will drop the survival craft down while survivors are climbing up a ladder or net. Otherwise, there is the danger of the boat or raft being raised up by the wave and hitting the survivors.

It has been found that survivors are often unable to assist in their own rescue because of fatigue or numbness from exposure. The Navy and Coast Guard consider that for all practical purposes survivors will be unable to help themselves. Military vessels have trained men who can go over the side in life jackets with lifelines attached and swim to assist the survivors. On a merchant ship, if there are expert swimmers in the crew, a similar course can be followed. The greatest care must be taken that volunteers or people detailed to this task are not exposed to grave risks themselves.

If large numbers of survivors have to be rescued, rescue ships may hang cargo nets over the side for survivors to cling to and to climb up if they are capable of doing so. Heaving lines and gantlines should be available to assist in the rescue. The problem of getting survivors aboard the rescuing vessel, when a lifeboat is not used, is a serious one. Forethought and initiative in this matter can save lives.

### RESCUE BY HELICOPTER

You could be rescued directly from the survival craft or from a rescue ship by a helicopter. *The suggestions which follow pertain to rescue from a ship but can be modified as appropriate to apply to the survival craft.*

The wind developed by the helicopter rotor system can be over 70 knots. That is why it is important to have all loose gear on deck securely tied down or stowed below decks. The rotor system could be destroyed if any loose objects are blown into the rotor during the hoist.

Your voice cannot be heard over the noise made by the helicopter engine, so it is important to plan ahead. Work out problems which may occur before the helicopter hovers overhead.

Remember to wear your life jacket! The U.S. Coast Guard usually uses a rescue basket (figure 8-1) for survivors who can help themselves. The basket is very easy to use. Just climb into the basket after it touches the deck (to discharge static electricity), sit down, and keep hands and arms inside. A Navy rescue net may be utilized by Navy helicopters and is also illustrated in figure 8-1.

A "horse collar" sling may be carried on board helicopters. It is used by rescue helos from other countries more often than it is used by the U.S. Coast Guard. The "horse collar" is just a padded loop which is placed over the body and underneath the armpits. The hoist is made with the line in front of the face as illustrated in figure 8-2.

A litter will usually be used to hoist those who have serious injuries or illnesses or who are unable to walk. To use the litter it is necessary to get help from other crew members. The straps must be disconnected and spread out. The blankets must be removed. The patient should be put in and covered with the blanket. The straps are then snugly fastened with the pad on top of the chest.

Navy Rescue Net     Horse Collar Rescue Sling     Coast Guard Rescue Basket

Fig. 8-1. Helicopter rescue devices. From *Able Seaman and Lifeboatman.* Courtesy of Marine Education Textbooks, Houma, LA.

If the litter has to be taken below decks to the victim, it must be unhooked from the cable. This hook must *not* be attached to any part of the vessel. There is always a possibility that there may be an emergency aboard the helo itself. The helo may have to move unexpectedly. To decrease this type of danger, the pilot may hover off to one side of the vessel while waiting.

It is suggested that if both ships and helicopters are in the area, rescue ships pick up all survivors and only those most in need of medical attention be removed by helicopter from the rescue ship. In that eventuality the following guidelines are provided.

## When Requesting Helicopter Assistance

1. Give accurate position, time, speed, course, weather conditions, wind direction and velocity, voice and CW frequencies.
2. If not already provided, give complete medical information, including whether or not the patient is ambulatory.
3. If you are beyond helicopter range, advise your diversion intentions so that a rendezvous point may be arranged.
4. If there are any changes, advise immediately. Should the patient expire prior to arrival of the helicopter, be sure to advise. Remember, the flight crew are risking their lives attempting to help you.

Fig. 8-2. Horse collar sling rescue by a helicopter. Courtesy of U.S. Coast Guard.

## Preparations Prior to Arrival of the Helicopter

1. Provide continuous radio guard on 2182 kHz, or specified *voice* frequency if possible. The helicopter cannot operate CW.
2. Select and clear the hoist area, preferably aft, with a minimum 50-foot radius. This must include the securing of loose gear, awnings, and antenna wires. Trice up running rigging and booms. If the hoist is aft, lower flagstaff.
3. If hoist is at night, light the pickup area as well as possible. *Be sure you do not shine any lights on the helicopter* so the pilot is not blinded. If there are obstructions in the vicinity, put a light on them so the pilot will be aware of their positions.
4. Point searchlights vertically to aid in locating the ship, and secure them when the helicopter is on scene.
5. Advise location of pickup area before the helicopter arrives so that the pilot may make the approach aft, amidships, or forward, as required.
6. There will be a high noise level under the helicopter, making voice communication almost impossible. Arrange a set of hand signals among the crew who will assist.

## Hoist Operations

1. If possible, move the victim to a position as close to the hoist area as his or her condition permits—*time is important.*
2. Normally, if a litter is required, it will be necessary to move the patient to the special litter which will be lowered by the helicopter. Be prepared to do this as quickly as possible. Be sure the victim is strapped in, face up, *wearing a life jacket, if his or her condition permits.*
3. Be sure the victim is tagged to indicate what medication, if any, was administered, and when.
4. Have the victim's medical record and necessary papers in an envelope or package ready for transfer *with* him or her.
5. Change course so the ship rides as easily as possible with the wind on the bow, preferably on the port bow. Try to choose a course to keep stack gases clear of the hoist area. Once established, maintain course and speed.
6. Reduce speed if necessary to ease the ship's motion, but maintain steerageway.

7. If you do not have radio contact with the helicopter, when you are in all respects ready for the hoist, signal the helicopter in with a "come on" by hand, or at night by flashlight.

8. *Allow the basket or stretcher to touch deck prior to handling to avoid static shock.*

9. If a trail line is dropped by the helicopter, guide the basket or stretcher to deck with the line—keep line clear at all times.

10. Place the victim in the basket, sitting with hands clear of sides, or in the litter as described above. Signal the hoist operator when ready for hoist. The victim signals by nodding his or her head if able. Deck personnel give thumbs up.

11. If it is necessary to take the litter away from the hoist point, unhook the hoist cable and keep it free for the helicopter to haul in. *Do not secure the cable to the vessel or attempt to move the stretcher without unhooking it first.*

12. When the victim is strapped in the stretcher, signal the helicopter to lower cable, hook up, and signal the hoist operator when ready to hoist. Steady the stretcher from turning or swinging.

13. If a trail line is attached to the basket or stretcher, use it to steady. Keep your feet clear of the line.

## CARE OF SURVIVORS

When a person has been in a life raft for some days, and especially when the water intake has been low, the blood circulation suffers and he or she will therefore easily develop shock. The victim's condition is like that of astronauts who have been in a weightless situation for a longer period.

If the survivor suddenly rises to his or her feet, the blood pressure will drop suddenly, and the survivor will faint.

*It is important that survivors are helped and supported during rescue.*

As soon as possible survivors should be put in a horizontal position in order to keep the blood pressure up.

*Liquids should be administered in small quantities.*

The first days after rescue, food should be light until the bowel again functions normally.

Survivors may be nervous and upset. Treat them gently and quietly. They may want someone to stay with them for reassurance—they can't believe that they are safe. They often wake up terrified, thinking that they are still on the raft. Loud or sudden noises and thunder often terrify them.

Speak to them quietly. If a person is confused, explain where the person is and how he or she was picked up. Convince the survivor that he or she is being taken care of. If a survivor weeps, don't try to stop him or her. Wait patiently until the person is through. If a survivor gets aggressive, let him or her yell and encourage the person to get it out of his or her system. Don't try to stop this behavior unless it is disturbing to others or too exhausting for the survivor. Being rough with a person who has been through an ordeal does not help that person to forget it or get over it. It makes him or her angry and increases the survivor's nervousness.

The leaders may try to continue a brave front after the rescue. Give them a chance to break down too—it will help them come back to normal more quickly.

Finally, survivors could feel depressed because they made it and their shipmates may not have lived. Psychological care may be necessary for such survivors.

## GETTING HOME

As the time approaches for landing, eagerness to get on shore is coupled with exhilaration. You just can't wait to get away from the ship. Well, sometimes it's as rosy as one pictures it, but sometimes it's not so easy. It's a different way of life to get used to. The people you meet haven't shared your experiences. Their point of view may seem so different that you feel like an outsider.

These experiences are common. People have longed to see their families only to find that the noise of the children irritates them. Their friends annoy them. They are cross, blame themselves, then feel worse.

Continued psychological care may be necessary until the survivor completely recovers from the trauma of abandoning his or her vessel and the rescue.

## CONCLUSION

For survival at sea the will to survive is paramount. This will to survive is reinforced with knowledge of the environment, self-control, and training. Today, with the Global Maritime Distress and Safety System the probability of rescue within 24 hours is close to 100 percent. Once in your survival craft, it would be best to stay in the area by use of a sea anchor and ensure the EPIRB is activated. The immediate action required to be taken after abandoning ship was published by the U.S. Coast Guard in their NVIC 2-92 and is in support of IMO Resolution A.657(16) which was adopted by the SOLAS Convention on 19 October 1989. These instructions are prioritized in figure 8-3. The survival craft commander must maintain a log and make a casualty report. An example of such report and log for a life raft is illustrated in figure 8-4.

The greatest obstacle that is faced at sea is fear of the unknown. Fear is natural, but it can be controlled and overcome. Survival at sea is determined by your knowledge, equipment, and morale. Although the master or captain is responsible for the vessel's safety, responsibility also lies with each seafarer. The best possible safety devices will be worthless if you don't know how and when to use them.

**Part A**

INSTRUCTIONS FOR IMMEDIATE ACTION IN A LIFERAFT

The instructions concerning immediate action upon entering the liferaft should be written in easily legible type on waterproof material, and displayed so as to be easily seen by a person entering the liferaft. The instructions should be written in one of the official languages of the Organization in addition to the official language of the country.

1 Cut painter and get clear of ship.

2 Look for and pick up other survivors.

3 Ensure sea-anchor streamed when clear of ship.

4 Close up entrances.

5 Read survival instructions.

**Part B**

INSTRUCTIONS ON HOW TO SURVIVE IN A LIFERAFT

1 Identify person in charge of liferaft.

2 Post a look-out.

3 Open equipment pack.

4 Issue anti-seasickness medicine and seasickness bags.

5 Dry liferaft floor and inflate, if appropriate.

6 Administer first aid, if appropriate.

Fig. 8-3. Life raft survival instructions. (*Continued on following page*). Courtesy of U.S. Coast Guard.

7   Manoeuvre towards other liferafts, secure liferafts together and distribute survivors and equipment between survival craft.

8   Arrange watches and duties.

9   Check liferaft for correct operation and any damage and repair as appropriate (ventilate if $CO_2$ leaking into liferaft).

10  Check functioning of canopy light and if possible conserve power during daylight.

11  Adjust canopy openings to give protection from weather or to ventilate the liferaft as appropriate.

12  Prepare and use detection equipment including radio equipment.

13  Gather up any useful floating objects.

14  Protect against heat, cold and wet conditions.

15  Decide on food and water rations.

16  Take measures to maintain morale.

17  Make sanitary arrangements to keep liferaft habitable.

18  Maintain liferaft including topping up of buoyancy tubes and canopy supports.

19  Make proper use of available survival equipment.

20  Prepare action for:

.1   arrival of rescue units;

.2   being taken in tow;

.3   rescue by helicopter; and

.4   landing and beaching.

Notes: 1 The order in which the above instructions are followed will depend on the particular circumstances.

2 The above instructions can stand alone or can be amplified as appropriate to the satisfaction of the Administration.

Fig. 8-3 *(continued)*.

## SURVIVOR'S REPORT

Please complete as much as you can of this report. It will help you to answer the questions you will be asked when rescued.

(1) DATE OF CASUALTY ———————— TIME ————————

(2) DETAILS OF VESSEL: -
    (a) Name of vessel          ———————————————
    (b) Official number (if any) ———————————————
    (c) Gross Tonnage         ———————————————
    (d) Number in Crew        ———————————————

(3) POSITION OF VESSEL: -
    (a) Latitude             ———————————————
    (b) Longitude           ———————————————
    (c) Nearest Land         ———————————————
    (d) Last port of call      ———————————————
    (e) Where bound         ———————————————

(4) OWNERS OF VESSEL (Give name and address)

————————————————————————————————————

(5) MASTER OF VESSEL (Give name and address)

————————————————————————————————————

(6) NATURE OF CASUALTY
    (Give brief description of the incident. If another vessel was involved give details of its name, etc. if known.)

————————————————————————————————————
————————————————————————————————————
————————————————————————————————————
————————————————————————————————————
————————————————————————————————————

(7) DETAILS OF LIFERAFT LAUNCHING: -
    (a) From which part of the ship   ———————————————
    (b) Height above water        ———————————————
    (c) Weather conditions        ———————————————

(8) DETAILS OF BOARDING
    (a) Was raft boarded by jumping or from water? ———————
    (b) Any difficulty experienced in boarding     ———————
    (c) Were lifejackets worn?            ———————

Fig. 8-4. Casualty report and log. (*Continued on following page*). Courtesy of Switlik Parachute Company, Inc., Trenton, NJ.

(9) NUMBER OF PEOPLE IN THE RAFT?     —————

(10) WAS THE FLOOR INFLATED?     —————

(11) COMMENTS ON FUNCTIONAL USE OF: -

   (a) The sea anchor          ————————————
   (b) Pump                    ————————————
   (c) Sea light               ————————————
   (d) Emergency pack contents ————————————
   (e) Repair kit              ————————————

(12) HOW WAS ATTENTION ATTRACTED?

————————————————————————————————————

————————————————————————————————————

————————————————————————————————————

(13) WEATHER CONDITION WHEN RESCUED:-

   (a) Visibility     ————————————————
   (b) Sea state      ————————————————

(14) METHOD OF RESCUE

   (a) Ship (give name)   ————————————
   (b) Lifeboat           ————————————
   (c) Beaching           ————————————
   (d) Aircraft           ————————————

(15) DATE, TIME AND POSITION OF RESCUE

————————————————————————————————————

————————————————————————————————————

————————————————————————————————————

————————————————————————————————————

## DAILY LOG

Fig. 8-4. (*continued*).

# Lifeboat, Rescue Boat, and Rigid Life Raft Equipment; Description, Recommendations, and Inspection Guidelines*

*Because equipment quantities and stowage arrangements may vary slightly from boat to boat, the Coast Guard recommends that a chart be posted in a prominent location inside the boat which lists the equipment and the quantity of each required in the boat. A diagram of the stowage location of each item should be included.*

Lifeboat Equipment for U.S. Registered Vessels Equipped to
Requirements in Effect Prior to the 1983 SOLAS Amendments†

| Item | Ocean and Coastwise | | | Great Lakes | | Lakes, bays, sounds, and rivers |
| | All except MODUs and seagoing barges | Mobile Offshore Drilling Units | Seagoing barges | Passenger vessels and vessels carrying cargo | Other vessels | |
|---|---|---|---|---|---|---|
| Bailer | 1 | 1 | None | 1 | None | None |
| Bilge pump | 1[1] | 1[1] | None | None | None | None |
| Boathook | 2 | 2 | 2 | 1 | 1 | 1 |
| Bucket | 2 | 2 | 1 | 1 | 1 | 1 |
| Compass | 1 | 1 | None | None | None | None |
| Cover, protecting | 1[2] | None | None | None | None | None |
| Ditty bag | 1 | None | None | None | None | None |
| Drinking cup | 1 | 1 | 1 | None | None | None |
| EPIRB (FCC Class S) | 2 per ship[3] | None | None | None | None | None |
| Fire extinguisher | 2[4] | 2[4] | 24 | 2[4] | 2[4] | 2[4] |
| First-aid kit | 1 | 1 | None | None | None | None |
| Fishing kit | 1 | 1 | None | None | None | None |

\* Courtesy of U.S. Coast Guard.
† Continued on pages 188 and 189. See numbered footnotes on page 189.

| Item | Ocean and Coastwise | | | Great Lakes | | Lakes, bays, sounds, and rivers |
|---|---|---|---|---|---|---|
| | All except MODUs and seagoing barges | Mobile Offshore Drilling Units | Seagoing barges | Passenger vessels and vessels carrying cargo | Other vessels | |
| Flare—hand red flare | 12 | 12 | None | 6 | None | None |
| Flare—rocket parachute flare | 12[5] | 12 | None | 6 | None | None |
| Flashlight | 1 | 1 | None | 1 | None | None |
| Hard bread | 2 lb per person[6] | 2 lb per person[6, 7] | None | None | None | None |
| Hatchet | 2 | 2 | None | 2 | 1 | 1 |
| Heaving line | 2 | 2 | None | None | None | None |
| Jackknife | 1 | 1 | 1 | None | None | None |
| Ladder | 1 | 1 | None | None | None | None |
| Lifejacket | 2 | 2 | 2 | 2 | 2 | 2 |
| Lifeline | 1 | 1 | 1 | 1 | 1 | 1 |
| Lighting system/lantern | 1 | 1 | 1 | 1 | 1 | 1 |
| Locker | 1 | 1 | None | 1 | None | None |
| Mast and sail | 1[8] | None | None | None | None | None |
| Milk | 1 lb per person | 1 lb per person[7] | None | None | None | None |
| Mirror | 2 | 2 | None | None | None | None |
| Oars/oarlocks | 1 unit | 1 unit[7] | 1 unit | 1 unit | 1 unit | 1 unit |
| Painter | 2 | 2 | 1 | 2 | 1 | 1 |
| Plug | 1 | 1 | 1 | 1 | 1 | 1 |
| Rudder and tiller | 1 | 1 | 1 | 1 | 1 | None |
| Sea anchor | 1 | 1 | None | 1 | None | None |
| Searchlight | None[9] | None | None | None | None | None |
| Smoke signal | 2 | 2 | None | None | None | None |
| Storm oil | 1 gal | 1 gal[7] | None | 1 gal | None | None |
| Table of lifesaving signals | 1 | 1 | None | None | None | None |
| Tool kit | 1[4] | 1[4] | 14 | 1[4] | 1[4] | 1[4] |
| Two-way radiotelephone | 3 per ship[3] | None | None | None | None | None |

| Item | Ocean and Coastwise | | | Great Lakes | | Lakes, bays, sounds, and rivers |
|---|---|---|---|---|---|---|
| | All except MODUs and seagoing barges | Mobile Offshore Drilling Units | Seagoing barges | Passenger vessels and vessels carrying cargo | Other vessels | |
| Water | 3 quarts per person | 3 quarts per person | 1 quart per person | None | None | None |
| Whistle | 1 | 1 | None | None | None | None |

[1] Each lifeboat with a capacity of 100 persons or more, must carry an additional bilge pump, or be equipped with a powered bilge pump.

[2] Not required for totally enclosed lifeboats.

[3] Applies only to SOLAS Convention ships. See NVIC 9-91 for details and alternatives.

[4] Required for motor lifeboats only. Fire extinguishers may be of any approved size.

[5] Vessels in coastwise service need only carry 12 flares for each 5 lifeboats or fraction thereof.

[6] One unit of lifeboat provisions consists of 3,600 calories (equivalent to 2 lb of hard bread).

[7] Required only on MODUs in international service.

[8] Oar-propelled lifeboats only.

[9] One searchlight required only on passenger ship emergency lifeboats.

## Lifeboat, Rescue Boat, and Rigid Liferaft Equipment for Ships Equipped to Meet 1983 SOLAS Amendments*†

| Item | Lifeboat | Rescue boat[1] | Rigid liferaft[2] |
|---|---|---|---|
| Bailer | 1 | 1 | 1 or 2 [19] |
| Bilge pump | 1[3] | 1[3] | None |
| Boathook | 2 | 1 | None |
| Bucket | 2 | 1[15] | None |
| Can opener | 3[4] | None | 3[4, 8] |
| Compass | 1 | 1 | None |
| Cover, protecting | None[5] | None | None |
| Dipper | 1 | None | None |
| Ditty bag | None[6] | None | None |
| Drinking cup | 1 | None | 1[9] |
| EPIRB (FCC Class S) | 2 per ship[7] | None | 2 per ship[7] |
| Emergency provisions | 10,000 kJ per person[8] | None | 10,000 kJ per person[8] |
| Fire extinguisher | 1[9] | None | 1[9] |

* Courtesy of U.S. Coast Guard.
† Continued on pages 190 and 191. See numbered footnotes on page 191.

| Item | Lifeboat | Rescue boat[1] | Rigid liferaft[2] |
|---|---|---|---|
| First-aid kit | 1 | 1 | None |
| Fishing kit | 1[8] | None | None |
| Flare—hand red flare | 12[11] or 6[10] | None | 12[11] or 6[10] |
| Flare—rocket parachute flare | 12[11] or 4[10] | None | 4[10] |
| Flashlight | 1 | 1 | 1 |
| Hatchet | 2 | None | None |
| Heaving line | 2 | 2 | 1 |
| Instruction card | None | None | None |
| Jackknife | 1 | None | None |
| Knife | None | 1[16] | 1 or 2[19] |
| Ladder | 1 | None | 1 |
| Lighting system/lantern | 1 | None | 1 |
| Mast and sail | None[6] | None | None |
| Mirror | 2 or 1[11] | None | 2 or 1[11] |
| Oars/oarlocks | 1 unit [12] | 1 unit | None |
| Paddle | None | None | 2 |
| Painter | 2 | 1 | 1 |
| Position-indicating light | 1 | 1[17] | 1 |
| Pump | None | 1[18] | None |
| Radar reflector | 1 | 1 | 1 |
| Rainwater collection equipment | 1[5, 13] | None | None |
| Repair kit | None | 1[18] | None |
| Rudder and tiller | None[14] | None[14] | None |
| Sea anchor | 1 | 1 | 2 |
| Searchlight | 1 | 1 | None |
| Seasickness kit | 1 per person | None | 1 per person |
| Skates and fenders | 1 set | None | None |
| Smoke signal | 2 | None | 2[10] |
| Sponge | None | 2[18] | 2 |
| Survival manual | 1 | None | 1 |
| Table of lifesaving signals | 1 | None | 1 |
| Thermal protective aid | 10% × number of persons; 2 minimum | 10% × number of persons; 2 minimum | 10% × number of persons; 2 minimum |
| Tool kit | 1[6] | None | None |
| Towline | None | 1 | None |

| Item | Lifeboat | Rescue boat[1] | Rigid liferaft[2] |
|---|---|---|---|
| Two-way radiotelephone | 3 per ship[7] | 3 per ship[7] | 3 per ship7 |
| Water | 3 liters per person | None | 1.5 liters per person[8] |
| Whistle | 1 | 1 | 1 |

[1] A rescue boat which is also one of the ship's lifeboats must carry the equipment listed in both the lifeboat and rescue boat columns. Where the quantities are different, the largest number in either column is the minimum quantity required. A lifeboat which is also approved as a rescue boat does not have to carry rescue boat equipment if it is not the ship's designated rescue boat.

[2] At time of publication, there were no rigid liferafts meeting the 1983 SOLAS Amendments, which had been approved by the Coast Guard. Liferafts equipped with all indicated equipment in the column are marked "SOLAS A PACK." Those with the indicated reductions for short international voyages are marked "SOLAS B PACK."

[3] Bilge pump not required for boats of self-bailing design. Each lifeboat with a capacity of 100 persons or more must carry an additional bilge pump, or be equipped with a powered bilge pump.

[4] Can openers may be omitted if they are not required to open any of the containers carried as survival equipment.

[5] Approved partially enclosed lifeboats include a foldable canopy which must be maintained in serviceable condition. An open lifeboat voluntarily equipped to the 1983 SOLAS standards must also carry an approved protecting cover. The foldable canopy and protecting cover for these boats are required to include a means for collecting rainwater. No additional rainwater collection equipment is required.

[6] An open oar-propelled lifeboat voluntarily equipped to the 1983 SOLAS standards must also carry mast and sail, and a ditty bag. A tool kit is not required on an oar-propelled or hand-propelled lifeboat.

[7] See NVIC 9-91 for details and alternatives.

[8] Not required on ships in short international voyage service.

[9] Extinguisher Type B:C Size II. Alternately 2 Type B:C Size I extinguishers may be carried.

[10] One-half of this quantity required on ships in short international voyage service.

[11] Larger number is current U.S. requirement which applies to U.S. vessels. Lower number is current SOLAS requirement. Coast Guard will accept Class S EPIRB *carried or installed on board* the lifeboat or liferaft as equivalent to the signaling devices required in excess of the SOLAS requirements. Lifeboats or liferafts equipped with Class S EPIRBS may carry the smaller number of other signaling devices.

[12] Oars not required in free-fall lifeboats.

[13] SOLAS requirement for this equipment on totally enclosed lifeboats is vague. SOLAS regulation III/41.7.5 requires that means shall be provided for the storage of collected rainwater, but means for collecting rainwater is explicitly required only for partially enclosed lifeboats. Coast Guard interpretation is that rainwater collection equipment is required on totally enclosed boats and is implied by the requirement to provide for the storage of collected rainwater. As an alternative to rainwater collection equipment, Coast Guard will accept an approved hand-operated reverse osmosis desalinator.

[14] An open lifeboat voluntarily equipped to the 1983 SOLAS standards must also carry a rudder and tiller. Totally enclosed and partially enclosed lifeboats are equipped with permanently installed steering systems. Rescue boats also have permanently installed steering systems, or else are powered by outboard motors which incorporate rudder and tiller functions.

[15] Required only in a rigid rescue boat.

[16] A hatchet may be carried instead of a knife in a rigid rescue boat.

[17] Instead of a position-indicating light, a rescue boat which is not also a lifeboat, should be equipped with navigation lights in accordance with the 1972 COLREGS.

[18] Required only in an inflated or rigid/inflated rescue boat.

[19] Larger number required for liferafts with a capacity of 13 persons or more.

## Bailer

The bailer must be buoyant, except for a bailer with a lanyard used in the lifeboat or rescue boat before July 1, 1986 and continued in use thereafter.

## Bilge pump

Bilge pumps in lifeboats approved under the 1983 SOLAS Amendments must be installed in the lifeboat in a ready-to-use condition. Ready-to-use installation is recommended, but not required, in other lifeboats.

1. A size 3 bilge pump may be used in any lifeboat.
2. Size 2 bilge pumps are intended for lifeboats of less than 70 persons capacity.
3. No approved size 1 bilge pumps have been made since 1967. Any still in good and serviceable condition may be used in lifeboats of less than 330 cubic foot capacity.

*Inspection:* The bilge pump should be visually inspected to confirm parts are in good condition, especially rubber parts and mounting arrangements. The pump should be operated to show that it pumps water efficiently.

## Boathook

Each boathook should be kept free and ready for use at all times. The recommended style is a single hook and ball-point, however, a different style may be used on an inflated rescue boat if intended to minimize the possibility of damage to an inflatable hull. The handle should be at least 2.4 m (8 ft.) long, except that for boats 9 m (30 ft.) long or longer, the handle should be at least 3.6 m (12 ft.) long. Handles need to be at least 38 mm (1½ in) diameter in order to be properly gripped.

## Bucket

Buckets should be of corrosion resistant material and have a nominal capacity of at least 7.5 liters (2 gallons). A lanyard at least 2 m (6 ft.) long and 4 mm (5⁄32 in) in diameter, should be attached to the bail of each bucket.

## Can opener

Each can opener must be suitable for opening the cans carried in the lifeboat or liferaft. The can opener in an approved jackknife counts toward this requirement. If the boat carries no cans which require the use of can openers, the can openers need not be carried.

## Compass

The compass must either be in an illuminated binnacle or have a luminous dial. The compass in totally enclosed lifeboats must be permanently mounted at the steering station. Permanent mounting at the steering station is also recommended for partially enclosed lifeboats, but a removable compass may be used. The mounting base for a removable compass must be installed in a location where the compass will be in sight of the helmsman.

*Inspection:* The compass bowl should be filled with fluid and the card free to rotate. Markings should be legible. If the boat is operated in the course of an inspection, the compass reading should be compared with a few known bearings. If large errors are evident, the compensating mechanism should be used to reduce the errors, or a compass deviation card should be prepared and mounted on or near the compass.

## Cover, protecting

The protecting cover for a partially enclosed lifeboat is approved as a component of the lifeboat. Protecting covers on SOLAS ship lifeboats must be equipped with retroreflective material.

*Note:* These protecting covers provide shelter for persons in lifeboats. Any cover used on the lifeboat while it is stowed in the davits is used at the option of the operator, and is not regulated by the Coast Guard. Any such cover must be able to be quickly removed in order to make the boat ready for launching in an emergency.

*Inspection:* The cover should be free of unrepaired rips and holes. All framework for erecting the cover should be complete and suitable for its intended purpose. The rainwater collection device in a protecting cover should be in good condition and have a length of tubing sufficient to reach the water storage tanks.

## Dipper

Each dipper must be of corrosion resistant material. A lanyard approximately 1 m (3 ft.) long or longer should be attached to the dipper. The dipper must be suitable for dipping collected water from the lifeboat's water storage tanks.

## Ditty bag

The ditty bag should be canvas or equivalent material, and must contain a sailmaker's palm, needles for repairing a sail, sail twine, marline, and marline spike.

## Drinking cup

The drinking cup must be of corrosion resistant material and graduated with column markings in milliliters or ounces, or both. A lanyard approximately 1 m (3 ft.) long or longer should be attached to the drinking cup.

## EPIRB

An EPIRB carried as boat equipment must be either a class S EPIRB, or a Category 2 Satellite EPIRB. The EPIRB may be carried in an equipment locker, but the preferred stowage arrangement is mounting in a position where it is ready to be used.

1. The class S EPIRB must be a type which meets the regulations of the Federal Communications Commission.
2. The Category 2 Satellite EPIRB must be a type which meets the regulations of the Federal Communications Commission.

*Inspection:* Each EPIRB must be tested monthly using the integrated test circuit and output indicator to determine that it is operative, and by checking the battery expiration date. EPIRB batteries must be replaced when their expiration date has passed.

## Emergency provisions

One lifeboat ration is required for each person the boat is equipped to accommodate. One ration consists of 10,000 kJ (2400 calories) of approved emergency provisions. Some emergency provisions will be packed in sizes other than 10,000 kJ, so total kJ counts rather than package counts, should be used to determine the quantity of emergency provisions required.

*Inspection:* Canned emergency provisions can be checked only by visual examination of the condition of the container. Emergency provisions in vacuum packed flexible pouches should have packaging material tightly compressed against the contents. Loose contents indicate a loss of the vacuum seal, and such pouches should be replaced. Non-vacuum packed pouches should be squeezed to check for air leakage. Approved emergency provisions are marked with a packing date, and some may have an expiration date. All packages past their expiration date should be replaced during the annual stripping and cleaning of the lifeboat or rigid liferaft. Packages without an expiration date should be replaced if they are more than five years old.

## Fire extinguisher

Each fire extinguisher must be listed by an independent laboratory and be marked with a Coast Guard approval number.

*Inspection:* Fire extinguishers must be inspected periodically as a condition of their independent laboratory listing. Inspection instructions are on the extinguisher label.

## First-aid kit

The first-aid kit in a lifeboat, rescue boat and in a rigid liferaft must be U.S. Coast Guard approved.

*Inspection:* The required contents of an approved first aid kit are listed in the instructions provided with the kit. These contents may vary depending upon the age of the kit and the manufacturer. Various substitutions have been approved since the Coast Guard approval regulations were first published. Each unit carton must be in an intact water- proof package. If it is not, it must be replaced with a waterproof unit from a supplier of approved first aid kits. Standard cellophane-wrapped unit cartons are not waterproof. Any dated medications in the kit must be replaced during the annual stripping and cleaning of the lifeboat or rigid liferaft if their expiration date has passed.

## Fishing kit

The fishing kit must be approved.

*Inspection:* The fishing kit should not be opened for inspection. If the sealed package is intact, and the package markings legible, the fishing kit is acceptable for continued use.

## Flare—hand red flare

Hand red flares to SOLAS standards are Coast Guard approved.

*Inspection:* Approved flares are marked with an expiration date. All flares past their expiration date must be replaced during the annual stripping and cleaning of the lifeboat or rigid liferaft.

## Flare—rocket parachute flare

Rocket parachute flares to SOLAS standards are Coast Guard approved.

*Inspection:* Approved flares are marked with an expiration date. All flares past their expiration date must be replaced during the annual stripping and cleaning of the lifeboat or rigid liferaft.

## Flashlight

The flashlight must be a Type I or Type III. Three spare batteries and two spare bulbs, stored in a watertight container, must be provided for each flashlight. Three-cell size flashlights bearing Coast Guard approval numbers may continue to be used as long as they are in good and serviceable condition.

*Inspection:* Flashlight batteries must be replaced at each annual stripping and cleaning of the lifeboat or rigid liferaft, unless they are marked with an expiration date. Batteries with an expiration date must be replaced if their expiration date has passed.

## Hard bread

Hard bread provisions have evolved into modern approved emergency provisions. Lifeboats required to carry two pounds of hard bread per person should carry the equivalent in approved emergency provisions, instead. The equivalent of two pounds of hard bread is 15,000 kJ (3600 calories) in approved emergency rations. Note that this is 50% more than the requirements under the 1983 SOLAS Amendments. If emergency provisions are also substituted for milk, there will be more than twice the quantity emergency provisions carried as compared to the 1983 SOLAS Amendment requirements. Substitutions should not be made for the lesser quantity, unless the lifeboat is completely equipped to the 1983 SOLAS standard.

## Hatchet

Hatchets should be stowed in brackets near the release hooks. On boats with only one release hook, the second hatchet should be stowed near the towing point. Each hatchet should be secured to the lifeboat by a 4 mm ($5/32$ in) minimum diameter lanyard long enough to allow a hatchet to reach the falls and painter.

*Inspection:* Hatchets should be reasonably free of rust. The edge should be sufficiently sharp to cut wood cleanly from a board when the hatchet strikes the board in a direction nearly parallel to the grain.

## Heaving line

Each heaving line must be buoyant and have a buoyant rescue quoit attached to one end. The heaving line must be at least 8 mm ($5/16$ in) in diameter, and at least 30 m (100 ft.) long.

## Instruction card

The instruction card must be printed on plastic or other stiff waterproof material, and must be suspended from the inside canopy. The instruction card must contain information on the immediate steps to be taken by survivors upon entering the liferaft.

## Jackknife

The jackknife must be secured to the boat by a lanyard.

*Inspection.* Jackknives should be free of rust. The edge of the blade should be sufficiently sharp to shave wood cleanly from a hardwood board.

## Knife

The knife must be of the non-folding type with a buoyant handle. The knife in an inflated or rigid/inflated rescue boat must be a type designed to minimize the possibility of damage to the fabric portions of the hull.

1. The knife for a rigid liferaft must be secured to the liferaft by a lanyard and stowed in a pocket on the exterior of the canopy near the point where the painter is attached to the liferaft. The lanyard must be long enough to permit the knife to be used to cut the painter.
2. An approved jackknife secured by a lanyard may be substituted for the knife required in a rescue boat or for the second knife required on a liferaft equipped for 13 or more persons.

## Ladder

The boarding ladder for a lifeboat must be capable of being used on either side of the boat to enable persons in the water to board the boat. A boarding ladder for a rigid liferaft is used at any entrance without a boarding ramp. The ladder must be a permanently installed rigid type or a flexible ladder kept rigged ready for use. The flexible ladder may be kept rigged over the side, so that it is immediately ready for use. The lowest step of the ladder must be at least 0.4 m (15¾ in) below the light waterline of the lifeboat or liferaft.

The recommended ladder is a short pilot ladder or rope embarkation ladder.

Another acceptable configuration for a flexible ladder is as follows:

1. The ladder should have flat steps with handhold openings in them.
2. Each step should have a bare wood surface, or a nonskid surface.
3. The steps of the ladder should be spaced approximately 0.3 m (12 in) apart.
4. Each suspension member should be at least 15 mm ($\frac{5}{8}$ in) diameter manila rope, or another material provided it is at least 15 mm in diameter and has a breaking strength of at least 17.6 kN (3,960 lb). Synthetic rope should not be used unless it is ultraviolet light resistant, or is pigmented in a dark color.

*Inspection:* Boarding ladders should be carefully inspected for condition, especially those which are assembled with tarred marline which can loosen as it dries out. Steps should be securely attached to side ropes, and there should be no broken or cracked steps.

### Lifejacket
Each lifejacket must be approved. After July 1, 1986, each *new* lifejacket on a SOLAS ship, including those stowed in the lifeboats, must meet the 1983 SOLAS Amendment requirements.

### Lifeline
Each lifeboat must have a lifeline secured near the gunwale. The lifeline must be of a material and secured in a manner similar to that which was approved as the lifeboat's original equipment.

### Lighting system/lantern
Each totally enclosed and partially enclosed lifeboat, and each rigid liferaft must have an operating interior lighting system that is approved as a component of the lifeboat or liferaft.

Open lifeboats must carry a lantern containing sufficient oil to burn for at least 9 hours. The lantern must be kept ready for use. Each lifeboat equipped with a lantern must also carry:

1. At least 100 wooden friction matches with striking surface, in a watertight container.
2. A quantity of at least 0.94 liter (1 quart) of illuminating oil in a durable container in addition to the oil provided in the lantern.

### Locker
The locker must be suitable for the storage and preservation of the small items of equipment.

## Mast and sail

The mast and sail unit must be substantially equivalent to that originally specified by the lifeboat manufacturer and approved by the Coast Guard. The mast and sail unit normally consists of:

1. One standing lug sail of good quality canvas or equivalent material, international orange in color.
2. Spars.
3. Rigging at least 4.75 mm ($\frac{3}{16}$ in) in diameter of either galvanized or stainless steel wire rope.
4. Cover or storage container.

## Milk

The milk required is condensed milk in cans. The Coast Guard recommends operators substitute additional emergency rations for the required milk. Substitution should be on the basis of 5800 kJ of emergency rations per pound of milk required (1400 calories/lb).

*Inspection:* Unless otherwise indicated on its container, canned condensed milk is not intended for long term storage, and should be replaced each year during the annual stripping and cleaning of the lifeboat.

## Mirror

The signaling mirror must be approved.

*Inspection:* The signaling mirror package should not be opened for inspection. If the sealed package is intact, and the package markings legible, the mirror is acceptable for continued use.

## Oars/oarlocks

Each unit of oars must consist of sufficient buoyant oars or paddles to make headway in calm seas.

1. The number and type of oars required for a motor lifeboat is determined during the manufacturer's approval testing. If not specified on an equipment chart in the boat, the number should be specified in the operation or maintenance manual provided by the manufacturer with the boat. If not specified by the manufacturer, the complement of oars for motor lifeboats and hand-propelled lifeboats is four rowing oars and one steering oar of the length specified in the following table.

| Length of lifeboat in meters (feet) | | Numbers of oars for oar-propelled boats | | Length of oars in meters (feet) | |
|---|---|---|---|---|---|
| *Over* | *Not over* | *Rowing* | *Steering* | *Rowing* | *Steering* |
| – | 4.5 (15) | 4 | 1 | 2.4  (8) | 2.7  (9) |
| 4.5 (15) | 5.8 (19) | 6 | 1 | 3.0 (10) | 3.3 (11) |
| 5.8 (19) | 6.4 (21) | 6 | 1 | 3.3 (11) | 3.6 (12) |
| 6.4 (21) | 7.0 (23) | 6 | 1 | 3.6 (12) | 4.0 (13) |
| 7.0 (23) | 7.6 (25) | 8 | 1 | 4.0 (13) | 4.3 (14) |
| 7.6 (25) | 8.2 (27) | 8 | 1 | 4.3 (14) | 4.5 (15) |
| 8.2 (27) | – | 8 | 1 | 4.5 (15) | 4.8 (16) |

2. On small motor lifeboats, the manufacturer may be able to meet the requirement with buoyant paddles, rather than conventional oars.
3. An oarlock or equivalent device, either permanently installed or attached to the boat by a lanyard or chain, must be provided for each oar. Removable oarlocks must be attached to the boat by lanyards or chains. SOLAS describes these as "thole pins, crutches, or equivalent arrangements." In some cases, this requirement might be met by oar ports in the canopy of the boat. If paddles are provided instead of oars, no oarlocks are needed.
4. A rescue boat is not required to carry oars if the boat is equipped with a motor and carries two paddles.

## Paddle
Each paddle must be buoyant.

## Painter
If the painter is of synthetic material, it must be of a dark color or of a type certified to be resistant to deterioration from ultraviolet light.

1. *Lifeboat painters.* Painters must be of a length equal to and not less than twice the distance from the stowage position of the lifeboat to the waterline in the lightest seagoing condition, or 15 m (50 ft.), whichever is the greater. One painter must be attached to a painter release device capable of quickly releasing the painter when the painter is being used to tow the boat. This painter shall be placed at the forward end of the lifeboat. The other painter shall be firmly secured at or near the bow of the lifeboat ready for use. The painter should have a strength of at least 34 kN (7,700 lb).

2. *Rescue boat (SOLAS) painters.* The painter must be of a sufficient length to properly launch and recover the rescue boat. The painter must be attached to the boat's painter release device and shall be placed at the forward end of the rescue boat. The painter should have a strength of at least 34 nK (7,700 lb).

3. *Rescue boat (Subpart 160.056) painters.* Each painter for a rescue boat meeting 46 CFR Subpart 160.056 must be firmly secured at or near the bow ready for use. The painter must be at least 9 m (30 ft.) long, at least 9.5 mm (⅜ in) diameter, and have a breaking strength of at least 5.5 kN (1,220 lb).

4. *Liferaft painters.* The painter for a rigid liferaft must be of a length equal to and not less than two times the distance from the stowage position of the liferaft to the waterline in the lightest seagoing condition or 15 m (59 ft.), whichever is the greater. The painter must have a breaking strength of not less than 10.0 kN (2,250 lb) for liferafts approved for nine persons or more, and not less than 7.5 kN (1,687 lb) for any other liferaft. A float-free link meeting 46 CFR Subpart 160.073 must be secured to the end of the painter that is attached to the vessel. The breaking strength of float-free link must be between 1800 N (400 lb) and 2400 N (536 lb).

### Position-indicating light

The position-indicating light provided with a Coast Guard approved lifeboat or rigid liferaft meets SOLAS requirements and may be used as long as it is maintained in good and serviceable condition, regardless of whether or not Coast Guard approval marking is evident. Any position-indicating light added to a lifeboat or rigid liferaft must be approved.

### Plug

The automatic drain required in the lifeboat must be provided with a cap or plug attached to the lifeboat with a suitable chain.

### Pump

The pump or bellows must be manually operated and arranged to be capable of inflating any part of the inflatable structure of the rescue boat.

### Radar reflector

As a minimum, the radar reflector must be certified by its manufacturer to have a detection range of at least 4 nm in calm sea conditions. The radar reflector must also have mounting provisions to install it on the boat in its proper orientation.

Higher performing radar reflectors are recommended but not presently required. Such radar reflectors should have an apparent cross sectional area of at least 10 square meters (107 square feet) over 65% of the horizontal plane, using a radar system operating in the 9300-9500 MHz band.

### Rainwater collection equipment

SOLAS requires that "means shall be provided for the stowage of collected rainwater." Each lifeboat has at least one watertight compartment arranged to hold collected water. In order to meet the SOLAS requirement, the boat must also have a means to collect the rainwater and drain it to the watertight compartment. This may be incorporated into the design of the canopy, or may be a separate device to be mounted outside the lifeboat, with a drain tube leading to the compartment. In any case, the device should have a projected horizontal area of at least a 1 square meter (10.7 square feet) collection area, and be designed to function unattended. Alternatively, a reverse osmosis desalinator approved by the Coast Guard may be substituted for the rainwater collection device as an acceptable equivalent. Note that other types of approved desalinators are not acceptable alternatives to rainwater collection equipment. This same device may be counted as a substitution for some of the emergency drinking water (see *Water*).

### Repair kit

The repair kit for inflated and rigid/inflated rescue boats must contain at least:

1. Six sealing clamps.
2. Five 50 mm (2 in) diameter tube patches.
3. Roughing tool.
4. Cement compatible with the tube fabric. The cement must have an expiration date on its container that is not more than 24 months after the date of manufacture of the cement.

   *Inspection:* The cement must be replaced during the annual stripping and cleaning of an inflatable or rigid/inflatable rescue boat, if the expiration date of the cement has passed.

### Rudder and tiller

Lifeboats with a removable rudder and tiller must have the rudder and tiller stowed in the lifeboat ready to be set in place once the boat is launched. The rudder and tiller must be as specified by the manufacturer for the approved lifeboat.

### Sea anchor

1. *Lifeboat sea anchor.* It is a type designed to accept a storm oil distribution can, but storm oil is not required on lifeboats equipped to the 1983 SOLAS Amendments. The sea anchor must be on a shock-resistant hawser (normally nylon) and must be equipped with a tripping line which provides a firm hand grip when wet. The hawser should be at least 10 m (33 ft.) long.
2. *Liferaft sea anchors.* On each rigid liferaft, one sea anchor must be permanently attached to the liferaft in such a way that when the liferaft is waterborne, the sea anchor will cause the liferaft to lie oriented to the wind in the most stable manner. The second sea anchor must be stowed in the rigid liferaft as a spare. Each sea anchor on a rigid liferaft must be fitted with a swivel at each end of the line and must be of a type that is unlikely to turn inside-out between its shroud lines. The sea anchors must be as specified by the liferaft manufacturer and accepted by the Coast Guard when the liferaft is approved.
3. *Rescue boat sea anchor.* If the rescue boat is also one of the ship's lifeboats, the sea anchor must be as described under "lifeboat sea anchor." A rescue boat which is not a lifeboat may carry a Coast Guard approved sea anchor as specified by the boat manufacturer and accepted by the Coast Guard when the rescue boat is approved. The sea anchor must be on a shock-resistant hawser (normally nylon) and must be equipped with a tripping line which provides a firm hand grip when wet. The hawser should be at least 10 m (33 ft.) long.

### Searchlight

Each lifeboat built to the 1983 SOLAS Amendments includes a search-light which the lifeboat manufacturer has determined to be in compliance with the SOLAS requirements. If the searchlight must be replaced, it should be replaced with the same make and model, or else with a search-light certified by its manufacturer. For lifeboats built before July 1, 1986, a searchlight formerly approved is also acceptable.

1. The searchlight must be permanently mounted on the canopy, or must have a stanchion type or collapsible type portable mount-

ing on the canopy. The mounting must be located to enable operation of the searchlight by the boat operator.

2. The searchlight's power source must be capable of operating the light without charging or recharging, for not less than 3 hours continuous operation, or 6 hours total "on" time in cycles consisting of 15 minutes on and 5 minutes off.

3. If the power source is an engine starting battery, there must be sufficient battery capacity to start the engine at the end of either operating period specified in the preceding paragraph.

4. The power source must be connected to the searchlight using watertight electrical fittings.

5. The lifeboat must carry two spare bulbs.

### *Seasickness kit*
Each seasickness kit must be in a waterproof package and must include one waterproof seasickness bag, six doses of anti-seasickness medication, and instructions for using the medication. In totally enclosed and partially enclosed lifeboats, each seasickness kit should be stowed within reach of the seat it is intended for. Any medication considered safe and effective for motion sickness by the U.S. Food and Drug Administration is acceptable, but the following are recommended:

1. A combination of 25 mg of promethazine hydrochloride and 25 mg of ephedrine sulfate comprising a single dose, to be taken at six-hour intervals.

2. A transdermal patch containing scopolamine suitable for at least 2 days use. One patch is considered to comprise six doses for the purposes of this requirement.

*Inspection:* If their expiration date has passed, dated medications in the kit must be replaced during the annual stripping and cleaning of the lifeboat or rigid liferaft.

### *Skates and fenders*
Any skates and fenders must be as specified by the lifeboat manufacturer to facilitate launching and prevent damage to a lifeboat intended for launching down the side of a vessel.

### *Smoke signal*
Smoke signals to SOLAS standards are Coast Guard approved.

*Inspection:* Approved smoke signals are marked with an expiration date. All signals past their expiration date must be replaced during the annual stripping and cleaning of the lifeboat or rigid liferaft.

## Sponge
Each sponge should have a volume of at least 1000 cubic centimeters (62 cubic inches) when fully expanded.

## Storm oil
At least 3.75 liters (1 U.S. gallon) of storm oil must be carried, consisting of vegetable, fish, or animal oil. The storm oil must be in a container suitable for attachment to the sea anchor and designed to distribute a controlled amount of oil on the water.

## Survival manual
The manual is normally provided by the boat or liferaft manufacturer, printed on waterproof paper or plastic. The manual must be in English, but additional languages may be included. Manuals should be substantially in compliance with IMO Resolution A.657(16).

## Table of lifesaving signals
The table of lifesaving signals must be those in the current version of Regulation V/16 of the SOLAS Convention, printed on a waterproof card.

## Thermal protective aid
Each thermal protective aid must be approved.

## Tool kit
The tool kit must contain sufficient tools for minor adjustments to the engine and its accessories. As a minimum, the tool kit must include:

1. A container large enough to hold all the items in the kit.
2. One 340 g (12 oz.) ball peen hammer.
3. One screwdriver with a 150 mm (6 in) flat blade.
4. One pair of 200 mm (8 in) slip-joint pliers.
5. One 200 mm (8 in) adjustable wrench.

## Towline
The towline for a rescue boat must be at least the same size and length as its painter. The towline for all other rescue boats and lifeboats must

be buoyant, not less than 50 m (164 ft.) in length, and must have a breaking strength of not less than 13.3 kN (3,000 lb).

### *Two-way radiotelephone apparatus*
Three or more two-way radiotelephone apparatus for survival craft are required on the ship, but these do not necessarily have to be carried in the lifeboats or rescue boats.

### *Water*
Emergency drinking water is Coast Guard approved. Up to one-third of the required water may be replaced by desalting apparatus capable of producing an equal amount of fresh water in 2 days. Desalting apparatus is Coast Guard approved.

   *Inspection:* Canned water should be checked for vacuum by the "slap test." Any clicking sound is evidence of an acceptable vacuum. Doubtful cans can be checked by opening some of them. If a hiss is heard consistently as these cans are opened, the rest of the doubtful cans may be accepted, and only the open cans replaced. Water in flexible pouches should be checked by squeezing the pouch. Any leaking water or air is cause for rejection. All approved water containers are marked with a packing date, and some may have an expiration date. All containers past their expiration date should be replaced during the annual stripping and cleaning of the lifeboat or rigid liferaft. Containers without an expiration date should be replaced if they are more than five years old.

### *Whistle*
The whistle must be a ball-type or multi-tone whistle of corrosion-resistant construction, attached to a lanyard at least 0.9 m (3 ft.) long. An equivalent sound signal, such as a horn, may be provided instead.

# Sample U.S. Coast Guard Questions and Answers for Lifeboatman

1. The proper oar command to be given when you wish to take all the way off the lifeboat is:
   A. Way enough
   B. Trail oars
   C. Hold water
   D. Give way
2. What is the purpose of the limit switch on gravity davits?
   A. It stops the boat at the embarkation deck so passengers may board
   B. It limits the total number of passengers on the boat
   C. It cuts off all power when lowering the boat
   D. When hoisting the boat, it cuts off all power to the winch before the davits reach the stops
3. To determine which lifeboat you are assigned to, you should check the:
   A. Certificate of inspection
   B. Station bill
   C. Operating procedures manual
   D. None of the above
4. You have pulled up on shore. What signal do you give to guide the other boats in?
   A. Wave arms
   B. Red star signal
   C. Horizontal motion of white flag
   D. Vertical motion of white flag
5. When underway rowing a lifeboat and getting close to the ship you want the two forward oarsmen to standby to take the sea painter. What command would you give?
   A. Trail oars
   B. In bows

    C. Way enough

    D. Toss oars

6. When adrift in a liferaft near land what is the best time of day to pull in the sea anchor and let the prevailing winds blow you ashore?

    A. Morning

    B. Afternoon

    C. Evening

    D. Night

7. Lifesaving equipment shall be stowed so that it will be:

    A. Easily accessible

    B. Permit liferafts and lifefloats to float free

    C. Protected from the elements

    D. All of the above

8. The purpose of the tripping line on a sea anchor is to:

    A. Aid in casting off

    B. Direct the draft of the vessel

    C. Aid in its recovery

    D. Maintain maximum resistance to broaching

9. Upon which of the below listed commands will a lifeboat crew lift their oars to a vertical position with the handles resting on the footings?

    A. Oars

    B. Way enough

    C. Up oars

    D. Let fall

10. The proper command to have the crew row in an astern motion is:

    A. Row backwards

    B. Back water

    C. Give way backwards

    D. Way enough

11. Which of the following is not required equipment for an inflatable liferaft?

    A. Jackknife (1)

    B. Repair kit (1)

    C. Hatchet (2)

    D. Paddles (1 pair)

12. After launching the inflatable liferaft, why do we leave the operating cord attached to the vessel?
    A. To steady the raft alongside
    B. To keep it near the vessel for boarding
    C. To keep it on the lee of the vessel to avoid list caused by the wind
    D. To balance the pressures in the buoyancy compartments

13. When rowing a lifeboat and the coxswain gives the command "oars," you should:
    A. Complete the stroke, bring the oars horizontal at right angles to the keel, blades feathered
    B. Immediately stop rowing
    C. Put your oars in the boat
    D. Raise the oars in the air vertically

14. When would you pull the trip line to release the tricing pendant?
    A. As soon as you get in the boat
    B. After the boat is in the water
    C. When all passengers are on board and you are ready to lower to the water
    D. Never, it releases automatically

15. The length of a heaving line in the lifeboat is?
    A. 5 fathoms
    B. 10 fathoms
    C. 15 fathoms
    D. 20 fathoms

16. What kind of davit would you find a limit switch on?
    A. Gravity
    B. Radial
    C. Quadrantal
    D. Sheath-screw

17. When approaching the vessel, you want the bowmen to stop rowing and standby with boat hooks, which boat command would you use?
    A. Up oars
    B. Boat the oars
    C. Way enough
    D. In bows

18. In a lifeboat the hatchets are found:
    - A. In the equipment locker on board the ship
    - B. In the bosun's locker under lock and key
    - C. Inside the equipment locker next to the coxswain's position
    - D. On the bow and on the stern on a lanyard
19. A line passed around the falls to prevent fore and aftmotion is called?
    - A. A tricing pendant
    - B. A frapping line
    - C. A guy line
    - D. A forestay
20. When taking a bearing with a lifeboat compass one should:
    - A. Keep all metal objects away from compass
    - B. Use the compass on the centerline of the boat
    - C. Apply compass error
    - D. All the above
21. What is the purpose of a span wire on a gravity davit?
    - A. To support the davits
    - B. To secure the manropes
    - C. It is part of the falls
    - D. It keeps davits from surging
22. Which of the following would make the best storm oil?
    - A. Fish oil
    - B. Lubrication oil
    - C. Diesel oil
    - D. Crude oil
23. Which davit can be operated by one man?
    - A. Radial
    - B. Gravity
    - C. Quadrantal
    - D. Sheath and screw
24. The proper oar command to be given when you wish to turn the lifeboat quickly to starboard is:
    - A. Give way port, backwater starboard
    - B. Give way starboard, backwater port
    - C. Stern all
    - D. Standby to give way

25. On which type davit do the davit heads remain horizontal while launching?
    A. The radial type davit
    B. The quadrantal type davit
    C. The sheath and screw type davit
    D. The gravity type davit
26. The service life or service use of distress flares and signals is:
    A. 1 year
    B. 2 years
    C. 3 years
    D. 5 years
27. What is the lifeboat landing signal for a safe place to bring other boats in?
    A. White flag moved horizontally
    B. Green star signal
    C. Orange smoke
    D. White smoke
28. When a vessel underway is recovering a lifeboat at sea, the sea painter is to be attached by using:
    A. The stern post
    B. The amidships thwart
    C. The falls and releasing hooks
    D. A long eye splice passed around the thwart and held in place by a wooden toggle which is attached by a small lanyard to the boat
29. The primary purpose of a thwart is:
    A. Seat
    B. To provide rigidity to the sides
    C. For stowage
    D. Prevents backwash
30. What color are the sails on a lifeboat?
    A. Indian orange
    B. Red, white and blue
    C. White and orange
    D. Yellow

31. How many spare life preservers are in a lifeboat?
    A. One
    B. Two
    C. Four
    D. One for every person allowed by the capacity limit of the lifeboat.

32. The parts on the rudder stock that fit into the gudgeons are called?
    A. Posts
    B. Pintles
    C. Nipples
    D. Knobs

33. How many pounds of food are required per person on a lifeboat?
    A. 5 pounds
    B. 2 pounds
    C. 3 pounds
    D. 1 pound

34. One thing to remember about a lifeboat compass is that:
    A. It must be checked for error each day at noon
    B. You can forget compass error because you are steering a short course
    C. It should be on the center line of the lifeboat
    D. You should always compensate for west variation

35. How much condensed milk per person is stowed on the lifeboat?
    A. One quart
    B. One pint
    C. One gallon
    D. One pound

36. How much fuel must a lifeboat carry?
    A. 5 gallons
    B. Enough for 12 hours
    C. 10 gallons
    D. Enough for 24 hours

37. How often do you inspect limit switches on the gravity davit?
    A. 30 days
    B. 60 days
    C. 90 days
    D. Every year

38. When do you release the lifeboat falls?
    A. When the lifeboat is waterborne
    B. At the embarkation deck
    C. Before loading the passengers
    D. They must remain attached
39. What is used to hold the lifeboat in at the embarkation deck?
    A. Preventer bar
    B. Tricing line
    C. Tripping lines
    D. The sea painter
40. If you hear one blast on the ship's whistle when at lifeboat stations, it means:
    A. Stop lowering the boat
    B. Dismissed from stations
    C. Lower the boat
    D. Hoist the boat
41. What is the most commonly used davit on commercial ships?
    A. Radial
    B. Sheath and screw
    C. Quadrantal
    D. Gravity
42. What is the most important thing to remember when lowering a lifeboat?
    A. Check for life preservers
    B. Check the drain plug
    C. Secure the sea painter
    D. Check the oars
43. When are you supposed to put the cap on the drain plug in the lifeboat?
    A. Before you get in the boat
    B. Before the launch
    C. On the way down
    D. After you get in the water
44. What is the first thing you would attach to a lifeboat when recovering?
    A. The falls
    B. Tricing pendant
    C. The floating blocks
    D. The sea painter

45. When rigging the emergency radio transmitter while adrift in a lifeboat, how should it be grounded?
    A. No grounding is necessary
    B. Place ground wire in the water
    C. Ground it to the gunwale
    D. It is internally grounded to the radio's metal shell with a wing screw

46. What is another name for a steering oar?
    A. Sweep
    B. Bow
    C. Stern
    D. Side

47. The athwartship pieces of wood attached to the footings in a lifeboat against which oarsmen brace their feet are called:
    A. Stringers
    B. Stretchers
    C. Bracers
    D. Spreaders

48. If your lifeboat rudder is disabled, what could be used as an emergency rudder?
    A. Steering oar
    B. Trowel
    C. Bucket with a painter attached
    D. Emergency rudder

49. Where is the ladder on a lifeboat?
    A. Bow only
    B. Stern only
    C. A and B
    D. Midship on gunwale

50. When in a lifeboat, you should not smoke because it will:
    A. Give you cramps
    B. Make you vomit
    C. Make you thirsty
    D. Make you seasick

51. What is the purpose of the limber hole?
    A. Drain lifeboat over the side
    B. Keep water from being trapped between the floors
    C. Makes the boat flexible
    D. No special purpose

52. While in a lifeboat what could be used to prevent the boat from broaching?
    A. Balance weight
    B. The sea anchor
    C. The center board
    D. The broach block

53. If you are in a lifeboat during daylight hours, what would you have to give a signal to a plane or vessel?
    A. Yellow flag
    B. Signal mirror
    C. Fog horn
    D. Bell

54. In vessel construction what is the garboard strake?
    A. It is located next to and parallel to the keel
    B. It is located next to and parallel to the gunwale
    C. It is another term for the bilge keel
    D. It is another term for the rub rail

55. How do you repair punctures of an inflatable liferaft (under water)?
    A. Vulcanizing patch with sail twine
    B. Use a patch plug
    C. Use sealing clamps
    D. Use a tube patch

56. Liferafts are light and tend to skim across the water. The equipment located on the bottom of the raft to prevent this is:
    A. Sea anchor
    B. Two skin keels
    C. Ballast bags (stabilizers or scoops)
    D. An anchor

57. How do you hoist an inflatable liferaft onto a rescuing vessel?
    A. By the hand line
    B. By the towing bridle
    C. By the righting straps
    D. By two slings under the liferaft

58. In the event that a ship sinks, what should be done if there is more than one raft in the water?
    A. Tie them together
    B. Disperse so you can be seen over a greater area
    C. Use rockets
    D. Invert all rafts

59. Inflatable liferafts must be serviced:
    A. Every six months
    B. Every year
    C. Every two years
    D. Only if used
60. Which of the following statements is true about the steering oar on a lifeboat?
    A. It is longer than a standard oar
    B. It is shorter than a standard oar
    C. It is lashed to the stern
    D. It is located in the bow and used by the bow man
61. What is the best way to release a liferaft from a cradle?
    A. Unhook the shackle
    B. Cut the straps
    C. Push the plunger in the middle of the hydrostatic release mechanism
    D. Break the weak link
62. Where is the personnel capacity printed on a liferaft?
    A. On the outside of container
    B. Metal tag on bottom
    C. Equipment list
    D. On a forward thwart
63. How deep would a vessel sink before the inflatable liferafts automatically release?
    A. 15 to 20 feet
    B. 10 to 15 feet
    C. 30 to 50 feet
    D. None of the above
64. Approximately what pressure is required to activate the hydrostatic release mechanism?
    A. 65 pounds force
    B. 100 PSI
    C. 6 PSI
    D. 60 PSI
65. The line (painter or operating cord) attached to a rubber raft is:
    A. Used to inflate the rubber raft after it is in the water
    B. To hold the raft alongside the ship after it has been inflated
    C. Used to assist in launching the raft
    D. Both A and B

66. On an inflatable liferaft another name for the weak link is:
    A. The weakest link
    B. A breakable link
    C. The float free link
    D. The missing link

67. Which of the below is built into the inflatable liferaft?
    A. Overhead lines
    B. Built in seats
    C. Ballast bags
    D. Sea anchor

68. From what side of a vessel should you launch a liferaft?
    A. Windward
    B. Bow
    C. Aft
    D. Leeward

69. With which type of lifeboat davit must you use a hand crank to swing the lifeboat out over the water?
    A. Gravity
    B. Radial
    C. Sheath and screw
    D. Welin

70. When using the hand crank on the gravity davits make sure that:
    A. The brake is disengaged
    B. The limit switch is off
    C. The windlass power is off
    D. The crank handle is in the locked position

71. What is true about the floor of a liferaft?
    A. It is rigid
    B. It is inflatable
    C. It is painted international orange
    D. It can be removed

72. When you desire that the boat crew commence rowing, which boat command do you give?
    A. Oars
    B. Let fall
    C. Hold water
    D. Give way

73. What do you pull after the raft is in the water to inflate the raft?
    A. Sea painter
    B. Hydrostatic release
    C. Weak link
    D. Lifeline

74. If a ship sinks below 100′ of water, what will prevent the loss of the liferaft?
    A. Weak link
    B. Hydraulic valves
    C. Hydrostatic release
    D. Missing link

75. The releasing gear, which releases the stowed raft from its cradle is of the _____ type.
    A. Electric
    B. Rottmer
    C. Hydrostatic
    D. Pneumatic

## ANSWERS

| | | | |
|---|---|---|---|
| 1. C | 20. D | 39. B | 58. A |
| 2. D | 21. B | 40. C | 59. B |
| 3. B | 22. A | 41. D | 60. A |
| 4. D | 23. B | 42. B | 61. C |
| 5. B | 24. A | 43. B | 62. A |
| 6. B | 25. A | 44. D | 63. B |
| 7. D | 26. C | 45. B | 64. C |
| 8. C | 27. B | 46. A | 65. D |
| 9. C | 28. D | 47. B | 66. C |
| 10. B | 29. B | 48. A | 67. C |
| 11. C | 30. A | 49. D | 68. D |
| 12. B | 31. B | 50. C | 69. C |
| 13. A | 32. B | 51. B | 70. C |
| 14. C | 33. B | 52. B | 71. B |
| 15. B | 34. C | 53. B | 72. D |
| 16. A | 35. D | 54. A | 73. A |
| 17. D | 36. D | 55. C | 74. A |
| 18. D | 37. C | 56. C | 75. C |
| 19. B | 38. A | 57. B | |

# Table of Life-Saving Signals

**1**  Landing signals for the guidance of small boats with crews or persons in distress.

| | MANUAL SIGNALS | LIGHT SIGNALS | OTHER SIGNALS | SIGNIFICATION |
|---|---|---|---|---|
| Day signals | Vertical motion of a white flag or of the arms | or firing of a green star signal | ▬ • ▬<br>or code letter **K** given by light or sound-signal apparatus | This is the best place to land |
| Night signals | Vertical motion of a white light or flare | or firing of a green star signal | ▬ • ▬<br>or code letter **K** given by light or sound-signal apparatus | |

A range (indication of direction) may be given by placing a steady white light or flare at a lower level and in line with the observer.

| | MANUAL SIGNALS | LIGHT SIGNALS | OTHER SIGNALS | SIGNIFICATION |
|---|---|---|---|---|
| Day signals | **Horizontal** motion of a white flag or of the arms extended horizontally | or firing of a red star signal | • • •<br>or code letter **S** given by light or sound-signal apparatus | Landing here highly dangerous |
| Night signals | **Horizontal** motion of a light or flare | or firing of a red star signal | • • •<br>or code letter **S** given by light or sound-signal apparatus | |
| Day signals | 1 **Horizontal** motion of a white flag, followed by<br>2 the placing of the white flag in the ground and<br>3 by the carrying of another white flag in the direction to be indicated | 1 or firing of a red star signal vertically and<br>2 a white star signal in the direction towards the better landing place | 1 or signalling the code letter **S** (...) followed by the code letter **R** (.‒.) if a better landing place for the craft in distress is located more to the *right* in the direction of approach<br>2 or signalling the code letter **S** (...) followed by the code letter **L** (.‒..) if a better landing place for the craft in distress is located more to the *left* in the direction of approach | Landing here highly dangerous. A more favourable location for landing is in the direction indicated |
| Night signals | 1 **Horizontal** motion of a white light, or flare<br>2 followed by the placing of the white light or flare on the ground and<br>3 the carrying of another white light or flare in the direction to be indicated | 1 or firing of a red star signal vertically and a<br>2 white star signal in the direction towards the better landing place | 1 or signalling the code letter **S** (...) followed by the code letter **R** (.‒.) if a better landing place for the craft in distress is located more to the *right* in the direction of approach<br>2 or signalling the code letter **S** (...) followed by the code letter **L** (.‒..) if a better landing place for the craft in distress is located more to the *left* in the direction of approach | |

Courtesy of IMO *Search and Rescue Manual,* Vol. I, Appendix C.

**2**   Signals to be employed in connection with the use of shore life-saving apparatus.

| | MANUAL SIGNALS | LIGHT SIGNALS | OTHER SIGNALS | SIGNIFICATION |
|---|---|---|---|---|
| Day signals | Vertical motion of a white flag or of the arms | or firing of a green star signal | | In general: affirmative<br>Specifically: rocket line is held –<br>tail block is made fast –<br>hawser is made fast –<br>man is in the breeches buoy –<br>haul away |
| Night signals | Vertical motion of a white light or flare | or firing of a green star signal | | |
| Day signals | Horizontal motion of a white flag or of the arms extended horizontally | or firing of a red star signal | | In general: negative<br>Specifically: slack away – avast hauling |
| Night signals | Horizontal motion of a white light or flare | or firing of a red star signal | | |

**3**   Replies from life-saving stations or maritime rescue units to distress signals made by a ship or person.

| | | | | |
|---|---|---|---|---|
| Day signals | Orange smoke signal | or combined *light and sound* signal (thunder-light) consisting of 3 single signals which are fired at intervals of approximately one minute | | You are seen – assistance will be given as soon as possible<br><br>(Repetition of such signal shall have the same meaning) |
| Night signals | White star rocket consisting of 3 single signals which are fired at intervals of approximately one minute | | | |

If necessary, the day signals may be given at night or the night signals by day.

**4** Air-to-surface visual signals.

Signals used by aircraft engaged in search and rescue operations to direct ships towards an aircraft, ship or person in distress

**PROCEDURES PERFORMED IN SEQUENCE BY AN AIRCRAFT**          **SIGNIFICATION**

| <br>1 CIRCLE the vessel at least once. | <br>2 CROSS the vessel's projected course close AHEAD at a low altitude while ROCKING the wings. (See Note). | 3 HEAD in the direction in which the vessel is to be directed. | The aircraft is directing a vessel towards an aircraft or vessel in distress.<br><br>(Repetition of such signals shall have the same meaning) |
|---|---|---|---|

4 CROSS the vessel's wake close ASTERN at low altitude while ROCKING the wings. (See Note)

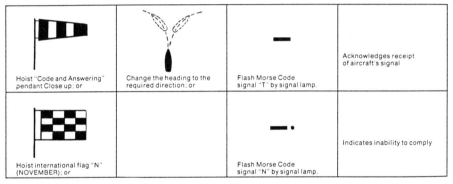

| | The assistance of the vessel is no longer required. |
|---|---|
| NOTE  Opening and closing the throttle or changing the propeller pitch may also be practiced as an alternative means of attracting attention to that of rocking the wings. However, this form of sound signal may be less effective than the visual signal of rocking the wings owing to high noise level on board the vessel. | (Repetition of such signals shall have the same meaning) |

Signals used by a vessel in response to an aircraft engaged in search and rescue operations

**SIGNIFICATION**

| Hoist "Code and Answering" pendant Close up; or | Change the heading to the required direction; or | Flash Morse Code signal "T" by signal lamp. | Acknowledges receipt of aircraft's signal |
|---|---|---|---|
| Hoist international flag "N" (NOVEMBER); or | | Flash Morse Code signal "N" by signal lamp. | Indicates inability to comply |

**5** Surface-to-air visual signals.

Communication from surface craft or survivors to an aircraft.

| Use the following surface-to-air visual signals by displaying the appropriate signal on the deck or on the ground | |
|---|---|
| **Message** | **ICAO\*/IMO\*\* visual signals** |
| – Require assistance | V |
| – Require medical assistance | X |
| – No or negative | N |
| – Yes or affirmative | Y |
| – Proceeding in this direction | ↑ |

\*  ICAO annex 12 – Search and rescue.
\*\* IMOSAR and MERSAR Manuals .

Reply from an aircraft observing the above signals from surface craft or survivors.                    **SIGNIFICATION**

| Drop a message or | Rock the wings (during daylight) or | Flash the landing lights or navigation lights on and off twice (during hours of darkness) or | Flash Morse Code signal "T" or "R" by light or | Use any other suitable signal | Message understood |
|---|---|---|---|---|---|
| Fly straight and level without rocking wings or | Flash Morse Code signal "RPT" by light or | Use any other suitable signal | | | Message not understood (repeat) |

## 6    Signals to survivors.
Procedures performed by an aircraft.                                              **SIGNIFICATION**

| Drop a message or | Drop communication equipment suitable for establishing direct contact | | The aircraft wishes to inform or instruct survivors |
|---|---|---|---|

Signals used by survivors in response to a message dropped by an aircraft          **SIGNIFICATION**

| Flash Morse Code signal "T" or "R" by light or | use any other suitable signal | | Dropped message is understood by the survivors |
|---|---|---|---|
| Flash Morse Code signal "RPT" by light | | | Dropped message is not understood by the survivors |

\* High visibility coloured streamer

# Index

# About the Author

Robert J. Meurn, master mariner and captain, U.S. Naval Reserve (Ret.), received his bachelor of science in nautical science from the U.S. Merchant Marine Academy (USMMA), Kings Point, New York, and his master of arts in higher education from the George Washington University. He taught at Texas Maritime Academy, was commandant of cadets and executive officer of the TS *Texas Clipper,* and was selected as teacher of the year in 1978. In 1983 he was honored again as teacher of the year at the U.S. Merchant Marine Academy, where he served as head, Nautical Science Division. He coauthored the second edition of *Marine Cargo Operations* in 1985 and authored *Watchstanding Guide for the Merchant Officer* in 1990.

Meurn has sailed with U.S. Lines, Farrell Lines, American Export Lines, Moore McCormick Lines, Grace Lines, and Military Sealift Command. In the U.S. Navy he had active duty as a gunnery officer aboard a destroyer and executive officer aboard an LST.

A relief chief mate and master with Military Sealift Command, Atlantic, he was an active member of the U.S. Naval Reserve, where he was commanding officer of Convoy Commodore and Naval Control of Shipping Units in addition to two other commands. His last active duty was as a vice commodore during a convoy exercise in December 1989 in Diego Garcia. Meurn is a member of, and has presented papers to, the International Marine Simulation Forum (IMSF) and the International Radar and Navigation Simulator Lecturers Conference (IRNSLC). He is also a member of the SNAME Maritime Safety Panel (0-44); the accreditation panel for the Sandy Hook Pilots Association; the examining panel for qualifications of assistant captains and captains of the Staten Island Ferries of New York; the International Maritime Lecturers Association (IMLA); the Nautical Institute (where he is treasurer of the northeast coast, USA branch); and the Marine Board, National Research Council's committee on ship/bridge simulation training. Currently, he is full professor in the department of marine transportation at USMMA.

ISBN 0-87033-444-1

52500

9 780870 334443